Kenneth P. Norwick is a member of the New York law firm of Norwick & Schad and specializes in publishing and communications law. He is the author of *Lobbying for Freedom: A Citizen's Guide to Fighting Censorship at the State Level*, published in 1975, and the editor and principal author of a revised and expanded edition of that book, *Lobbying for Freedom in the 1980s: A Grass-Roots Guide to Protecting Your Rights*, published in 1983. He is also the editor of *Your Legal Rights: Making the Law Work for You*, published in 1975. He is an Adjunct Professor of Law at New York Law School, teaching Publishing Law, and has served as Legislative Director of the New York Civil Liberties Union. He is a 1965 graduate of the University of Chicago Law School where he was an editor of the *Law Review* and the founder and editor in chief of the law school's newspaper.

Jerry Simon Chasen is a member of the firm of Chasen & Lichter and is resident in the firm's Santa Fe, New Mexico, office. A member of the bars of California, New York, New Mexico, and Florida, Mr. Chasen specializes in entertainment, publishing, and arts-related matters. He has served as counsel to the P.E.N. American Center and on the Committee on Arts Related Law of the New York County Lawyers Association and the Copyright Committee of the Association of the Bar of the City of New York. Mr. Chasen is an honors graduate of the New York University School of Law where he was a law review editor. He is also a trained mediator, with a particular expertise in resolving disputes concerning creative projects and productions.

Also in this series

AN AMERICAN CIVIL LIBERTIES UNION HANDBOOK

THE RIGHTS OF AUTHORS, ARTISTS, AND OTHER CREATIVE PEOPLE

THE BASIC ACLU GUIDE TO AUTHOR AND ARTIST RIGHTS

SECOND EDITION
Completely Revised and Up-to-Date

Kenneth P. Norwick
Jerry Simon Chasen

General Editor of the Handbook Series
Norman Dorsen, President ACLU 1976–1991

SOUTHERN ILLINOIS UNIVERSITY PRESS
CARBONDALE AND EDWARDSVILLE

95 94 93 92   4 3 2 1

Library of Congress Cataloging-in-Publication Data

Norwick, Kenneth P.
    The rights of authors, artists, and other creative people: the
    basic ACLU guide to author and artist rights / Kenneth P. Norwick,
    Jerry Simon Chasen.—2d ed., completely rev. and up-to-date.
        p.   cm.—(An American Civil Liberties Union handbook)
    Rev. ed. of: The rights of authors and artists. 1984, © 1983.
    Includes bibliographical references.
    1. Authors—Legal status, laws, etc.—United States.
2. Artists—Legal status, laws, etc.—United States. 3. n-us.
I. Chasen, Jerry Simon. II. Norwick, Kenneth P. Rights
of authors and artists. III. American Civil Liberties Union.
IV. Title. V. Series.
KF390.A96N67   1992
344.73′017617—dc20
[347.30417617]   91-23721
ISBN 0-8093-1773-7   CIP

The paper used in this publication meets the minimum requirements of
American National Standard for Information Sciences—Permanence of
Paper for Printed Library Materials, ANSI Z39.48-1984. ∞

Contents

Preface

This guide sets forth your rights under the present law and offers suggestions on how they can be protected. It is one of a continuing series of handbooks published in cooperation with the American Civil Liberties Union (ACLU).

Surrounding these publications is the hope that Americans, informed of their rights, will be encouraged to exercise them. Through their exercise, rights are given life. If they are rarely used, they may be forgotten and violations may become routine.

This guide offers no assurances that your rights will be respected. The laws may change, and in some of the subjects covered in these pages they change quite rapidly. An effort has been made to note those parts of the law where movement is taking place, but it is not always possible to predict accurately when the law *will* change.

Even if the laws remain the same, their interpretations by courts and administrative officials often vary. In a federal system such as ours, there is a built-in problem, since state and federal law differ, not to speak of the confusion between states. In addition, there are wide variations in the ways in which particular courts and administrative officials will interpret the same law at any given moment.

If you encounter what you consider to be a specific abuse of your rights, you should seek legal assistance. There are a number of agencies that may help you, among them ACLU affiliate offices, but bear in mind that the ACLU is a limited-purpose organization. In many communities, there are federally funded legal service offices that provide assistance to persons who cannot afford the costs of legal representation. In general, the rights that the ACLU defends are freedom of inquiry and expression; due process of law; equal protection of the laws; and privacy. The authors in this series have discussed other rights (even though they sometimes fall outside the ACLU's usual concern) in order to provide as much guidance as possible.

These books have been planned as guides for the people directly affected: thus the question-and-answer format. (In some areas there are more detailed works available for experts.) These guides seek to raise the major issues and inform the nonspecialist of the basic law on the subject. The authors of these books are themselves specialists who understand the need for information at "street level."

If you encounter a specific legal problem in an area discussed in one of these handbooks, show the book to your attorney. Of course, he or she will not be able to rely exclusively on the handbook to provide you with adequate representation. But if your attorney hasn't had a great deal of experience in the specific area, the handbook can provide helpful suggestions on how to proceed.

Norman Dorsen, General Editor
Stokes Professor of Law
New York University School of Law

Acknowledgments

Several of our colleagues graciously agreed to review portions of this book and give us the benefit of their comments, and the book has been significantly enhanced by their contributions. In addition, several organizations provided invaluable assistance and resource materials. We are especially grateful to Elliot Brown, Robert Cavallo, Tim Knowlton, Thomas Levine, Maxwell J. Lillienstein, and Susan Victor, and to the Libel Defense Resource Center, the Media Coalition, and the Writer's Guild of America. We also wish to acknowledge the enormous research assistance provided by Michael Benjamin, Pete Lobel, and Tom Mallon. Finally, we each want to pay special tribute to our respective partners, Tennyson Schad and Rosalind Lichter, for their support, encouragement, forbearance, and assistance during the preparation of this book.

In the earlier edition of this book, we acknowledged with gratitude and affection the guidance, support, and friendship we have each received over the years from Harriet F. Pilpel. This very special person died suddenly in 1991, and this edition is dedicated to her memory. We also want to acknowledge our deep respect and appreciation for the extraordinary contribution that one individual has made to the legal rights of not only creative people but all Americans—Supreme Court Justice William J. Brennan, Jr., who retired from the Court in 1990 and who will be greatly missed on that Court.

Kenneth P. Norwick
Jerry Simon Chasen

Introduction

This book is a revised, expanded, and updated edition of *The Rights of Authors and Artists*, which was published in 1983. Although much of that earlier book remains accurate and has been carried forward into this one, the ever-changing nature of the law and the publishing, communications, and entertainment businesses has required substantial revisions to that book. It is the authors' hope and intention that this book is as accurate and reliable as they could make it for readers in the 1990s.

Because this book is entitled *The Rights of Authors, Artists, and Other Creative People*, a few disclaimers are necessary. First, although portions of the book should prove useful to all creative people, the book does not address the legal rights and problems of all creators. Of necessity, lines had to be drawn and categories of creators excluded. Thus, the book does not deal separately with performing artists, those who compose or arrange music, choreographers, or directors, among others. Instead, the book concentrates on those who write articles, books, plays, and motion pictures and those who create works of visual art.

Second, the book does not purport to provide the last word on most of the issues it discusses. Especially where the applicable law can vary markedly from state to state, such an undertaking would have been impossible. Instead, the book attempts to provide an introduction to and overview of the basic legal rights of authors, artists, and other creative people. Readers who are confronted with specific legal problems may well find guidance in this book but should nevertheless obtain the assistance of a lawyer familiar with the applicable law in resolving those problems. Appendix A contains a listing of organizations that may provide assistance and recommend qualified lawyers in your area.

I

The Constitutional Foundation

The Constitution of the United States is not only "the supreme law of the land"; it is also the original source of all other law in this country. In Article I, for example, the Constitution spells out the "legislative powers" that are vested in Congress. It is this article that grants to Congress the principal power to enact the laws that ultimately affect the business and personal lives of all of us. And in the Bill of Rights, the Constitution sets forth the fundamental rights and freedoms of all people in this country, rights and freedoms that cannot be denied or abridged by Congress in its laws or by any other branch or level of government.

Unlike most groups or categories of Americans who do not find specific reference to their callings in the Constitution, creative people are doubly blessed: They can point to two separate, and most important, references to their activities in the Constitution. Indeed, these two constitutional provisions establish the foundation for the most important legal rights of all creative people.

The first reference, in Clause 8 of Section 8 of Article I, grants Congress the legislative power "to promote the progress of science and useful arts, by securing for limited times to authors and inventors the exclusive right to their respective writings and discoveries."[1]

This clause has empowered Congress to enact copyright laws, which have provided creative people the essential protection they need to continue to create since the first Congress. And although the clause refers only to "authors" and "writings," it is clear that, as the Supreme Court has put it, the copyright clause "may be interpreted to include any physical rendering of the fruits of creative, intellectual or aesthetic labor."[2] However, as will be discussed in Chapter II, it is clear that in the copyright laws it has passed, Congress has not protected all the fruits of such labor it might have.

The second reference to the activities of creative people is in the First Amendment, which provides that "Congress shall make no law . . . abridging the freedom of speech, or of the press." Especially since it is now clear that this provision applies as fully to state and local governments as it does to the federal government,[3] it is not difficult to agree with the Supreme Court that the First Amendment is "the matrix, the indispensable condition, of nearly every other form of freedom."[4]

The scope of the First Amendment is extensive. Most obviously, it applies to speech and writings on "political" matters. As Justice Hugo L. Black put it: "In the First Amendment the Founding Fathers gave the free press the protection it must have to fulfill its essential role in our democracy. The press was to serve the governed, not the governors. The Government's power to censor the press was abolished so that the press would remain forever free to censure the Government."[5]

Perhaps of equal importance to most authors and artists, it is clear that the First Amendment is not limited to such "political speech." As the Supreme Court confirmed in a 1981 decision: "Entertainment, as well as political and ideological speech, is protected; motion pictures, programs broadcast by radio and television and live entertainment, such as musical and dramatic works, fall within the First Amendment guarantee."[6]

Read literally, the First Amendment prohibits any law that would abridge the "freedom of speech, or of the press," which presumably includes all the creations of all authors and artists. But if anything is clear about the meaning of those words, it is that they do not mean what they seem to say and that the First Amendment has never been construed as "absolute" in its force and effect. Instead, as will be discussed more fully in Chapters IV and V, the First Amendment does not necessarily protect all speech and writings. Nevertheless, it and the copyright clause, with the laws they have engendered, are the sources and bulwarks of the most fundamental rights of authors and artists.

There is at least a potential conflict between the copyright clause and the First Amendment. Thus, the latter's prohibitions could be read to encompass the freedom to write or speak whatever one wishes, including the writings of others, while the copyright clause makes clear that Congress can prevent such borrowing. The late Professor Melville Nimmer, a leading authority on copyright, has posed the dilemma: "Does not the Copyright Act fly directly in the face of [the First Amendment's] command? Is it not precisely a 'law' made by Congress which abridges the 'freedom of speech' and 'of the press' in that it punishes expressions by speech and press when such expressions consist of the unauthorized use of material protected by copyright?"[7]

Somewhat surprisingly, the courts have not found it necessary to determine whether these two constitutional provisions conflict. However, it is generally assumed that if and when that effort becomes necessary, the courts will not find that the legal protections afforded authors and artists by copyright laws violate the First Amendment but will reconcile whatever conflict exists. Indeed, many courts have at least implicitly done so through the "fair-use" exception built into copyright law, by reference to the constitutional purpose of the copyright clause—to promote knowledge—and by adhering to the well-established rule that copyright does not protect "ideas" but only "the particular selection and arrangement of ideas, as well as a given specificity in the form of their expression."[8]

It seems clear that authors and artists will continue to be able to claim the protection of both the copyright law and the First Amendment. We shall now turn to the rights afforded under the copyright law.

NOTES

1. The derivation and history of the copyright clause has been summarized as follows: "When the framers of the United States Constitution met in Philadelphia to consider which powers might best be entrusted to the national government, there appears to have been virtual unanimity in determining that copyright should be included within the federal sphere. Although the committee proceedings which considered the copyright clause were conducted in secret, it is known that the final form of the clause was adopted without debate. Moreover, in *Federalist Paper No. 43* James Madison found it necessary to devote but a single paragraph to the efficacy of both the copyright and patent powers. Stating that 'the utility of this power will scarcely be questioned,' he put the case for federal authority with respect to both copyrights and patents on the ground that 'The States cannot separately make effectual provision for either of the cases.'" *Nimmer on Copyright*, §1.01 (1980) (hereinafter, Nimmer).

2. *Goldstein v. California*, 412 U.S. 546, 561 (1973).

3. *See, e.g., Gitlow v. New York*, 268 U.S. 652 (1925).
4. *Palko v. Connecticut*, 302 U.S. 319, 326 (1937) (opinion by Justice Cardozo). A recent history of the First Amendment written for the layperson is Hentoff, *The First Freedom: The Tumultuous History of Free Speech in America* (1980), which contains a useful bibliography.
5. *New York Times Co. v. United States*, 403 U.S. 713, 720 (1971) (the Pentagon Papers case) (concurring opinion).
6. *Schad v. Borough of Mount Ephraim*, 452 U.S. 61, 66 (1981).
7. Nimmer §1.1O[A].
8. Nimmer §1.1O[B].

II
Copyright and Other Legal Rights

Pursuant to the power granted to it in Article I of the Constitution,[1] Congress enacted the first Copyright Act in 1790. Since then, there has always been such a law, with major revisions made when developments in communications rendered the existing law inapplicable or anachronistic. On January 1, 1978, the first major revision of our law in almost 70 years took general effect. The Copyright Act of 1976 was the result of more than 20 years of study, drafting, and compromise by the various (often conflicting) interests directly affected by copyright law. The previous Copyright Act had been enacted in 1909, before sound motion pictures, radio, television, and computers; it was not relevant to modern communications and had not been for a long time.

This chapter will review the kinds of works that are eligible for copyright protection, the nature of the rights that copyright confers, the "fair use" doctrine, and the formalities that must be complied with to secure copyright protection. Where necessary, it will refer to the law as it existed prior to January 1, 1978, which in several respects was quite different from the present law. It will also discuss some of the other kinds of legal protection available to authors and artists.

What do we mean by *copyright?*
Copyright is a form of legal protection given to a wide variety of creative works. It is a property right that one "owns," much as one owns a car, a horse, or shares of stock, a kind of monopoly the law gives to creative people for their creations.

Under current law, only one kind of copyright is available to creative people for virtually all creative works: the protection afforded by the federal Copyright Act of 1976. Creative works either enjoy the protection of the Act or they have no copyright protection. Before 1978, there were two systems of copyright available to authors and artists. The first, known as common-law copyright, was available through *state* decisional law and applied to works that had never been published or otherwise publicly disseminated. The second, the federal Copyright

Act of 1909, applied mainly to published works.[2] With the enactment of the 1976 Act, virtually all prior systems of common law copyright were abolished.[3] In legal parlance, the new act substantially "preempted" common-law copyright protection.

The protection of the Copyright Act is extensive.[4] Anyone who without the authority of its owner uses a copyrighted work in a way that constitutes an infringement may be subject to civil remedies, including an injunction,[5] forfeiture of the infringing items,[6] and the obligation to pay the copyright owner all profits from the infringement,[7] money damages,[8] and the owner's attorneys' fees.[9] In appropriate cases, the infringer is also subject to criminal penalties.[10] Further questions in this chapter deal with infringement.

What kinds of works can be protected by copyright under the Act?

Section 102 of the Act states: "Copyright protection subsists in original works of authorship fixed in any tangible medium of expression, now known or later developed, from which they can be perceived, reproduced, or otherwise communicated, either directly or with the aid of a machine or device."[11]

There are two fundamental requirements for copyright protection: the work must be "original," and it must be "fixed" in a "tangible medium of expression."

What is the "originality" requirement?

This requirement is relatively undemanding. To be sufficiently original, a work does not have to be novel, unique, or ingenious, as a patentable invention must be.[12] It must simply have been created or originated by an "author" rather than found or identically copied from another work, and it must present more than a trivial variation on prior works from which it is derived.[13] Perhaps the best summation of originality was provided by Judge Learned Hand, who wrote that "if by some magic a man who had never known it were to compose anew Keats's Ode on a Grecian Urn, he would be an 'author,' and, if he copyrighted it, others might not copy that poem, though they might of course copy Keats's."[14]

To illustrate how limited the requirement of originality is, the Copyright Act states that compilations or anthologies of previously copyrighted (or public domain) works are eligible for copyright, originality being in the selection and ordering of the works. Similarly, a collage composed of found objects is the original work of an artist who has created the work through a process of selection and arrangement, and is copyrightable.

A recent decision by the Supreme Court illustrates the point.[15] Rural Telephone Service Co., the only telephone company serving a small rural area of Kansas, was required by law to publish a telephone directory. Feist Publications, Inc., published a competing directory for parts of Kansas that included the area served by Rural. Rural refused Feist permission to use its directory in the preparation of Feist's, but Feist used Rural's directory anyway. Rural sued for copyright infringement and won in the lower courts.[16]

The Supreme Court unanimously reversed those holdings. Emphasizing the requirement of originality, the Court said, "The distinction is one between creation and discovery: The first person to find and report a particular fact has not created the fact; he or she has just discovered its existence."[17] Copyright protection for a compilation in which the facts speak for themselves, the Court held, is "thin" because the "only conceivable expression is the manner in which the compiler has selected and arranged the facts."[18] The Court specifically rejected a line of lower-court cases that upheld copyright protection for works that were derived from "the sweat of [the compiler's] brow," holding that "the principal focus should be on whether the selection, coordination, and arrangement are sufficiently original to merit protection."[19] Finding that Rural's directory did not have that degree of originality and thus was not entitled to copyright protection, the Court overturned the lower courts' findings of infringement against Feist.

Every work must be evaluated to determine if it is sufficiently original. There is no one formulation or standard that articulates the requirement. The courts have found that mezzotint reproductions of eighteenth- and nineteenth-century paintings,[20] a scale-model reproduction of Rodin's *Hands of God* sculpture,[21] and computer answer sheets for standardized tests[22] needed some degree of judgment, skill, and expertise for their creation and were "original" enough for copyright.

What is required for a work to be "fixed in a tangible medium of expression"?

According to the Copyright Act, "A work is 'fixed' in a tangible medium of expression when its *embodiment in a copy . . . by or under the authority of the author, is sufficiently permanent or stable to permit it to be perceived, reproduced, or otherwise communicated for a period of more than transitory duration.*" (Emphasis added.)[23] The statutory definition is intentionally broad so that it will be applicable to modes of expression developed in the future that are unknown today. Preparatory works such as sketches, drafts, models, and notes, as well as finished works such as manuscripts, paintings, sculptures, motion pictures, and audio- and videotapes, satisfy the fixation requirement. But oral recitations or performances, however original and otherwise eligible for federal copyright, do not satisfy the fixation test. An unauthorized taping of an oral recitation would not be eligible for copyright since the statutory definition requires the "embodiment" to be "by or under the authority of the author." (Even though such an unfixed rendition will not qualify for federal copyright protection, it may—as is discussed later in this chapter—qualify for other forms of legal protection.)

What kinds of works are protected?

Section 102 of the Act provides a partial answer: "Works of authorship include the following categories: (1) literary works; (2) musical works, including any accompanying words; (3) dramatic works, including any accompanying music; (4) pantomimes and choreographic works; (5) pictorial, graphic, and sculptural works; (6) motion pictures and other audiovisual works; and (7) sound recordings."[24] Most of those terms (e.g., "literary works" and "pictorial, graphic, and sculptural works") are given more specific definitions in the Act. "Literary works" are defined as "works, other than audiovisual works, expressed in words, numbers, or other verbal or numerical symbols or indicia, regardless of the nature of the material objects, such as books, periodicals, manuscripts, phonorecords, film, tape, disks, or cards, in which they are embodied."[25]

Significantly, the seven categories listed in Section 102 do not exhaust the kinds of works that may qualify for copyright protection. The introduction to the listing contains the word *include,* which the Act defines as "illustrative and not limitative." Still, not every creative work qualifies for copyright protection.

What is not protected by copyright?

Unfortunately, there is no clear and concise answer. The 1976 Copyright Act provides several categories or descriptions of works that are not subject to copyright protection. But the precise meaning of the statutory language is frequently difficult to discern and is open to interpretation and debate.

Section 102(b) provides: "In no case does copyright protection extend to any idea, procedure, process, system, method of operation, concept, principle, or discovery, regardless of the form in which it is described, explained, illustrated, or embodied in such work."[26]

This is a very important limitation on copyright protection. The traditional statement of this rule is that copyright protects only the "expression" of an idea and not the idea itself.[27] It is often far from clear just when the noncopyrightable "idea" becomes the copyrightable "expression" of that idea. For example, in one famous case, the author of the play *Abie's Irish Rose* sued the producer of the motion picture *The Cohens and the Kellys* for copyright infringement. Both works involve the marriage of a Jewish man to an Irish woman; their fathers oppose the marriage but ultimately come to bless it. The court rejected the copyright claim, declaring:

> Upon any work, and especially upon a play, a great number of patterns of increasing generality will fit equally well, as more and more of the incident is left out. The last may perhaps be no more than the most general statement of what the play is about, and at times might consist only of its title; but there is a point in this series of abstractions where they are no longer protected, since otherwise the playwright could prevent the use of his ideas, to which, apart from their expression, his property is never extended.[28]

Hypothetically, a novel dealing with the life and times of a Mafia "godfather" would not necessarily infringe the copyright of Mario Puzo's *The Godfather*, and a comic strip or motion picture about a man of extraordinary strength who can fly would not necessarily infringe the copyrights protecting Superman.[29]

On a more prosaic level, the U.S. Copyright Office, the federal agency responsible for administering the Copyright Act, has articulated the idea-expression distinction as follows:

> Copyright protection extends to a description, explanation, or illustration of an idea or system assuming that the requirements of the copyright law are met. Copyright in such a case protects the particular literary or pictorial form in which an author chooses to express himself. However, it gives the copyright owner no exclusive rights in the idea, plan, method, or system involved.
>
> Suppose, for example, that an author copyrights a book explaining a new system for food processing. The copyright in the book . . . will prevent others from publishing the author's text and illustrations describing the author's ideas for machinery, processes, and merchandising methods. However, it will not give him any rights against others who adopt the ideas for commercial purposes, or who develop or use the machinery, processes, or methods described in the book.[30]

At some point, a subsequent author's use of another author's "ideas" may well violate the copyright, since at some point the first author's combination of "ideas" becomes protectable expression for copyright purposes. Just when that point will be reached is impossible to say in general. Each case depends on its circumstances.

What about an author's research and the discovery of facts?
As noted above, facts as such are not protectable by copyright, even if they are newly discovered by an author. Copyright protects only the original creative work of an author. Discovered facts do not meet that requirement. As a recent case put it:

> Obviously, a fact does not originate with the author of a book describing the fact. Neither does it originate with one who "discovers" the fact. "The discoverer merely finds and records. He may not claim that the facts are 'original'

with him although there may be originality and hence authorship in the manner of reporting, i.e., the 'expression' of the facts." . . . Thus, since facts do not owe their origin to any individual, they may not be copyrighted and are part of the public domain available to every person.[31]

Similarly, most courts have decided that an author's research, no matter how diligent or important, cannot be copyrighted. As that recent case explained:

> The valuable distinction in copyright law between facts and the expression of facts cannot be maintained if research is held to be copyrightable. There is no rational basis for distinguishing between facts and the research involved in obtaining facts. To hold that research is copyrightable is no more or no less than to hold that the facts discovered as a result of research are entitled to copyright protection.[32]

In its 1991 decision in the telephone directory case,[33] the Supreme Court conclusively laid to rest the notion that an author's effort in assembling facts could itself merit copyright protection.

But what must be added to facts to merit protection is not always clear. *Hoehling v. Universal City Studios, Inc.* involved a nonfiction book, *Who Destroyed the Hindenberg?* in which the author presented the results of his exhaustive research and his theory of what happened to the German dirigible. When a movie was produced on the same subject propounding the same theory, the author sued for copyright infringement. Even though it was admitted that the book was used in the making of the movie, the federal court of appeals rejected the suit, holding that neither the author's research nor his theory were protected by copyright. As the court put it:

> In works devoted to historical subjects, it is our view that a second author may make significant use of prior work, so long as he does not bodily appropriate the expression of another. This principle is justified by the fundamental policy undergirding the copyright laws—the encouragement of contributions to recorded knowledge. The "financial reward guaranteed to the copyright holder is but an incident of this general objective, rather than an end in

itself." . . . Knowledge is expanded as well, by granting new authors of historical works a relatively free hand to build upon the work of their predecessors.[34]

But the *Hoehling* case has not been uniformly followed. In federal courts in Chicago, books presenting the theory that bank robber John Dillinger was not killed by the FBI in 1934 as generally believed were held copyrightable as "historical nonfiction." In the key case, the court held that the author's interpretive story—that Dillinger did not die but lived on the West Coast for many years after the FBI killed the wrong man—was protectable by copyright even if the idea and facts used in support of the theory were not.[35] The court held that "interpretative theories based on historical facts are copyrightable."[36]

Thus, as the Supreme Court has acknowledged, "In the realm of factual narrative, the law is currently unsettled regarding the ways in which uncopyrightable elements combine with the author's contributions to form protected expression."[37] This difficulty may be due in part to a recognition of the dilemma facing nonfiction writers—there may be only limited ways to express the facts. Thus a direct rendition of those facts may not entail the requisite creativity for copyright purposes. However, protection could still be available for the "association, presentation, and combination of the ideas and thought which go to make up the [author's] literary combination."[38] So although the "ordinary" phrase may not be protected, "its use in a sequence of expressive words doesn't cause the entire passage to lose protection."

Legal protection for ideas apart from copyright is discussed later in this chapter.

What about names, titles, and short phrases?

According to the Copyright Office, "To be protected by copyright, a work must contain at least a certain minimum amount of authorship in the form of original literary, musical, or graphic expression. Names, titles, and other short phrases do not meet these requirements."[39]

The office has provided a listing of kinds of phrases that do not qualify for copyright. It includes "names or pseudonyms of individuals (including a pen name or stage name)," "titles of works," and "catchwords, catch phrases, mottoes, slogans, or short advertising expressions." To emphasize the point, the office states that this ineligibility "is true even if the name, title, or short phrase is novel, distinctive, or lends itself to a play on words."

But here too, at some point a short phrase, perhaps even a title, will be long enough to qualify for copyright. Just how long is "long enough" is impossible to state in a single formulation. The determination whether any particular phrase or title will qualify for copyright protection requires a case-by-case evaluation.

What about works of the U.S. government?

The Copyright Act expressly provides that "copyright protection . . . is not available for any work of the United States Government," which the Act defines as "a work prepared by an officer or employee of the United States Government as a part of that person's official duties."[40]

It should usually be fairly easy to determine whether a work merits this exclusion. Statements and reports issued by congressional committees or federal agencies and opinions of the federal courts are clearly not eligible for copyright and may be used freely. Sometimes the determination may not be so easy. One leading case involved the copyrightability of speeches by an admiral of the U.S. Navy that were written and delivered on his own time but typed by his navy assistant on navy equipment and stationery on navy time. The court ruled that the speeches did not qualify as "works of the United States Government" and thus could be copyrighted by the admiral because they were not given as a part of his official duties but as an individual.[41] Presumably, then, a congressman's speech on the floor of the House would not be eligible for copyright, but his speech to a college audience might be. However, the mere fact that material is included in the *Congressional Record* does not mean anyone can use it; it may have been quoted there and created by someone other than an officer or employee of the U.S. government.

A more difficult issue is whether copyright can be secured in works prepared under a government contract or grant. The Act is deliberately silent on this point; it was Congress's intent to allow each government agency to make a determination on copyrightability for each situation. Congress anticipated that if the agency hired an outside person or firm to do the work "merely as an alternative to having one of its own employees prepare the work," the right to copyright would not be granted.[42] It is foreseeable, however, that many contracted works will be eligible for copyright. The matter is open to negotiation, and authors who are considering doing work under the auspices of the federal government should ensure that their work will be copyrightable.

What about works in the "public domain"?

This answer is somewhat circular: Works that are in the public domain are not eligible for copyright protection. A work is in the public domain when it is not protected by copyright, either because its copyright term has expired or because it failed to obtain or was otherwise ineligible for copyright protection. Generally, works in the public domain can be freely copied. All of Shakespeare's works, for example, are in the public domain. Once a work falls into the public domain, there is no way to return it to copyright protection.

Can characters be protected by copyright?

Definitely, if they are in pictorial form. Pictorial renditions of Mickey Mouse, Dick Tracy, Wonder Woman, and other created characters are eligible.[43]

It is more difficult for literary characters, those depicted in words but not pictorially, to meet the level of expression required for copyright protection. Some courts have held that such characters are protectable if they "constitute the story being told" rather than being just the "vehicle" for telling the story.[44]

Applying this reasoning, one court held that Dashiell Hammett's transfer to Warner Brothers of the copyright in his first Sam Spade story, *The Maltese Falcon*, did not transfer a copyright in the Spade character, so that Hammett was free to continue to use Spade in his work.[45] One of the most famous judicial statements on the issue came from Judge Learned Hand in the *Abie's Irish Rose* case:

> If Twelfth Night were copyrighted, it is quite possible that a second comer might so closely imitate Sir Toby Belch or

Malvolio as to infringe, but it would not be enough that for one of his characters he cast a riotous knight who kept wassail to the discomfort of the household, or a vain and foppish steward who became amorous of his mistress. These would be no more than Shakespeare's "ideas" in the play, as little capable of monopoly as Einstein's Doctrine of Relativity, or Darwin's theory of the Origin of Species. It follows that the less developed the characters, the less they can be copyrighted; that is the penalty an author must bear for marking them too indistinctly.[46]

Thus, a well-delineated literary character will be protectable by copyright.

What about three-dimensional works?

Three-dimensional works, such as sculptural works, are generally copyrightable under the protection for pictorial, graphic, and sculptural works,[47] but with one critical exception: Works that are "utilitarian" or "useful articles" are generally not copyrightable. Section 101 of the Copyright Act provides that

such works shall include works of artistic craftsmanship insofar as their form but not their mechanical or utilitarian aspects are concerned; the design of a useful article, as defined in this section, shall be considered a pictorial, graphic, or sculptural work only if, and only to the extent that, such design incorporates pictorial, graphic, or sculptural features that can be identified separately from and are capable of existing independently of, the utilitarian aspects of the article.

Courts have struggled to determine when something is utilitarian (hence not protected by copyright) and when there is additional artistic expression (thus permitting protection).[48]

An initial question is whether the separate identification and existence of the "design" must be physical or simply conceptual. Although "physical" separability was adopted by at least one court,[49] the preferred view seems to be that "the features only need to be conceptually separable from the utilitarian functions of the garments to be entitled to protection under the copyright law."[50] Under that view, a useful article will be denied protection "if the design elements reflect a merger of aesthetic and functional considerations. Conversely, where design elements can be identified as reflecting the designer's artistic judgment exercised independently of functional influences, conceptual separability exists." The test does not require that applied art be completely divorced from utilitarian concerns, but only that the artistic form not be influenced "in significant measure" by functional considerations.[51]

In other words, the design process will be examined carefully. But too literal an application of this test may make an article's copyrightability determined by where in the creative *process* an artist considered functional elements.[52] Copyrightability ultimately "should depend on the extent to which the work reflects artistic expression uninhibited by functional considerations."[53]

What is a "derivative" work?

One of the five "exclusive rights" (discussed more fully below) that copyright confers on a copyright owner is the right "to prepare derivative works based upon the copyrighted work."[54] The Act defines a *derivative work* as "a work based upon one or more preexisting works, such as a translation, musical arrangement, dramatization, fictionalization, motion picture version, sound recording, art reproduction, abridgment, condensation, or any other form in which a work may be recast, transformed, or adapted." It adds that "a work consisting of editorial revisions, annotations, elaborations, or other modifications which, as a whole, represent an original work of authorship, is a 'derivative work.'"[55]

Thus, whenever a book is translated into another language or abridged, a movie is based on a book or a play, a television series is based on a movie, or a book is based on a short story or magazine article, the resulting works are derivative works the original copyright owner can control. Conversely, derivative works created without the consent of the copyright owner infringe the copyright in the original work.

The derivative work is entitled to a separate copyright. However, the Act states that the copyright in the derivative work "extends only to the material contributed by the author of such work, as distinguished from the preexisting material employed in the work, and does not imply any exclusive right in the preexisting material," and that it "is independent of, and does not affect or enlarge the scope, duration, ownership, or subsistence of, any copyright protection in the preexisting material."[56] In other words, only the new matter in the derivative work is protected by its copyright.

As a result of these provisions, it is possible that a derivative work (such as a movie version or translation of a book) can be protected by its own copyright even if the underlying book is no longer copyrighted. This protection is limited: Others are free to create movie versions or translations of the same underlying book—as long as they do not copy from a previously copyrighted movie version or translation. And the right of the owner of the copyright in a derivative work to continue to exploit that work may be limited by the terms of the underlying grant and the terms of the Copyright Act.

What about collections of separate works, such as an almanac, an anthology, or an issue of a magazine?
The Copyright Act has provisions for "compilations" and "collective works." A *compilation* is "a work formed by the collection and assembling of preexisting materials or of data that are selected, coordinated, or arranged in such a way that the resulting work as a whole constitutes an original work of authorship." Furthermore, "the term 'compilation' includes collective works."[57]

A *collective work* is "a work, such as a periodical issue, anthology, or encyclopedia, in which a number of contributions, constituting separate and independent works in themselves, are assembled into a collective whole."[58]

Thus, unlike derivative works (which by definition require adaptation and change of the underlying copyrighted work), a compilation or collective work presumably involves no changes to the underlying material. As with derivative works, compilations (including collective works) can have their own copyrights, but the copyrights are independent from and do not affect the existence, duration, or effectiveness of the copyright in the underlying material.[59]

What specific rights does a copyright confer?

Copyright grants its owner a form of legal monopoly over her work. It is not an absolute monopoly, however; it consists of specific "exclusive rights."

The Copyright Act lists five exclusive rights that belong to a copyright owner:

(1) to reproduce the copyrighted work in copies;
(2) to prepare derivative works based upon the copyrighted work;
(3) to distribute copies of the copyrighted work to the public by sale or other transfer of ownership, or by rental, lease, or lending;
(4) in the case of literary, musical, dramatic, and choreographic works, pantomimes, and motion pictures and other audiovisual works, to perform the copyrighted work publicly; and
(5) in the case of literary, musical, dramatic, and choreographic works, pantomimes, and pictorial, graphic, or sculptural works . . . to display the copyrighted work publicly.[60]

Thus the copyright grants its owner the right to control the destiny of the copyrighted work. The owner can determine whether to expose it to the public, and if it is exposed, the owner can control (at least initially) the persons and means through which the exposure will take place.[61] Any right the copyright owner possesses can be transferred to others.

These exclusive rights do not give the copyright owner complete control. The Act provides specified limitations; for example, libraries and archives have certain rights to reproduce copyrighted works without the copyright owner's consent.[62] In addition, the owner of an authorized copy of a copyrighted work (e.g., a book purchased in a bookstore) can do whatever he or she wishes with the copy, including reselling it, without the copyright owner's consent.[63] Probably the most significant limitation on the exclusive rights of the copyright owner is "fair use."

What is "fair use"?

Although the concept of "fair use" was not expressly recognized in the copyright acts before the current one, it has long been an integral part of the law as interpreted by the courts.[64] Faced with claims of infringement that seemed unfair, unrealistic, or inconsistent with the constitutional purpose of copyright to promote knowledge, and perhaps with the spirit of the First Amendment, the courts had little difficulty creating a fair-use limitation on the rights of copyright owners to prevent unauthorized use. Thus, a judicially created doctrine of fair use was well established in the law of copyright before the 1976 Copyright Act was enacted.

That Act expressly recognized a fair-use limitation, providing that notwithstanding the grant of exclusive rights enumerated in the law, "the fair use of a copyrighted work . . . for purposes such as criticism, comment, news reporting, teaching (including multiple copies for classroom use), scholarship, or research, is not an infringement of copyright."[65] In the congressional reports accompanying the 1976 Act, the drafters of the law provided other, more explicit examples of fair use:

Quotation of excerpts in a review or criticism for purposes of illustration or comment; quotation of short passages in a scholarly or technical work, for illustration or clarification of the author's observations; use in a parody of some of the content of the work parodied; summary of an address or article, with brief quotations, in a news report; reproduction by a library of a portion of a work to replace part of a damaged copy; reproduction by a teacher or student of a small part of a work to illustrate a lesson; reproduction of a work in legislative or judicial proceedings or reports; incidental and fortuitous reproduction, in a news reel or broadcast, of a work located in the scene of an event being reported.[66]

As with many other concepts at the heart of copyright law, it is much easier to describe fair use in general than to give it a specific definition. Indeed, it has been stated that "since the doctrine is an equitable rule of reason, no generally applicable definition is possible, and each case raising the question must be decided on its own facts."[67]

To assist in this effort, Congress has provided in the 1976 Act four factors "to be considered" in "determining whether the use made of a work in any particular case is a fair use":

1. the purpose and character of the use, including whether such use is of a commercial nature or is for nonprofit educational purposes
2. the nature of the copyrighted work
3. the amount and substantiality of the portion used in relation to the copyrighted work as a whole
4. the effect of the use upon the potential market for or value of the copyrighted work.[68]

The first factor is self-explanatory. Even an extensive use for the purpose of criticism or scholarship will be viewed differently than the same or lesser use for the purpose of competing with the original copyrighted work or saving the second user the bother of having to create his original work. The Supreme Court has held that a commercial use (i.e., a use where the user stands to profit from exploitation of the copyrighted material) is presumptively unfair."[69] The crux of the "profit/nonprofit distinction is not whether the sole motive of the use is monetary gain, but whether the user stands to profit from exploitation of the copyrighted material without paying the customary price."[70]

The second factor, the nature of the copyrighted work, also requires little comment. In works eligible for copyright, some obviously lend themselves far more readily than others to unauthorized use. A newspaper article or photograph reporting a political debate or a police raid, although entitled to copyright protection, seems far more susceptible to fair use than a poem, painting, or letter to one's spouse. If a copyrighted work is out of print or otherwise not readily accessible, unauthorized use of the work is more likely to be fair use.[71] But conversely, if a work is unpublished, it is far more unlikely that a court will consider any use to be fair, even if similar use after publication might be deemed fair.[72]

The third factor, the amount and substantiality of the portion used, generates the most questions by potential users (e.g., writers and publishers who want to include portions of the copyrighted work of others in their work). Invariably they ask "How many words, how many pages, how many illustrations can we use without having to get permission from the copyright owner?" There is no one answer to this question. Fair-use determination can be made only after evaluating all the factors in the surrounding circumstances. Nevertheless, it is obvious that the more one takes (especially as that taking represents an increasingly significant portion of the entire copyrighted work), the less likely it is that the use will be found fair. And quantity alone is not determinative of this factor. The quality or significance of what is taken is also relevant.[73]

The final factor, "undoubtedly the single most important element of fair use,"[74] is "the effect of the use upon the potential market for or value of the copyrighted work." Actual damage to the market does not have to be demonstrated; it is sufficient if the use has the potential to damage the market.

The Supreme Court's best-known fair-use case involved the memoirs of former president Gerald Ford.[75] *Time* magazine had been granted the exclusive right to publish excerpts from the memoirs by Harper & Row, the book's hardcover publisher, which controlled the rights. However, just prior to *Time*'s publication, the *Nation* magazine published extensive excerpts from the book, which it had obtained from an unidentified source. *Time* canceled its agreement with Harper & Row; Harper sued the *Nation*, which claimed the use was fair.

The *Nation*'s fair-use defense was rejected by the Supreme Court. On the first test, purpose and character of the use, the Court found that the *Nation*'s motive for the use was profit; it was using the copyrighted material without paying the customary fees for doing so. The excerpts that were selected were critical to the copyrighted work; thus qualitatively, what was taken was significant, which weighed against a fair-use finding on the third factor. And finally there was the cancellation by *Time* of its agreement to publish excerpts, providing an unusual instance of actual damage to the market for the copyrighted work.

But what really seems to have tipped the balance in Harper & Row's direction was the Court's evaluation of the second test, the nature of the protected material. The material taken by the *Nation* was unpublished. The Court noted that "fair use traditionally was not recognized as a defense to charges of copying from an author's as yet unpublished works."[76] In the Court's view, "Because the potential damage to the author from judicially enforced 'sharing' of the first publication right with unauthorized users of his manuscript is substantial, the balance of equities in evaluating such a claim of fair use inevitably shifts." Consequently, "under ordinary circumstances, the au-

thor's right to control the first public appearance of his undis-
seminated expression will outweigh a claim of fair use."

Is using unpublished material ever permissible?

Under the applicable law in early 1992, the answer would be
maybe, but extremely rarely. However, if proposed legislation
in Congress is enacted, the answer could be significantly more
affirmative.

In either event, the answer depends on how and why the
material is being used. Three recent cases illustrate this point.
In the first,[77] Random House planned to publish an unauthorized biography of author J. D. Salinger that included a large
number of quotations from unpublished letters written by Salinger that had been donated by recipients to various university
libraries.[78] Salinger was sent a set of galley proofs of the book,
and when he learned of its use of those letters, he registered
all of them with the Copyright Office and instructed his counsel
to object to the book's publication by Random House. Although
the publisher made certain changes to the manuscript, Salinger
deemed them inadequate and sued for an injunction under
the Copyright Act barring use of the letters. Random House
claimed fair use.

Although the trial court found the use fair, the appeals court
disagreed and reversed the lower court's denial of the injunction. The appeals court relied heavily on the Supreme Court's
decision in the *Harper & Row* case and the fact that "unpublished letters normally enjoy insulation from fair use copying."
It also found that its application of the four fair-use factors to
the case before it defeated the fair-use claim. As to the first
factor, the court noted that even though the biographer and
publisher anticipated profits, the use in a biography was the
kind of use favored under the statute, a factor favoring the
biographer. With respect to the second factor, the court reiterated that by its nature, unpublished material was unlikely to
be appropriate for fair use (weighing in Salinger's favor). On
the third factor, amount and substantiality of the portion used,
the court noted that even if the quantity of the material used
was not great, its quality—Salinger's actual or paraphrased
expression—was a significant element of the book (another
point for Salinger). Finally, regarding effect on the market, the
court speculated that because the "biography copies virtually

all of the most interesting passages of the letters, including several highly expressive insights about writing and literary criticism, . . . some impairment of the market seems likely." With two factors weighing heavily for Salinger, and a third only less so, the claim of fair use failed. In closing, however, the court seemed to stress that it was the biographer's use of Salinger's "expressive content" that led to its decision, not just his use of the material itself, even though it was unpublished.

A second case involved an unauthorized biography of the founder of the Church of Scientology, L. Ron Hubbard.[79] The book was a "hostile, critical biography using fragmentary extracts to demonstrate critical conclusions about him."[80] Some use was made of Hubbard's unpublished diary and correspondence. The owner of Hubbard's copyrights sued the book's publisher, which responded with a fair-use defense. With some apparent reluctance, the trial court found that at least with respect to the unpublished material used in the book, the book infringed the copyrights in those works. But the court refused to grant the requested injunction. The court attempted to distinguish the holding in *Salinger* by noting that in that case the author's use of the material "enlivened the text"; here, the specific passages were used to demonstrate Hubbard's boastfulness, pomposity, grandiosity, pretension, and self-importance, which was crucial to the biographer's effort to convey Hubbard's perception of himself. "It is incompatible with the ends of fair research and criticism to accuse of dishonesty without being permitted to specify what were the dishonest words."[81] The trial judge considered all four fair-use factors and with respect to the fourth test, market impact, he found no negative impact on the market for publication of the unpublished material.

Two of the three judges on the appellate court disagreed completely with the trial judge's analysis, although all three agreed with the decision to deny the injunction. The majority applied the fair-use factors, and while it determined that the nature of the use, critical biography, favored the publisher, it also found that the fourth factor, market impact, favored the copyright owner. In perhaps the most important sentence in its opinion, the majority indicated just how unlikely a finding of fair use would be for unpublished material: "Where use is made of materials of an 'unpublished nature,' the second fair use factor [nature of the copyrighted work] has yet to be applied in favor of an infringer, and we do not do so here."[82] The third judge essentially agreed with the trial court's analysis; all the judges agreed that no injunction should be granted against the book. But the majority based that conclusion solely on its finding that the copyright owner waited too long to sue.

The fair-use defense continues to be raised for the unauthorized use of unpublished material, and in rare instances it has been successful. In late 1991 the same federal appeals court upheld a trial court's conclusion that a biography of the writer Richard Wright, published in 1988, did not violate the copyright law, even though it quoted and paraphrased unpublished materials written by Mr. Wright.[83] The appeals court found that the first fair-use factor, the purpose and character of the defendants' work, a serious biography, clearly favored the defendants, even though they "anticipated profits." The court then found that the second factor, the nature of the copyrighted work, favored the plaintiff because of the unpublished nature of that work. Emphasizing that "a very small portion" of Wright's materials were used, and that "qualitatively" the material used did not represent the "heart" of those materials, the court found that the third factor, the amount and substantiality of the material used, favored the defendants. Finally, the court held that the fourth factor, the effect of the use upon the potential market for or value of the copyrighted work, also favored the defendants because the biography "does not pose a significant threat to the potential market for Wright's letters or journals."

Weighing all the factors, and acutely aware of the same court's earlier decisions involving unpublished works, the court found that the fair-use defense protected the biography: "In short, this is not a reprise of [the *Salinger* or *Hubbard* cases]. The biography's use of Wright's expressive work is modest and serves either to illustrate factual points or to establish [the biographer's] relationship with the author, not to 'enliven' her prose." Although this decision was a welcome victory, the very limited uses of unpublished material involved in the case, and the court's narrow approach, mean that the decision has not really changed a writer's ability safely to make use of unpublished materials in more than the most cramped and insignificant ways.

In 1991, separate bills were introduced in both houses of Congress to amend the fair use provisions of the Copyright Act to permit greater leeway for the use of unpublished material.[84] However, in part because each House has its own approach to the problem, and also because writers' and publishers' groups are unclear as to which approach is preferable (and less fraught with unanticipated risks), the prospects in 1992 for legislative relief were uncertain at best.

What about satire and parody?

Anyone familiar with television programs like "The Tonight Show" and "Saturday Night Live," or magazines like *Mad*, is aware that satire and parody of popular (and copyrighted) works is an important aspect of contemporary entertainment and communication. Whether such satires and parodies violate the copyrights in the underlying works is a serious and not necessarily easy question, and again requires an analysis of the four fair-use factors set forth in the Copyright Act.[85]

In many cases a copyright owner has claimed that a satire or parody of his work infringed his copyright, including a Jack Benny spoof of the Charles Boyer-Ingrid Bergman movie *Gaslight*;[86] pornographic versions of such characters as Mickey and Minnie Mouse;[87] *Mad* magazine's versions of the lyrics to such classic songs as "A Pretty Girl Is Like a Melody" ("Louella Schwartz Describes Her Malady");[88] a musical play entitled *Scarlett Fever* that offended the owners of *Gone with the Wind*;[89] and the use of Pillsbury's jingle and doughdolls by *Screw* magazine.[90] The results in these cases have been anything but consistent, some courts finding infringement and others finding fair use.

The courts recognize that to be effective, a parody must "conjure up" the original, frequently needing to be "more than a fleeting evocation of an original in order to make its humorous point."[91] But even more than is minimally necessary to "conjure up" the original might still be fair use, provided the parody "builds upon the original, using the original as a known element of modern culture and contributing something new for humorous effect or commentary." Again, each case depends upon its own facts and the court's evaluation of the four fair-use factors.

Are there any users who are not subject to the copyright laws?

The Eleventh Amendment to the Constitution bars suits in federal courts against states by citizens of that state or any other. Applying that amendment, a number of courts ruled that claims of copyright infringement against states and their instrumentalities (most significantly, their boards of education or regents groups) could not be brought in federal court. And since the only permissible forum for copyright claims is federal court, preventing a copyright owner from suing a state in federal court effectively prevents the suit from being brought. Although these courts have generally acknowledged the injustice of this result, they have felt bound by Supreme Court precedents involving federal statutes similar to the Copyright Act.[92] They have also invited Congress to correct the situation.

In 1990 Congress did just that. It passed a law providing that with respect to violations of the Copyright Act occurring on or after June 26, 1990, the states and their instrumentalities, officers, and employees were not immune under the Eleventh Amendment from suits for copyright infringement and that a copyright owner has all of the same rights against the states as she would have against a private person, including the right to seek injunctions, actual and/or statutory damages, and costs and attorneys' fees.[93]

Who owns the copyright?

With two exceptions, discussed below, the Act provides that "copyright in a work vests initially in the author or authors of the work."[94] Although the Act does not separately define the term *author*, it does refer to "works of authorship," which were discussed above. Thus the person who originally creates a work of authorship—the writer of an article or book, the painter of a painting, the sculptor of a sculpture—owns the copyright in that work.

The current Copyright Act changed the prior law so that copyright protection now attaches to a work automatically upon its creation. (Before, an unpublished work was protected if at all under the common-law copyright principles of the states, with federal copyright protection in the main available only after the work was published.)[95]

What are the two exceptions to the author's ownership in the copyright?

The first exception, works of the U.S. government, has already been discussed. Under the Act, such works are not entitled to copyright protection.[96] The second (and very important) exception is "works made for hire."

What is a "work made for hire," and who owns the copyright?

The Copyright Act describes two kinds of work made for hire. The first is "a work prepared by an employee within the scope of his or her employment."[97] The works of authors and artists who are employed by newspapers, magazine or book publishers, advertising agencies, TV or motion-picture producers, or any other employer are works made for hire if they are created in the course of employment (essentially, as a part of the job). In 1989 the Supreme Court clarified how to determine whether an author or artist is such an "employee." Some lower courts limited work-for-hire status to situations where the author or artist was a full-time salaried employee. Other lower courts concluded that the hiring party's right to control the manner and means by which the work was created was the conclusive test, regardless of the nature of the creator's employment relationship. The Supreme Court rejected both views, particularly the requirement that the creator had to be a full-time salaried employee. The Court held that the "right-to-control" factor "was but one a host of factors to be considered in determining whether the creator of a work was an employee, none of which alone is determinative:

> Among the other factors relevant to this inquiry are the skill required; the source of the instrumentalities and tools; the location of the work; the duration of the relationship between the parties; whether the hiring party has the right to assign additional projects to the hired party; the extent of the hired party's discretion over when and how long to work; the method of payment; the hired party's role in hiring and paying assistants; whether the work is part of the regular business of the hiring party; whether the hiring party is in business; the provision of employee benefits; and the tax treatment of the hired party.[98]

So where a freelance artist was commissioned to create art for an advertisement, the work was done at the artist's own studio, the ad was one project and not an ongoing series of different projects, the commissioning party had no right to assign the artist any additional work or determine when it would be done or by which assistants, and the payment and tax treatment was as an independent contractor, a court had no trouble finding that the work in question was not work for hire.[99] However, if some of the work was done in the commissioning party's offices, there was a more regular relationship, or the artist received a regular salary, the question can still be rather muddy.

The second kind of work for hire is defined as "work specially ordered or commissioned for use as a contribution to a collective work, as part of a motion picture or other audiovisual work, as a translation, as a supplementary work, as a compilation, as an instructional text, as a test, as answer material for a test, or as an atlas, if the parties expressly agree in a written instrument signed by them that the work shall be considered a work made for hire."[100] *Supplementary work* is defined as "a work prepared for publication as a secondary adjunct to a work by another author for the purpose of introducing, concluding, illustrating, explaining, revising, commenting upon, or assisting in the use of the other work, such as forewords, afterwords, pictorial illustrations, maps, charts, tables, editorial notes, musical arrangements, answer material for tests, bibliographies, appendices, and indexes."[101] An *instructional text* is a "literary, pictorial, or graphic work prepared for publication with the purpose of use in systematic instructional activities."[102]

This second kind of work for hire has three significant aspects. First, works for hire are limited to the kinds set forth in the definition. Full-length books (other than instructional texts), plays, motion pictures, musical compositions, and almost all kinds of works of visual art (except illustrations for another work) can never be works for hire, which most often are articles or chapters for inclusion in magazines or books, illustrations for magazines or books, translations, or secondary contributions to a longer work, as described in the definition.

Second, the work has to be "specially ordered or commissioned." It will usually be clear that this requirement has been satisfied, but sometimes an evaluation of the surrounding circumstances will be necessary. As Professor Nimmer put it,

"The key factor would appear to be whether the motivating factor in producing the work was the [person requesting preparation of the work] who induced [its] creation."[103]

Third, the for-hire status must be confirmed in writing by the creator and employer. The Act does not state whether the writing must be signed before the work is created. Some publishers believe it is enough if the writing is signed much later, including as an endorsement to the check used to pay for the work. But if the intention of the parties is to create a work-for-hire relationship, prudence suggests that the writing be signed when the work is first commissioned, at least pending court decisions on the matter. It is also best for the parties to state expressly that the work "shall be considered a work for hire." Certain publishers and other parties that commission work require artists to sign blanket work-for-hire agreements, acknowledging that all work prepared by the artist for that party is work for hire; indeed, some have made signing such agreements a precondition to being assigned any work by that party. Such blanket agreements can often vitiate the protections under the Copyright Act, and a bill has been introduced in the Senate that would not only prohibit blanket work-for-hire agreements but require that such agreements be signed prior to beginning the work.[104] That bill, however, has engendered considerable opposition from the publishing industry and has not yet reached the floor of either house.

The owner of the copyright in a work made for hire is the employer, not the creator. The creator has only the rights that may be contained in the contract between the parties.

What happens when a work has two or more authors?

Under the Act, "the authors of a joint work are co-owners of copyright in the work." A *joint work* is defined as "a work prepared by two or more authors with the intention that their contributions be merged into inseparable or interdependent parts of a unitary whole."[105] Co-owners are equal owners unless a contract between them says otherwise.[106]

In 1991, the federal appeals court in New York provided valuable guidance with respect to the meaning of this provision.[107] The defendant in the case, Clarice Taylor, was a veteran actress who had portrayed the legendary black comedian Jackie "Moms" Mabley in an off-Broadway skit, and who became interested in developing a play based on Mabley's life. She began assembling material on Mabley, and in 1985 she contacted the plaintiff, playwright Alice Childress, about writing such a play. Taylor turned over all her materials to Childress, and at Childress's request did further research. Although Childress indisputably wrote the play that was the subject of the case, Taylor claimed that in addition to turning over her research materials—which she said involved a process of sifting through facts and selecting pivotal and key elements—she also discussed with Childress the inclusion of certain general scenes and characters in the play as well as the progress of the play. As the court put it, "Essentially, Taylor contributed facts and details about 'Moms' Mabley's life and discussed some of them with Childress. However, Childress was responsible for the actual structure of the play and the dialogue." Taylor had paid Childress $2,500 at the outset of the project, but the parties were never able to reach final agreement on their respective rights with respect to the play. The Childress play, with the consent of both parties, was staged by two different production companies.

The parties' relationship deteriorated, and Taylor then arranged to have another play written on Mabley's life. The writer of that play had access to, and utilized material from, Childress' play. Childress sued for, among other things, infringement of her copyright in her play. In response, Taylor claimed that she was a "joint author" of Childress's play and thus had the right to use it as she did. Both the trial court and the appellate court rejected that claim.

The appeals court began its analysis as follows:

[T]he determination of whether to recognize joint authorship in a particular case requires a sensitive accommodation of competing demands advanced by at least two persons, both of whom have normally contributed in some way to the creation of a work of value. Care must be taken to ensure that true collaborators in the creative process are accorded the perquisites of co-authorship and to guard against the risk that a sole author is denied exclusive authorship status simply because another person rendered some form of assistance. Copyright law best serves the interests of creativity when it carefully draws the bounds of "joint authorship" so as to protect the legitimate claims of both sole authors and co-authors.[108]

Addressing the Copyright Act's definition of "joint work" (quoted above), the court declared:

Some aspects of the statutory definition of joint authorship are fairly straightforward. Parts of a unitary whole are "inseparable" when they have little or no independent meaning standing alone. That would often be true of a work of written text, such as the play that is the subject of the pending litigation. By contrast, parts of a unitary whole are "interdependent" when they have some meaning standing alone but achieve their primary significance because of their combined effect, as in the case of the words and music of a song.[109]

Then, with respect to the word "intent" in the definition, the court said:

[I]t is hard to imagine activity that would constitute meaningful "collaboration" unaccompanied by the requisite intent on the part of both participants that their contributions be merged into a unitary whole, and the case law has read the statutory language literally so that the intent requirement applies to all works of joint authorship.[110]

Next, the court answered in the affirmative what it called the "troublesome" question whether the contributions of all joint authors had to be separately "copyrightable":

The insistence on copyrightable contributions by all putative joint authors might serve to prevent some spurious claims by those who might otherwise try to share the fruits of the efforts of a sole author of a copyrightable work. . . . More important, [this] view strikes an appropriate balance in the domains of both copyright and contract law. In the absence of contract, the copyright remains with the one or more persons who created copyrightable material. Contract law enables a person to hire another to create a copyrightable work, and the copyright law will recognize the employer as "author." . . . Similarly, the person with non-copyrightable material who proposes to join forces with a skilled writer to produce a copyrightable work is free to make a contract to disclose his or her material in return for assignment of part ownership of the resulting copyright. . . . It seems more consistent with the spirit of copyright law to oblige all joint authors to make copyrightable contributions, leaving those with non-copyrightable contributions to protect their rights through contract.[111]

Finally, the court addressed the *nature* of the requisite "intent," referring specifically to the situation where an editor "makes numerous useful revisions to the first draft" and where research assistants contribute to the final work:

What distinguishes the writer-editor relationship and the writer-researcher relationship from the true joint author relationship is the lack of intent of both participants in the venture to regard themselves as joint authors. Focusing on whether the putative joint authors regarded themselves as joint authors is especially important in circumstances, such as in the instant case, where one person (Childress) is indisputably the dominant author of the work and the only issue is whether that person is the sole author or she and another (Taylor) are joint authors. [The trial judge] properly insisted that [Childress and Taylor] entertain in their minds the concept of joint authorship, whether or not they understood precisely the legal consequences of that relationship. . . . In many instances, a useful test will be whether in the absence of contractual agreements concerning listed authorship, each participant intended that all would be identified as co-authors.[112]

After—and based on—its elaborate, thoughtful, and precedent-setting discussion of the relevant factors, the court had no difficulty rejecting Taylor's claim to be a joint author of the play. In so doing, the court said it was unnecessary to determine whether Taylor's contribution to the play was separately copyrightable, since "there is no evidence from which [a jury] could infer that Childress had the state of mind required for joint authorship."[113]

Joint ownership of a work is discussed further in Chapter III.

What can a copyright owner do with his copyright?

Pretty much anything the owner wants to. A copyright is a form of property. Like other property, it may be sold, mortgaged, leased, licensed, bequeathed by will, or given away.[114]

The current Copyright Act, unlike the 1909 law, allows the rights that make up the copyright to be sold separately.[115] Under the 1909 law, separate rights emanating from the copyright could be "licensed," but the copyright itself was deemed "indivisible" and could be owned by only one party at a time. For example, the owner of the copyright in a novel can now sell (or otherwise transfer) the exclusive right to publish it in book form to one or more publishers, sell (or otherwise transfer) the right to base a movie on it to somebody else, and retain all other rights. When one exclusive right is transferred by the copyright owner, the recipient owns the right for all purposes, including the right to bring suit for infringement.

When a copyright owner wishes to sell (or otherwise transfer) one or more of the exclusive rights in the copyright, the Act provides that there must be "an instrument of conveyance, or a note or memorandum of the transfer in writing and signed by the owner of the rights conveyed or such owner's duly authorized agent."[116] Thus an attempted oral grant of exclusive rights was held invalid as a matter of law.[117] The transfer of a nonexclusive right, however, does not have to be in writing to be valid.[118]

Does ownership of the physical work carry with it ownership of its copyright?

No. It used to be presumed that ownership of a work of art included the right to reproduce it and own all other rights in the work.[119] But that presumption was changed by statute in some states,[120] and it was eliminated in the 1976 Copyright Act, which provides (1) that "transfer of ownership of any material object," including the original of a work of art, "does not of itself convey any rights in the copyrighted work embodied in the object," and (2) conversely, that "transfer of ownership of a copyright or of any exclusive rights under a copyright" does not "convey property rights in any material object."[121]

A significant exception involves the exclusive right "to display the copyrighted work [of visual art] publicly." The sale of the physical work does not automatically carry with it the copyright in the work, which the artist retains, but it does transfer the "display" part of the copyright.[122]

How long does copyright protection last?

The answer to this simple question is not so simple. It depends on whether the work was protected by federal statutory copyright before January 1, 1978, whether it is a work for hire, and whether it is an "anonymous" or "pseudonymous" work.

Except for works for hire and anonymous or pseudonymous works, the copyright term in works that were not published by January 1, 1978, or were created after that date, lasts for the *life of the author plus 50 years.*[123] In the case of joint authors, this means 50 years after the death of the last surviving author.[124] (Copyright for works that were unpublished on January 1, 1978, does not expire until December 31, 2002, even if the author has been dead for 50 years before then. If such works are published on or before December 31, 2002, the copyright will last until December 31, 2027.)[125] Anonymous or pseudonymous works and works made for hire keep their copyright for 75 years from the year of first publication or 100 years from the year of creation, whichever comes first.[126]

For works that were protected by federal statutory copyright *before* January 1, 1978 (which includes all works published with copyright before then), the term is different. The prior copyright law provided for two 28-year terms, generally beginning on the date of publication. Failure to renew for the second (renewal) term would cause the work to fall into the public domain.[127] The 1976 Act made two changes for such works. First, the second term was extended to 47 years, making the total term 75 years.[128] Second, the old law required renewal within the exact last year (i.e., between the 27th and 28th anniversaries of the initial publication date).[129] The 1976 Act extended the first term to the end of the calendar year during which it would otherwise have expired. The outside renewal date is thus the December 31 after the old date.[130]

Who is the beneficiary of the renewal term?

The answer requires an appreciation of the purpose of the renewal term. Because it is difficult to estimate accurately the commercial value of a work before its initial publication, the 1909 Copyright Act sought to protect the creator by providing two periods of copyright protection, the creator being able to reclaim the rights to the work at the end of the first term. Further, the Act sought to protect the creator's family by providing a succession of beneficiaries who would own the renewal term of copyright if the author died during the first term: "the author of such work, if still living, or the widow, widower, or children of the author, if the author be not living, or if such author, widow, widower, or children be not living, then the author's executors, or in the absence of a will, his or her next of kin."[131]

This system did not work well, for several reasons. First, failure to renew often resulted in unwitting forfeiture of copyright protection. Second, the courts held that authors' grants made during the first term to the expected renewal term, even in the very first grant of rights, were effective and enforceable if the grantor was alive when the renewal term began.[132] It then became common practice for the recipient of rights during the first term to obtain a grant of renewal rights at the same time. However, if the grantor did not survive to the commencement of the renewal term, any prior grants of the renewal term were ineffective, and the statutory beneficiary would be the owner of the copyright for all purposes.

The consequences of these provisions were made dramatically clear in an important 1990 Supreme Court case.[133] Cornell Woolrich sold the motion picture and television rights to his story "It Had to Be Murder" in 1945. At the same time, he sold to the same buyer the same rights for the renewal term, which would commence in 1970. The story was the basis of the 1954 film *Rear Window*, which starred James Stewart and Grace Kelly, was directed by Alfred Hitchcock, and was produced and distributed by Paramount Pictures. Woolrich died in 1968 before the renewal term was to begin, leaving no survivors under the Copyright Act. His executor, the Chase Manhattan Bank, renewed the copyright and sold the second-term rights to an independent producer, Sheldon Abend. When *Rear Window* continued to be televised and exploited on tape and disk during the second term, Abend sued. He claimed that the film was a derivative work based on the story, that the original license to exploit that work had terminated because Woolrich was not alive when the renewal term commenced, and that the owner for the renewal term had sold the rights to him. The Supreme Court agreed. Not only would the original buyer (in this case the producers of *Rear Window*) be unable to make any other derivative works (movies, TV programs, etc.) based on the copyrighted work (Woolrich's story); it would not even be able to continue to exploit those works prepared during the first term when the grant was effective, including the original *Rear Window*.

The 1976 Act retained this renewal-term system for works that were in their first term on January 1, 1978, but Congress was determined to revise the system for works that first acquired copyright under the new Act's provisions. The new Act therefore provides for a single term of copyright for works first copyrighted after January 1, 1978, but it also provides the copyright owner specific and important rights to terminate transfers of rights during that term.

How can a copyright owner terminate an earlier grant of rights?

The 1976 Act grants the copyright owner (or a specified list of beneficiaries) the right to terminate prior transfers at certain times and under certain circumstances. Its provisions are too complicated to be fully described here; instead, we shall summarize some of the most important elements.

There are different termination provisions for transfers before and transfers after January 1, 1978 (the day the 1976 Act took effect).[134]

With respect to *transfers* (the term includes sales of the entire copyright as well as exclusive and nonexclusive licenses of selected rights) by an individual author–copyright owner that were made before January 1, 1978, when the two-term system was in effect, the new Act, in the words of Barbara Ringer, the register of copyrights when the Act took effect,

> permits an author (or certain heirs of a dead author) to reclaim rights under a copyright after the copyright has run 56 years. Since the new law extends the length of subsisting copyrights from the 56-year maximum provided in the 1909 Act to a new maximum of 75 years, the potential period covered by these terminations will usually be 19 years. However, for those copyrights that have already been given interim extensions beyond the 56-year maximum (under nine Acts of Congress between 1962 and 1974), the years remaining to be covered by a possible termination will be less than 19, and in some cases as few as five.[135]

For transfers made after January 1, 1978, the 1976 Act

> establishes a system under which the author (or certain members of a dead author's family) can terminate the grant of rights and reclaim the copyright after a specified period. Generally the minimum period will be 35 years from the date the grant was executed, but it can be longer (up to 40 years) in certain cases involving publishing rights. Exercise of this right is optional and is subject to a number of conditions and qualifications. However the right cannot be assigned away or waived in advance; the statute says: "Termination of the grant may be effected notwithstanding any agreement to the contrary, including an agreement to make a will or to make any future grant."

Furthermore:

> The earliest date anyone might be able to file an advance notice of termination will be January 1, 2013. The day may seem a long way off, but this should not deter anyone from keeping accurate records or establishing appropriate tickler files now.[136]

Finally, the register observed that terminations of transfers made before and after 1978 "are subject to a complex assortment of conditions, time limits, and procedural requirements but, assuming these are met, the right to terminate will exist regardless of any contrary agreements."[137]

Are there any legal formalities that must be complied with to obtain and maintain copyright protection?

No, and yes. Upon creation of a work, nothing need be done to secure copyright protection, which is automatic. However, particularly for works that are of U.S. origin, the Act contains requirements that must be complied with if and when a work is published and an owner wants to be able to sue for infringement. These formalities relate to *notice, registration and deposit,* and *recordation.*

What are the notice requirements of the Copyright Act?

The Act formerly provided that "whenever a work is published in the United States or elsewhere by authority of the copyright owner, a notice of copyright shall be placed on all publicly distributed copies from which the work can be visually perceived, either directly or with the aid of a machine or device."[138] *Publication,* for these purposes, means "the distribution of copies of a work to the public by sale or other transfer of ownership, or by rental, lease, or lending."[139]

However, this notice requirement has always been a peculiar aspect of U.S. copyright law and is not part of the law of most countries. Thus, when in 1989 the United States joined the Berne Convention (the world's largest international copyright treaty, which prohibits any formalities as a requirement of copyright protection), certain changes were made to this country's Copyright Act. After March 1, 1989 (the effective date of the Berne Convention Implementation Act), the failure to place a copyright notice on copies will not result in loss of copyright protection.

Official U.S. policy, however, is to encourage the voluntary placement of notice on copies, with the incentive that the defense of "innocent infringement," which is available to reduce potential damages if the infringer can prove he wasn't aware that the work was protected by copyright, would be unavailable to infringers of works published with proper notices.

A proper notice of copyright consists of

(1) the symbol c (the letter C in a circle), or the word "Copyright," or the abbreviation "Copr."; and

(2) the year of first publication of the work; in the case of compilations or derivative works incorporating previously published material, the year date of first publication of the compilation or derivative work is sufficient. The year date may be omitted where a pictorial, graphic, or sculptural work, with the accompanying text matter, if any, is reproduced in or on greeting cards, postcards, stationery, jewelry, dolls, toys, or any useful articles; and

(3) the name of the owner of copyright in the work, or an abbreviation by which the name can be recognized, or a generally known alternative designation of the owner.[140]

The Act provides that the notice "shall be affixed to the copies in such manner and location as to give reasonable notice of the claim of copyright."[141] (The 1909 Copyright Act required that the notice appear at specified places on a work.) The Copyright Office has issued regulations that set forth permissible kinds of notice, but the Act makes clear that other means of notice may be sufficient. The office has also declared that the notice should be permanently legible to an ordinary user of the work and not concealed from view upon reasonable examination.

What happens if notice is omitted or in error?

Now, except for the loss of protection from "innocent infringers," nothing. Moreover, the consequences of improper or omitted notice under the 1976 Act were never as severe as under the 1909 law, where omission of notice caused the work to go into the public domain.[142] For works publicly distributed before March 1, 1989, the Copyright Act provides that if notice was omitted from "no more than a relatively small number copies distributed to the public" or the notice contained certain errors, the copyright owner can preserve the copyright by taking certain steps spelled out in the Act, including (1) registering the work with the Copyright Office within 5 years of the publication without notice and (2) attempting to correct the missing or erroneous notice.[143] For works publicly distributed after that date, the only consequence of failing to place proper notice will be the possible use of the defense of innocent infringement.

What are the notice requirements for a contribution to a magazine?

Subject to the changes discussed above in connection with works published after March 1, 1989, a contribution to a magazine may (but is not required to) bear its own notice of copyright. If the contribution does not contain its own notice, the Act provides that an overall notice for the entire work "is sufficient to satisfy the [notice] requirements . . . with respect to the separate contributions it contains regardless of the ownership of copyright in the contributions and whether or not they have been previously published."[144] The only exception to this rule is for advertisements placed by anyone other than the publisher, which must contain their own notice.[145] Moreover, the single notice does not affect the copyright in that contribution, which (unless the contribution is a work made for hire or an agreement provides otherwise) will be owned by the creator and not the publisher whose name almost always appears in the single notice. The Act also makes clear that "in the absence of an express transfer of the copyright or of any rights under it, the owner of copyright in the collective work is presumed to have acquired only the privilege of reproducing and distributing the contribution as part of that particular collective work, any revision of that collective work, and any later collective work in the same series."[146]

What does registration involve?

Registration means the filing of a prescribed form with the Copyright Office together with, in most cases, one or two copies of the work and the payment of the prescribed fee.[147] (Generally, unpublished works require one copy; published works require two.) If the Copyright Office determines that the work is eligible for copyright, it issues a certificate of copyright to the copyright owner. Published and unpublished works may be registered. The Copyright Office will upon request furnish copies of its numerous circulars on the Act and its procedures as well as copyright application forms; the office will also answer telephone inquiries:

Information and Publications Section
Copyright Office, Library of Congress
Washington, D.C. 20559
(202) 287-8700

Registration is not required for copyright, but it is required before an infringement lawsuit involving "a work of U.S. origin" can be commenced.[148] A work is of U.S. origin if it is published first in the United States, is simultaneously published in the United States and in either a Berne or non-Berne state, is an unpublished work whose authors are all U.S. nationals, or is an audiovisual work whose authors are all legal entities headquartered in the United States. A pictorial, graphic, or sculptural work incorporated in a permanent structure located in the United States and a work that is published first in a non-Berne state whose authors are all U.S. nationals are also works of U.S. origin.[149]

Even if registration is not required, there are specific inducements to early registration for both works of U.S. origin and Berne works. Timely registration creates a rebuttable presumption that the facts stated in the certificate of registration are true and that the copyright is valid. And although registration may take place after the infringement,[150] the copyright owner may not be entitled to an award of statutory damages or attorneys' fees in the infringement suit. (Under any circumstances, registration is required for recovery of statutory damages or attorneys' fees for infringement of a work originating in a Berne state.) If a copyright owner contemplates the possibility of an infringement action, it is important that the work be registered as early as possible.

How does one know what form to use?

The forms issued by the Copyright Office do not correspond to the enumeration of "works of authorship" set forth in the Copyright Act but relate generally to the nature of the work. Form TX is used for all kinds of printed textual material, Form VA for works of visual art, Form PA for works of the performing arts, and Form SR for sound recordings. Renewals use Form RE, and supplementary and correcting information is registered with Form CA. Some works fit into more than one category; the owner should choose the one that best applies (there are no penalties for using the wrong form). When the form is completed, it is sent, along with the necessary deposit and payment, to the Copyright Office.

Must a copy of a work of visual art be deposited?

No. The Act authorizes the Copyright Office to issue regulations pursuant to which "identifying material" may be deposited in lieu of a copy of the work.[151] The office's regulations state that it will accept "photographic prints, transparencies, photostats, drawings or similar two dimensional reproductions or renderings of the work, in a form visually perceivable without the aid of a machine or device."[152] For pictorial or graphic works, "such material shall reproduce the actual colors employed in the work," but for all other works, the material may be in black and white.[153]

Except for holograms, only one set of complete identifying material is required. A *set of complete identifying material* consists of "as many pieces of identifying material as are necessary to show clearly the copyrightable content of the work for which deposit is made or for which registration is sought." All the pieces of identifying material in a set must be of uniform size. Transparencies must be at least 35mm, and if they are less than 3″ × 3″, they must be fixed on cardboard, plastic, or similar mounts to facilitate identification and storage. Identifying material other than transparencies should be not less than 3″ × 3″ and not more than 9″ × 12″. The Copyright Office expresses a preference for 8″ × 10″. At least one piece of the set must indicate the title and dimensions of the work on the frame, back, mount, or elsewhere. If the work has been published with a notice of copyright, the notice and its position on the work must be shown clearly on at least one piece of identifying material. If the size or position of the notice makes it necessary, a separate drawing or similar reproduction may be submitted.

What is recordation?

Recordation is the filing—recording—of certain documents with the Copyright Office. It is not a condition of copyright protection, but it is a prerequisite to bringing a suit for infringement.

As the Act puts it, "Any transfer of copyright ownership or other document pertaining to a copyright may be recorded in the Copyright Office if the document . . . bears the actual signature of the person who executed it, or if it is accompanied by a sworn or official certification that it is a true copy of the original, signed document."[154] Recordation provides "constructive notice" of the facts stated in the document and will establish priority between conflicting transfers.[155]

The only document that the law requires to be recorded is a notice of termination of a previous transfer, which must "be recorded in the Copyright Office before the effective date of termination, as a condition to its taking effect."[156]

What are the consequences of the United States joining the Berne Convention (other than the changes in notice and registration requirements discussed above)?

Effective on March 1, 1989, the United States joined the largest (seventy-nine members), oldest (first formalized in 1886), and most important multilateral international copyright treaty, the Berne Convention for the Protection of Literary and Artistic Works. The United States had for years been a member of the Universal Copyright Convention, a separate and somewhat overlapping copyright treaty whose protections were not as great as those of the Berne Convention. Membership in Berne means that the United States will be able to participate in the formulation of international copyright policy. Because Berne has increasingly become the focal point for the discussion and development of international policy relating to new technologies and the cross-border exploitation of copyrighted works, this is of potentially great value. By joining Berne, the United States established copyright relations with twenty-four countries with which such relations did not exist previously.[157]

Protection under Berne is based on "national treatment": Each member state has to provide to nationals of other member nations the same level of copyright protection it gives to its own citizens. An author's rights are automatic and may not be subject to any required formalities (which is why the notice and deposit requirements of the U.S. law had to be modified). Interestingly, the law of the country in which protection is sought will govern, so that a copyright owner might be able to recover there for acts that would not constitute infringement in the country in which the work originated.[158]

The benefit of U.S. membership in Berne will be greatest for those whose works are widely circulated in foreign countries.

What constitutes infringement?

As defined by the Act, "Anyone who violates any of the exclusive rights of the copyright owner" (subject to the doctrine of fair use and the other express limitations on those rights contained in the Act) "is an infringer of the copyright."[159] The Act does not further define what constitutes such a violation. Plainly, a copyrighted work would be infringed by reproducing it in whole or in any substantial part and by duplicating it exactly or by simulation. It is also clear that adapting a copyrighted work into a different medium (e.g., basing a movie on a novel) will also constitute infringement.

However, as indicated above in the discussion of the "originality" needed for copyright protection, similarity is not enough to establish infringement. As Nimmer has put it, "The rights of a copyright owner are not infringed if a subsequent work, although substantially similar, has been independently created without reference to the prior work. Thus absent copying there can be no infringement of copyright regardless of the extent of similarity."[160]

It is not always easy to prove such copying, but it can be established by circumstantial evidence. Thus, if the plaintiff (owner) can show that the defendant (alleged infringer) had access to the copyrighted work and that there are substantial similarities between the two works, a finding of infringement could follow. But if the defendant can prove that she actually copied from a different work or that the parts copied from the plaintiff are not copyrightable, there can be no infringement. The copying need not be verbatim. "As long as the defendant's work is substantially similar to that of the plaintiff's, and is the product of copying rather than independent effort, it will constitute an infringement of the plaintiff's 'expression.' Similarity which is not 'substantial,' even if due to copying, is a noninfringing use of the plaintiff's 'ideas.'"[161]

What should a copyright owner do upon discovering an infringement?

First, try to stop it. Sometimes the infringement is innocent: For one reason or another, the infringer is not aware that his use constitutes an infringement. In most of these cases the infringer will readily agree to stop, and perhaps to make amends. Innocence is no defense to an infringement action, but it will probably affect the nature and extent of the recovery obtained by the copyright owner in an infringement action.

However, the owner will often conclude that a lawsuit must be brought. Indeed, it is the availability of such a suit that gives copyright protection its "teeth" and makes copyright a respected and valuable right.

What remedies are available to a copyright owner in an infringement action?

Under the Act, a copyright owner can secure an injunction against continuation of the infringement, including in appropriate cases a "preliminary injunction" before the case goes to trial;[162] the impoundment and destruction of the infringing items;[163] an award of the owner's damages and the infringer's profits,[164] or an award of "statutory damages";[165] and in the discretion of the court, an award of the owner's attorneys' fees.[166]

Regarding actual damages and the infringer's profits, the Act provides:

> The copyright owner is entitled to recover the actual damages suffered by him or her as a result of the infringement, and any profits of the infringer that are attributable to the infringement and are not taken into account in computing the actual damages. In establishing the infringer's profits, the copyright owner is required to present proof only of the infringer's gross revenue, and the infringer is required to prove his or her deductible expenses and the elements of profit attributable to factors other than the copyrighted work.[167]

It is often difficult for a copyright owner to prove actual damages and/or profits realized from the infringement. Recognizing this, Congress (in both the 1909 Copyright Act and the current one) allowed the owner to elect instead an award of "statutory damages." As the Act puts it,

> The copyright owner may elect, at any time before final judgment is rendered, to recover, instead of actual damages and profits, an award of statutory damages for all infringements involved in the action, with respect to any one work, for which any one infringer is liable individually, or for which any two or more infringers are liable jointly and severally, in a sum of not less than $500 or more than $20,000 as the court considers just.[168]

Although a finding of copyright infringement often results in an injunction stopping the infringing use, that is not always the case. Where a copyrighted photograph was used in a book without permission, no injunction was granted because the court concluded that the burden on the defendant in lost sales would far outweigh the damage to the plaintiff from the use, particularly since the plaintiff did not have a competing book.[169]

The Act also provides that if the infringement "was committed willfully," the maximum statutory damages can be $100,000, and if the infringement was innocent (i.e., "the infringer was not aware and had no reason to believe that his or her acts constituted an infringement of copyright"), the minimum award of statutory damages can be $200.[170] The Act also provides that the court may grant to the copyright owner an award of her costs of litigation, including attorneys' fees.

Statutory damages and attorneys' fees, it is important to remember, will not be available unless the copyright owner complies with the registration provisions and had registered the work before the infringement began.

Finally, under certain circumstances, including willful infringement "for purposes of commercial advantage or private financial gain," the infringer may also be subject to criminal penalties.[171]

Are there rights protecting the work of authors and artists other than those stemming from the Copyright Act?

Yes. The Copyright Act of 1976 preempts all other copyright protection for works that meet its requirements.[172] Thus an original work of authorship that is fixed in a tangible medium of expression will either have copyright protection under the federal Copyright Act or none at all.

But what about original works of authorship that are not so fixed, such as a recited poem or story, an improvised performance of a skit or play or dance, or an oral description of a visual design or work of art? Since these works are not eligible for protection under the Copyright Act, it seems likely that they are still protected from infringement under state common-law copyright or other similar provisions. For example, oral statements (in the context of an interview or otherwise) would not be protected by federal copyright law; however, no court to date has held such statements protected by such other laws, although no court has ruled out the possibility either.[173]

Similarly, rights that are not the legal equivalent of copyright may be protected by state and other federal laws. For example, when Bette Midler sued Ford Motor Company for using a "sound-alike" in a TV commercial (i.e., the commercial used someone who sounded like Ms. Midler singing a song similar to one which the Divine Miss M had made famous), the claim was held not preempted by the Copyright Act. The court found that California's common law protected the distinctive elements of a person's identity and that such factors, not those inherent in copyright, were the real basis for the claim.[174]

There are also certain rights long recognized in other countries that are becoming increasingly important in the United

States, including in particular the rights of *droit de suite* and *droit moral*.

What is *droit de suite?*

Droit de suite has been loosely translated as the "art-proceeds" right.[175] It gives the artist the right to continue to receive payment each time a work is sold, especially if the work is resold at a price higher than at the original sale. It is recognized in a number of European countries, with differences in the kinds of sales covered (auction, dealer, private), percentage of resale price to be paid to the artist, the length of time the right remains in effect, and whether the price must exceed the original price.[176] *Droit de suite* has gained at least some acceptance in this country.

To what extent has *droit de suite* been recognized in the United States?

In 1977 California became the first state to enact a statute giving artists the right to receive royalties on the resale of their works.[177] The statute applies to sales of original paintings, sculptures, and drawings (but not lithographs or prints) that take place during the artist's lifetime or within twenty years of the artist's death in California or in which the seller is a California resident. The artist or his heirs receives 5 percent of the proceeds, and dealers and agents are required to withhold that percentage from the purchase price and attempt to locate and pay the artist. If the artist cannot be found, the money goes to a state art fund. The statute does not apply to the initial sale, a resale within twenty years after the artist's death, or a resale where the gross price is less than the price paid by the seller or is less than $1,000.

Unfortunately, California remains the only state with such a provision. A bill introduced in Congress included a resale royalty provision but failed to pass. A bill similar to California's was introduced in New York and engendered considerable debate.[178] Supporters argued that collectors and dealers make large profits on the sale of artwork which artists do not share; that this protection would benefit struggling young artists; and that since the artist is often responsible for the increased value of his earlier works, it is only fair that the artist participate in profits realized from their resale. Those opposed argued that

collectors and dealers often lose money on the resale of artworks, particularly those by living artists; that the bill might
force reductions in the prices paid to beginning artists; that
dealers and collectors would purchase works of art outside New
York to avoid the statutory payments to the artist; and that
dealers and collectors are as much responsible for the artist's
development as the artist. They also argued that the bill would
substantially complicate the sale of art by auction.[179]

It has been suggested that instead of adopting a law like
California's *droit de suite* statute, states should tax the sale of
art,[180] with proceeds going to a central fund from which payments would be made to needy professional artists. Such tax
funds would assist artists, would be deductible from the purchaser's other taxes, and if the rate was small, would not materially interfere with the art market.

What is *droit moral?*

Droit moral (literally, "moral right") refers to the artist's right
to maintain the integrity of a work even after it has been
sold.[181] This principle has long been a cornerstone of artists' (and
authors') protection in many European countries. This right is
"perpetual, inalienable, and cannot be waived,"[182] and it has
been further described as "non-property attributes of an intellectual and moral character which exist between a literary or
artistic work and its author's personality; it is intended to protect his personality as well as his work."[183]

Droit moral is distinct from copyright. Copyright protects
the artist's right to exploit a work—it protects an artist's property right. *Droit moral* is a personal right, protecting an artist's
expression: "[An artist] does more than bring into the world a
unique object having only exploitive possibilities; he projects
onto the work part of his personality and subjects it to the
ravages of public use. There are possibilities of injury to the
creator other than mere economic ones."[184]

There are four major components of moral right: *integrity,
paternity, divulgation,*[185] and *withdrawal.*[186] The right of integrity assumes that the work of art is an expression of the artist's
personality and that distortion, dismemberment, or misrepresentation of the work can adversely affect the artist's identity,
personality, and honor. In a celebrated case in France, the
court ruled that the artist's *droit moral* prevented the owner of

a refrigerator that had been decorated by Bernard Buffet from taking the refrigerator apart and selling its six panels separately.[187]

The right of paternity gives the artist the right to insist that his or her name be associated with the work.[188] In France, the right cannot be waived, even by the artist. In one case where a painter had agreed to use a pseudonym in a contract commissioning works over a period of 10 years, the court ruled that the artist could not be prohibited from using his real name in connection with the sale of the works.[189]

The right of divulgation gives the artist the absolute right to determine whether and when a work is complete and ready to be shown to the public.[190] Similar to the right of divulgation is the right to control the creation of a work. Thus, when Rosa Bonheur refused to paint a canvas pursuant to a contract, she was held liable for damages, but the court refused to order her to paint it.[191]

Finally, the right of withdrawal gives the artist the exclusive right to withdraw a work from publication and subsequently to change the work.[192]

Has *droit moral* been adopted in the United States?

Until recently, America has not been receptive to this right.[193] When it has been asserted, the courts have noted that it has not generally been recognized in the United States and have suggested that if artists want its benefits, they should seek to secure them in contracts.[194]

But times are changing. Creative (and at times persuasive) arguments have been fashioned from other legal doctrines to secure for authors and artists some of the elements of *droit moral*.[195] For example, although the right of divulgation has not specifically been mentioned in any of the cases, the Copyright Act has been held to provide protection similar to that right, particularly as construed by the Supreme Court with respect to unpublished material.[196] And although the Court acknowledged the possibility that an unauthorized user could prove fair use of an unpublished work, it indicated that such circumstances would be rare since "publication of an author's expression before he has authorized its dissemination seriously infringes the author's right to decide when and whether it will be made public."[197]

The federal trademark law, the Lanham Act,[198] has been the source of successful arguments for protection akin to the right of paternity and particularly that law's prohibition against the dissemination of works that contain a "false designation of origin." The Lanham Act permits claims on behalf of authors where false authorship credit is being given, even if trademark rights and market competition are not directly involved. In one case,[199] the court held for a plaintiff who complained that credit was falsely given to the defendant as preparer and editor of a book.[200]

However, most of the effort to secure *droit moral* protection has involved rights akin to the right of integrity. Every state has laws against "unfair competition," and to some extent such laws may still operate against the "misappropriation" of another's work. In two cases involving motion pictures, a right similar to the *droit moral* right of integrity was found to protect filmmakers whose films were severely edited for television.[201] The question was whether the artist had contracted away "mutilation" rights. Other state laws that might come into play are those involving defamation—for example, where the attribution of a distorted version of a work to an artist damages her reputation. And the Lanham Act has also been useful with respect to the right of integrity.

In one important case,[202] the Monty Python group sought an injunction against a television network that intended to broadcast severely edited versions of three of its programs, even though the network had obtained permission from the group to air the programs. The group contended that the network's editing "impaired the integrity" of its work and that this violated the permission the network had obtained and the legal rights of the group.

The federal court of appeals in New York ruled that "the unauthorized editing of the underlying work, if proven, would constitute an infringement of the copyright in that work similar to any other use of a work that exceeded the license granted by the proprietor of the copyright."[203] Even more significantly, the court declared that it seemed likely the group would establish that "the cuts made constituted an actionable mutilation of Monty Python's work." This legal claim, the court said, "finds its roots in the continental concept of droit moral, or moral right, which may generally be summarized as including th right of the artist to have his work attributed to him in the form in which he created it."[204] The court continued:

American copyright law, as presently written, does not recognize moral rights or provide a cause of action for their violation, since the law seeks to vindicate the economic, rather than the personal rights of authors. Nevertheless, the economic incentive for artistic and intellectual creation that serves as the foundation for American copyright law . . . cannot be reconciled with the inability of artists to obtain relief for mutilation or misrepresentation of their work to the public on which the artists are financially dependent. Thus courts have long granted relief for misrepresentation of an artist's work by relying on theories outside the statutory law of copyright, such as contract law or the tort of unfair competition. Although such decisions are clothed in terms of proprietary right in one's creation, they also properly vindicate the author's personal right to prevent the presentation of his work to the public in a distorted form.[205]

The court indicated that the "garbled" editing of the group's work violated its rights under the Lanham Act, which protects against "misrepresentations that may injure [a person's] business or personal reputation, even where no registered trademark is concerned."[206] The court concluded, "It is sufficient to violate the [Lanham] Act that a representation of a product, although technically true, creates a false impression of the product's origin."[207]

Although the language the court used strongly suggests that authors and artists have significant legal protection for the integrity of their work apart from copyright, and although such protection is to be desired, this case is somewhat unusual, and alas, such protection is generally not available in this country today.[208] The broad declarations of the Monty Python case have not been applied to enough situations where creators have suffered similar injury to lead to many useful legal precedents. For these rights to be truly meaningful, legislative action is necessary.

Have any *droit moral* laws been passed in the United States?
In 1979, California passed its Art Preservation Act,[209] protecting works of "fine art" (defined to include "an original paint-

ing, sculpture, or drawing, or an original work of art in glass, of recognized quality" but which does not include work "prepared under contract for commercial use by its purchaser") and thus became the first state to provide its artists protection similar to, although less extensive than, *droit moral*. As long as a work fits within the statutory classification of fine art, the artist has a right of paternity,[210] and the integrity of the work is to remain intact. Significantly, the law prohibits any mutilation or defacement of a work by anyone other than the artist, regardless of where the work is displayed or presented. The courts of California have already determined, however, that architectural plans do not constitute "fine art" within the statutory classification,[211] although acknowledging that traditional *droit moral* "embraces architectural plans."[212]

In 1983, New York, declaring that "the physical state of a work of art is of enduring and crucial importance to the artist and the artist's reputation," enacted its Artists' Authorship Rights Act,[213] which also granted artists protection akin to *droit moral*. Although its right of paternity is the same as California's, New York's integrity protection is even more limited than California's since it prohibits only the public display or publication of a defaced or mutilated work, not the defacing or mutilation itself. Presumably, in New York, an owner could deface a Chagall, Dali, or Wyeth as long as it is not publicly displayed. Moreover, alterations caused solely by the passage of time or the inherent nature of the materials do not constitute violations of the law unless there was "gross negligence" in maintaining or protecting the work.[214]

Other states have followed suit. Some have adopted statutes similar to California's;[215] some have adopted statutes similar to New York's;[216] and a third group, though providing the same rights of paternity as California's, have limited the integrity protection even more than New York's, so that they prohibit only "physical defacement, mutilation, alteration, or destruction of a work of fine art in public view," or apply only to art in public buildings.[217]

On the national level, on December 1, 1990, the limited but nevertheless significant Visual Artists Rights Act of 1990 became law.[218] Among other things, that Act adds a new section (§106A) to the Copyright Act entitled "Rights of certain authors to attribution and integrity." With respect to the narrow category of works of visual art covered by that new section, the section grants several additional rights to the authors of those works, including

(1) . . . the right (A) to claim authorship of that work; and (B) to prevent the use of his or her name as the author of any work of visual art which he or she did not create;

(2) . . . the right to prevent the use of his or her name as the author of the work of visual art in the event of a distortion, mutilation, or other modification of that work which would be prejudicial to his or her honor or reputation; and

(3) [subject to specific limitations, the right] (A) to prevent any intentional distortion, mutilation, or other modification of that work which would be prejudicial to his or her honor or reputation, and any intentional distortion, mutilation, or modification of that work is a violation of that right, and (B) to prevent any destruction of a work of recognized stature, and any intentional or grossly negligent destruction of that work is a violation of that right.[219]

The new section makes clear that "only the author" of the work in question has these new rights, "whether or not the author is the copyright owner," and that "the authors of a joint work . . . are coowners" of those rights.

The 1990 Act includes a definition of "a work of visual art" to which these new rights might apply:

(1) a painting, drawing, print, or sculpture, existing in a single copy in a limited edition of 200 copies or fewer that are signed and consecutively numbered by the author, or, in the case of a sculpture, in multiple cast, carved, or fabricated sculptures of 200 or fewer that are consecutively numbered by the author and bear the signature or other identifying mark of the author; and

(2) a still photographic image produced for exhibition purposes only, existing in a single copy that is signed by the author, or in a limited edition of 200 copies or fewer that are signed and consecutively numbered by the author."[220]

Further, the Act also spells out the kinds of works not entitled to the protection of the new rights:

any poster, map, globe, chart, technical drawing, diagram, model, applied art, motion picture or other audio-visual work, book, magazine, newspaper, periodical, data base, electronic information service, electronic publication, or similar publication; . . . any merchandising item or advertising, promotional, descriptive, covering, or packaging material or container; [or] any work made for hire.

Thus, in brief, the new rights only apply to limited categories of works of visual art, and even then only to works existing in a single copy or in a limited, signed, consecutively numbered edition of 200 or fewer copies. Moreover, the new rights do not apply "to any reproduction, depiction, portrayal, or other use of a work in, upon, or in any connection with any item" included in the listing of exceptions set forth above.

The 1990 Act provides that the new rights shall apply only during the life of the author, and not—as in the case of most other rights under the Copyright Act—for a period of 50 additional years after the author's death.

Finally, the 1990 Act also states that the new rights "may not be transferred" but "may be waived if the author expressly agrees to such waiver in a written instrument signed by the author," and that any transfer of the underlying work "shall not constitute a waiver of [those] rights."

Although decidedly limited in its scope, the Visual Artists Rights Act of 1990 still represents the first recognition of *droit moral* rights on the federal level and could well pave the way for the development of more such rights, on the federal and state levels, in the future.

There seems to be a growing recognition that the creators of fine art deserve legal protection beyond the proprietary protection of the Copyright Act. But how far this recognition will go remains to be seen. Moreover, it should be remembered that these bills protect only visual artists and their works and do not apply to authors and other creators of nonvisual works.

Have there been judicial tests of these laws to see how far they will go?

One recent case involved the various state and federal theories described above and New York's artists-protection statute.[221] In an attempt to pressure the National Endowment for the Arts (NEA) to withhold funding from works he found unsuitable, the Reverend Donald Wildmon and his American Family Association prepared and mailed throughout the country a pamphlet that included images taken from the catalog of a show at Illinois State University, "Tongues of Flame," which was funded in part with an NEA grant. The images in the pamphlet were from works by David Wojnarowicz, a gay artist living with HIV disease, which the artist said were "assertedly directed at bringing attention to the devastation wrought upon the homosexual community by the AIDS epidemic" and were sexually explicit and homoerotic. Most significant for the case, the images reproduced in the pamphlet were only fragments of whole works ("complex, multi-imaged collages") and were taken out of context, consisting of reproductions of selected portions of the works. They were those fragments that Wildmon found most offensive and were introduced in the pamphlet by a statement that "the photographs appearing on this sheet were part of the David Wajnarowicz [*sic*] 'Tongues of Flame' exhibit catalog." The pamphlet was mailed in an envelope marked "Caution—Contains Extremely Offensive Material."

Wojnarowicz sued Wildmon and the American Family Association for violation of New York's Artists' Authorship Rights Act. He also claimed unfair competition under the Lanham Act, copyright infringement, and defamation. The court found that the defendants had made "fair use" of the material under the four-part test of the Copyright Act and that there was no unfair competition under federal law because there was no commercial practice "involving imitation, misrepresentation, or misappropriation in connection with the sale of goods or services by the defendant." Because the plaintiff was, for purposes of his defamation claim, a limited-purpose public figure, he had to demonstrate that the statements were made with "actual malice." This he could not do with convincing clarity because although the court found Wildmon's statements misleading in giving the impression that the fragments were the whole, they were "literally accurate" and did not exhibit "a high degree of awareness of [the communication's] probable falsity, or [that he] in fact entertained serious doubts as to the truth of his publication."[222]

The court did find a clear violation of the New York statute, and although it did not award the plaintiff monetary damages because the plaintiff had not proved any,[223] it granted an injunction and required the defendants to send a "corrective communication to all those to whom they sent the original pamphlet."[224]

What about all the controversy surrounding the "colorizing" of old movies? Did that involve *droit moral?*

Yes, although not directly in this country. Since the people doing the colorizing had acquired the necessary copyright rights to the films (or the films were in the public domain), no copyright-infringement issues were involved. Those opposing the practice—including in some cases the directors and writers of the films being colorized without their consent or approval—based their objections on artistic integrity. But while their objections were deeply felt and urgently expressed, no court challenge to the practice has been commenced in this country. However, John Huston's heirs did bring suit in France, objecting to the Turner Entertainment Company's plan to distribute there a colorized version of *The Asphalt Jungle*, which was directed by Huston. In 1991, France's highest court—reversing lower court decisions that permitted the televising of the colorized version with disclaimers stating that the film's writer and director objected—emphatically ruled that the creators' *droit moral* supported an injunction against the showing of the colorized movie.[225]

Are there any other ways trademark and unfair competition laws can be useful to creators?

Short phrases and titles, which are not eligible for federal copyright protection, may be protected by the federal trademark law and the trademark and unfair competition laws of the states. A phrase like "Heeeere's Johnny!" or a title like *Gone with the Wind* will almost certainly be entitled to protection by such non-copyright laws, which have as their purpose preventing customer confusion or the erosion of the value of a trade name or identity.[226] The principal requirement here is that the phrase or title be distinctive and that it be associated in the public's mind with a particular source or a particular work. This means that the title of a literary work is probably not entitled to protection unless and until it has achieved such a direct association, which the law calls *secondary meaning.*[227]

Woody Allen successfully used the federal Lanham Act in

arguing that the use of a look-alike in an advertisement (i.e., someone who looked like but was not Mr. Allen) violated his rights by falsely implying his endorsement of the defendant's services.[228] Even though the defendant had put a disclaimer in small print disclosing the use of a "celebrity double," the court felt the disclaimer was inadequate to dispel the false impression of an endorsement and resulting consumer confusion. The injunction the court issued, however, was limited to prohibiting the look-alike from passing himself off as the real thing unless the context made clear, by means of adequate disclaimers or the like, that he was not what he appeared to be and that there was no endorsement by Mr. Allen.

Can an author protect ideas, as such, before they are published?

Yes, to some extent. Copyright does not protect ideas, and once they are publicly disclosed, they are in the public domain. But this does not mean that those ideas have no value before they are disclosed or that an author is powerless to protect them from unauthorized use.

It is obvious that ideas can have enormous value. Countless books, movies, TV shows, and advertising campaigns owe much of their success to an underlying idea. Under certain circumstances, the law will protect the creators of such ideas from misappropriation, wholly apart from copyright. For example, if a creator discloses an idea under circumstances where it is understood (or should have been understood) that it would be kept confidential or that the creator would be compensated if it was used following disclosure, the law may treat those "understandings" as contracts and permit the creator to recover for their breach.

In some cases, these contracts will be "implied" by the conduct of the parties; in others, they will be "implied" by the law as construed by the courts.[229] It may also be possible in appropriate cases to recover for unauthorized use where there has been no disclosure (e.g., where the idea has truly been stolen from its creator), but there are few precedents to support such relief, and the burden of proof on the plaintiff would be very high since the courts recognize that the same or similar ideas can often be devised independently and that many people erroneously assume that an idea similar to theirs "must have been stolen."[230]

What can an author do to protect ideas before they are disclosed?

First, the creator should put the idea in writing as fully as possible. This will ensure that at least the creator's expression of the idea will be protected by copyright and may also discourage others from trying to distinguish between the copyrightable expression and the uncopyrightable idea. Second, the creator should date the writing and take steps to establish proof of that date—by mailing a copy to herself or another person and keeping the envelope sealed; by having the date notarized or otherwise confirmed by a trusted other person, such as an agent or lawyer; or by filing the writing with a group like the Authors Guild (if the creator is a member) that will be able to confirm the date of filing. This establishes when the creator had the idea, which may be crucial if the dispute involves who had the idea first. Third, the creator should be extremely careful to whom and under what circumstances the idea is disclosed. The idea should be disclosed only when it is understood that the creator is not gratuitously relinquishing it but expects to be compensated if it is used. If the creator signs a release waiving any such expectation (and such releases are frequently demanded) or makes the disclosure knowing that the recipient has no obligation to pay if the idea is used, the creator may be without legal recourse if the idea is used following that disclosure.

NOTES

1. U.S. Const. Art. I., §8, cl. 8.
2. *See generally Nimmer on Copyright*, ch. 4 (1981) (hereinafter, Nimmer).
3. 17 U.S.C. §301.
4. *See generally* 17 U.S.C. §106.
5. 17 U.S.C. §502.
6. 17 U.S.C. §509.

7. 17 U.S.C. §504(b).
8. 17 U.S.C. §§504(b), (c).
9. 17 U.S.C. §505.
10. 17 U.S.C. §506.
11. 17 U.S.C. §102(a).
12. *See generally* 35 U.S.C. §§101-3. Congress recognized this difference, the legislative history stating that the standard under the copyright (as opposed to the patent) law "does not include requirements of novelty." H. Rep. 94-l476, 94th Cong., 2d Sess. 5l, reprinted in U.S. Code Cong. & Ad. News 5659, 5664 (1976) (hereinafter "H. Rep."). In an important recent decision, the Supreme Court addressed the "originality" requirement in *Feist Publications, Inc. v. Rural Telephone Serv., Inc.*, 111 S. Ct. 1282, 59 U.S.L.W. 4251 (1991).
13. *Alfred Bell & Co., Ltd. v. Catalda Fine Arts, Inc.*, 191 F.2d 99, 102–3 (2d Cir. 1951).
14. *Sheldon v. Metro-Goldwyn Pictures Corp.*, 81 F.2d 49, 54 (2d Cir. 1936), *aff'd*, 309 U.S. 390 (1940).
15. *Feist, supra* note 12.
16. 663 F. Supp. 214 (D.Kan. 1988), *aff'd*, 916 F.2d 718 (10th Cir. 1990).
17. 59 U.S.L.W. at 4253.
18. *Ibid.*
19. *Ibid.*
20. *Alfred Bell & Co., Ltd. v. Catalda Fine Arts, Inc., supra* note 13.
21. *Alva Studies, Inc. v. Winninger*, 177 F. Supp. 265 (S.D.N.Y. 1959).
22. *Harcourt, Brace & World, Inc. v. Graphic Controls Corp.*, 329 F. Supp. 517 (S.D.N.Y. 1971).
23. 17 U.S.C. §101.
24. 17 U.S.C. §102(a).
25. l7 U.S.C. §101.
26. 17 U.S.C. §102(b).
27. *Dellar v. Samuel Goldwyn, Inc.*, 150 F.2d 612 (2d Cir. 1945); *see, e.g., Mazer v. Stein*, 347 U.S. 201 (1954); *Baker v. Seldon*, 101 U.S. 99 (1879); *Peter Pan Fabrics, Inc. v. Martin Weiner Corp.*, 274 F.2d 487, 489 (2d Cir. 1960).
28. *Nicholas v. Universal Pictures Corp.*, 45 F.2d 119, 121 (2d Cir. 1930), *cert. denied*, 282 U.S. 902 (1931).
29. Indeed, in *Warner Bros., Inc. v. ABC, Inc.*, 654 F.2d 204 (2d Cir. 1981), Warner Bros. contended that because a character in the defendant's show "The Greatest American Hero" also flew, had superhuman strength, did battle with villains, etc., the defendant had infringed Warner's copyright in the character of Superman. The court affirmed the trial court's refusal to grant a preliminary injunction on the claim.

30. U.S. Copyright Office, *Ideas, Plans, Methods or Systems*, Circular 31 (1982).

31. *Miller v. Universal City Studios, Inc.*, 650 F.2d 1365, 1368–69 (5th Cir. 1981), cited with approval in *Feist, supra* note 12.

32. *Id.* at 1372.

33. *Feist Publications, Inc. v. Rural Telephone Serv., Inc., supra* n. 12.

34. *Hoehling v. Universal City Studios, Inc.*, 618 F.2d 972, 980 (2d Cir. 1980).

35. *Nash v. CBS Inc.*, 691 F. Supp 140 (N.D. Ill.), *but see same case, later opinion*, 704 F. Supp. 823 (N.D. Ill. 1989).

36. *Id.* at 143.

37. *Harper & Row Publishers, Inc. v. Nation Enterprises*, 471 U.S. 539, 105 S. Ct 2218, 2224 (1985).

38. *Salinger v. Random House Inc.*, 811 F.2d 90, 98 (2d Cir. 1987).

39. U.S. Copyright Office, *Copyright Protection Not Available for Names, Titles or Short Phrases*, Circular R34 (1978).

40. 17 U.S.C. §§101, 105.

41. *Public Affairs Assocs., Inc. v. Rickover*, 268 F. Supp. 444 (D.D.C. 1967); *see generally Scherr v. Universal Match Corp.*, 417 F.2d 497 (2d Cir. 1969); *Public Affairs Assocs., Inc. v. Rickover*, 284 F.2d 262 (D.C. Cir. 1960), *vacated for insufficient record*, 369 U.S. 111 (1962).

42. H. Rep. at 59; U.S. Code Cong. & Ad. News at 5672.

43. *See Walt Disney Productions v. The Air Pirates*, 345 F. Supp. 108 (N.D. Cal. 1972), *aff'd*, 581 F.2d 751 (9th Cir. 1978), *cert. denied*, 439 U.S. 1132 (1979).

44. *E.g., Warner Bros. Pictures, Inc. v. CBS. Inc.*, 216 F.2d 945 (9th Cir. 1954), *cert. denied*, 348 U.S. 971 (1955); *cf. CBS v. DeCosta* [1], 377 F.2d 315 (1st Cir.), *cert. denied*, 389 U.S. 1007 (1967).

45. *Warner Bros. Pictures, Inc. v. CBS. Inc., supra* note 44.

46. *Nicholas v. Universal Pictures Corp., supra* note 28, at 121.

47. 17. U.S.C. §102(a)(5).

48. *See generally* Nimmer §2.08[B].

49. *Esquire, Inc. v. Ringer*, 591 F.2d 796, 804 (D.C. Cir. 1978).

50. *Kisselstein-Cord v. Accessories by Pearl, Inc.*, 632 F.2d 989, 993 (2d Cir. 1980).

51. *Brandir Intern. Inc. v. Cascade Pacific Lumber Co.*, 834 F.2d 1142, 1145 (2d Cir. 1987) (quoted in *National Theme Productions Inc. v. Jerry B. Beck, Inc.*, 696 F. Supp 1348, 1353 [S.D. Cal 1988]). This test adopts the one suggested by Professor Denicola in "Applied Art and Industrial Design: A Suggested Approach to Copyright in Useful Articles," 67 *Minn. L. Rev.* 707 (1983).

52. *National Theme Productions, Inc. v. Jerry B. Beck, Inc., supra* note 51 at 1353.

53. Denicola, *supra* note 51 at 741.

54. 17 U.S.C. §106.

55. 17 U.S.C. §101.

56. 17 U.S.C. §103(b).

57. 17 U.S.C. §101.

58. *Id.*

59. 17 U.S.C. §103(b).

60. 17 U.S.C. §106.

61. In *Harper & Row Publishers, Inc. v. Nation Enterprises*, 471 U.S. 539, 554–55 (1985), the Supreme Court rejected the fair-use defense of the magazine *The Nation* in connection with its unauthorized publication of former President Ford's then unpublished memoirs, in large measure because the material had not yet been published. *See also Salinger v. Random House, Inc., supra* note 38.

62. 17 U.S.C. §108.

63. 17 U.S.C. §109.

64. *See generally* Nimmer §13.05.

65. 17 U.S.C. §107.

66. H. Rep. at 65; Code Cong. & Ad. News at 567–79.

67. *Id.*

68. 17 U.S.C. §107.

69. *Sony Corp. of America v. Universal City Studios, Inc.*, 464 U.S. 417, 451 (1984).

70. *Harper & Row Publishers Inc. v. Nation Enterprises, supra* n. 61 at 562.

71. For example, in *Maxtone-Graham v. Burtchaell*, 803 F.2d 1253 (2d Cir. 1986), *cert. denied*, 107 S. Ct. 2201 (1987), an anti-abortion advocate used 7,000 words from a pro-choice book, amounting to 4.3 percent of her anti-abortion book. Among the various factors which led the court to uphold the fair-use defense was the fact that the plaintiff's book was out of print. *But see Craft v. Kobler*, 667 F. Supp. 120 (S.D.N.Y. 1987), discussed in note 73, below, where the court rejected a fair-use defense even though the material was no longer in print.

72. *Harper & Row Publishers Inc. v. Nation Enterprises, supra* note 61, at 551, 562.

73. *Id.* at 565. In *Craft v. Kobler, supra* note 71, the plaintiff, who was Igor Stravinsky's personal assistant, inheritor of his copyrights, and coauthor on a number of books, sued the author of an unauthorized biography of Stravinsky because of quotations and paraphrases taken from copyrighted material without permission. The material was taken from a variety of works by Stravinsky, many of which were out of print, and constituted only 3 percent of the defendant's work. In the

court's judgment, however, the qualitative importance of the taken material to the biography exceeded its quantitative percentage, because the material taken was "the liveliest and most entertaining part of the biography."

74. *Id.*

75. *Harper & Row Publishers Inc. v. Nation Enterprises, supra* note 61.

76. *Id.* at 550–51.

77. *Salinger v. Random House, Inc.*, 811 F.2d 90 (2d Cir. 1987).

78. Although this fact was apparently not critical to the court's decision, it is at least interesting to note that the quotes were used even though the biographer signed form agreements furnished by the various libraries restricting the use he could make of the letters without the library's permission or that of the copyright owner. In fact, one form required permission "to publish the contents of the manuscript or any excerpt therefrom," and in another the biographer agreed "not to copy, reproduce, circulate or publish" the manuscripts without permission. *Id.* at 93.

79. *New Era Publications Int'l, ApS v. Henry Holt & Co.*, 873 F.2d 576 (2d Cir.), *cert. denied*, 110 S. Ct. 1168 (1990).

80. *Id.* at 594 (Oakes, C.J., concurring, *quoting* 695 F. Supp. 1493, 1523 [S.D.N.Y. 1988]).

81. *Id.* at 581 (*quoting* 695 F. Supp. at 1510).

82. *Id.* at 583.

83. *Wright v. Warner Books, Inc.*, 19 Med. L. Rptr 1577 (2d Cir. 1991).

84. The texts of both bills are set out and discussed in Stephenson, "Guild Continues Fight for New Fair-Use Law," *Author's Guild Bulletin*, Winter 1992.

85. *Warner Bros. Inc. v. American Broadcasting, Inc.*, 720 F.2d 231, 242 (2d Cir. 1983).

86. *Benny v. Loews, Inc.*, 239 F.2d 532 (9th Cir. 1956), *aff'd by an equally div'd court*, 356 U.S. 543 (1958).

87. *Walt Disney Productions v. The Air Pirates, supra* note 43.

88. *Berlin v. E.C. Publications, Inc.*, 329 F.2d 541 (2d Cir.), *cert. denied*, 379 U.S. 822 (1964).

89. *Metro-Goldwyn-Mayer. Inc. v. Showcase Atlanta Cooperative Productions. Inc.*, 479 F. Supp. 351 (N.D. Ga. 1979).

90. *Pillsbury Co. v. Milky Way Productions Inc.*, 8 Med. L. Rptr. 1016 (N.D. Ga. 1981).

91. *Elsmere Music, Inc. v. National Broadcasting Co.*, 623 F.2d 252, 253 (2d Cir. 1980), *aff'g* 482 F. Supp. 741 (S.D.N.Y.).

92. *BV Engineering v. University of California, Los Angeles*, 858 F.2d 1394 (9th Cir. 1988), *cert. denied*, 109 S. Ct. 1557 (1989); *Richard Anderson Photography v. Brown*, 852 F.2d 114 (4th Cir. 1988), *cert.*

denied, 109 S. Ct. 1171 (1989); *Lane v. First National Bank of Boston*, 10 U.S.P.Q.2d 1268 (1st Cir. 1989).

93. Copyright Remedy Clarification Act, Public Law 101-553, 101st Cong., 2d Sess. (1990).
94. 17 U.S.C. §201(a).
95. *See generally* Nimmer, ch. 4.
96. 17 U.S.C. §105.
97. 17 U.S.C. §101.
98. *Community for Creative Non-Violence v. Reid*, 109 S. Ct. 2166, 2178–79 (1989).
99. *M.G.B. Homes, Inc. v. Ameron Homes, Inc.*, 903 F.2d 1486 (11th Cir. 1990).
100. 17 U.S.C. §101.
101. *Id.*
102. *Id.*
103. Nimmer at 5–25.
104. S. 1253, 101st Cong., 2d Sess. (1990).
105. 17 U.S.C. §§201(a), 101 (emphasis added).
106. H. Rep. at 120; U.S. Code Cong. & Ad. News at 5736.
107. *Childress v. Taylor*, 945 F.2d 500 (2d Cir. 1991).
108. *Id.* at 504.
109. *Id.* at 505.
110. *Id.* at 505–6.
111. *Id.* at 507.
112. *Id.* at 507–8.
113. *Id.* at 509.
114. *See* 17 U.S.C. §201(d)(1).
115. *See generally* Latman, *The Copyright Law* at 99–101 (5th ed. 1979).
116. 17 U.S.C. §204(a).
117. *Library Publications, Inc. v. Medical Economics Co.*, 548 F. Supp. 1231 (E.D. Pa. 1982), *aff'd*, 714 F.2d 123 (1983) (unpub. dec.).
118. Latman, *supra* note 115, at 101.
119. *See, e.g.*, *Pushman v. New York Graphic Society, Inc.*, 25 N.Y.S.2d 32 (Sup. Ct. 1941), *aff'd*, 28 N.Y.S.2d 711 (1st Dept. 1941), *aff'd*, 287 N.Y. 302 (1942).
120. *E.g.*, N.Y. Gen. Bus. L. §219-g (McKinney 1982).
121. 17 U.S.C. §202.
122. *See* 17 U.S.C. §109(b).
123. 17 U.S.C. §302(a).
124. 17 U.S.C. §302(b).
125. 17 U.S.C. §303.
126. 17 U.S.C. §302(c).
127. *See generally* Latman, *supra* note 115, at 71–91.

128. 17 U.S.C. §304(a) (b).
129. *See generally* H. Rep. at 142–43; U.S. Code Cong. & Ad. News at 5758–59.
130. 17 U.S.C. §305.
131. 17 U.S.C. §304(a).
132. *Fred Fisher Music Co., Inc. v. W. Witmark & Sons*, 318 U.S. 643 (1943).
133. *Stewart v. Abend*, 110 S. Ct. 1750 (1990).
134. *Compare* 17 U.S.C. §203 (termination of grants made after January 1, 1978) *with* 17 U.S.C. §304(c) (termination of grants made before January 1, 1978).
135. Ringer, "Finding Your Way Around in the New Copyright Law," *Publishers Weekly*, Dec. 13, 1976, at 38.
136. *Id.*
137. *Id.*
138. 17 U.S.C. §401(a).
139. 17 U.S.C. §101.
140. 17 U.S.C. §401(b).
141. 17 U.S.C. §401(c).
142. H. Rep. at 146; U.S. Code Cong. & Ad. News at 5762.
143. 17 U.S.C. §405.
144. 17 U.S.C. §404(a).
145. *Id.*
146. 17 U.S.C. §201(c).
147. *See* 17 U.S.C. §408. Copyright registration fees have doubled from $10 to $20 per registration, and the register of copyrights has been given the authority to raise them every 5 years to reflect inflation and increased costs.
148. *See* 17 U.S.C. §411.
149. Copyright Law Reports (CCH) ¶6020 (1990).
150. *See* 17 U.S.C. §412.
151. *See* 17 U.S.C. §§408(b), 702.
152. Copyright Office Regs. §202.21, reprinted in Nimmer, app. 3.
153. *Id.*
154. 17 U.S.C. §205(a).
155. 17 U.S.C. §205(c).
156. 17 U.S.C. §§203(a)(4)(A), 304(c)(4)(A).
157. Copyright Law Reports (CCH) ¶6020 (1990).
158. *Id.*
159. 17 U.S.C. §501(a).
160. Nimmer §8.01[A].
161. *Id.* at §8.01[G].

162. 17 U.S.C. §502(a).
163. 17 U.S.C. §503.
164. 17 U.S.C. §504(b).
165. 17 U.S.C. §504(c).
166. 17 U.S.C. §505.
167. 17 U.S.C. §504(b).
168. 17 U.S.C. §504(c)(1).
169. *Belushi v. Woodward*, 598 F. Supp. 36 (D.D.C. 1984).
170. 17 U.S.C. §504(c)(2).
171. 17 U.S.C. §506.
172. 17 U.S.C. §301 (1990).
173. *See, e.g., Falwell v. Penthouse Int'l, Ltd.*, 521 F. Supp. 1204 (W.D. Va. 1981) (The Reverend Jerry Falwell sued because an interview he ostensibly gave for publication in another magazine appeared instead in *Penthouse*); *Hemingway v. Random House, Inc.*, 23 N.Y.2d 341, 296 N.Y.S.2d 771 (1969) (Ernest Hemingway's estate could not claim rights in conversations he had with the author of a book about him).
174. *Midler v. Ford Motor Co.*, 849 F.2d 460 (9th Cir. 1988).
175. Price & Price, "The Rights of Artists: The Case of the Droit de Suite," 31 *Art Journal* 144, reprinted in F. Feldman & S. Weil, *Art Works: Law, Policy, Practice*, at 67 (1974).
176. *See generally* R. Duffy, *Art Law: Representing Artists, Dealers, and Collectors*, at 265 (France), 269 (Germany). 270 (Italy) (1977).
177. Cal. Civ. Code §986 (West Supp. 1991). The statute was upheld despite challenges to its constitutionality in *Morseburg v. Balyon*, 621 F.2d 972 (9th Cir.), *cert. denied*, 449 U.S. 983 (1980).
178. *E.g.*, N.Y. Assy. 8171, 1977–78 Regular Session (1977).
179. The pros and cons of such legislation are discussed at length in Duffy, *supra* note 176, at 276–81.
180. Duffy, *supra* note 176, at 281–82.
181. *See generally* Duffy, *supra* note 176, at 291 *et seq.*; Feldman & Weil, *supra* note 175, at 8.
182. Duffy, *supra* note 176, at 292.
183. Sarraute, "Current Theory of the Moral Right of Authors and Artists under French Law," 16 *Am. J. Comp. L.* 465 (1968).
184. Roeder, "The Doctrine of Moral Right: A Study in the Law of Artists, Authors and Creators," 53 *Harv. L. Rev.* 554, 557 (1940).
185. Merryman, "The Refrigerator of Bernard Buffet," 27 *Hastings L. J.* 1023, 1027–28 (1976).
186. DaSilva, "Droit Moral Copyright: A Comparison of Artists' Rights in France and the United States," 28 *Journal of the Copyright Society of*

the U.S.A., No. 6 (August 1981); *Robert H. Jacobs, Inc. v. Westoaks Realtors, Inc.*, 159 Cal. App. 3d 637, 205 Cal. Rptr. 620 (2d Dist. 1984).

187. *Buffet v. Fersing*, Recueil Dalloz [D. Jur.] 570, 571 (Cour d'appel, Paris) (1962).

188. Merryman, *supra* note 185, at 1027.

189. *Guille v. Colmant*, Recueil Dalloz-Sirey [D.S. Jur.] 284, Gasette du Palais [Gaz.Pal.] I.17 (Cour d'appel, Paris) (1967).

190. Merryman, *supra* note 185, at 1028.

191. *Bonheur v. Pourchet*, Cour de Paris, D.P. 1865.2.201.

192. DaSilva, *supra* note 186; *Robert H. Jacobs, Inc. v. Westoaks Realtors, Inc.*, *supra* note 186.

193. Judge Jerome Frank once remarked that "the phrase 'moral rights' seems to have frightened some [American] courts to such an extent that some have unduly narrowed artists' rights." *Granz v. Harris*, 198 F.2d 585, 590 (2d Cir. 1952).

194. *See, e.g., Crimi v. Rutgers Presbyterian Church*, 194 Misc. 570, 89 N.Y.S.2d 813 (Sup. Ct. 1949).

195. *See generally* Duffy, *supra* note 176, at 299–300, 302–4, 306–11.

196. *Harper & Row, Inc. v. Nation Enterprises*, *supra* note 61. *See also Salinger v. Random House, Inc.*, *supra* note 77, at 95.

197. *Id.* at 551.

198. 15 U.S.C. §§ 1051 *et seq.*

199. *Dodd v. Fort Smith Special School District*, 666 F. Supp. 1278 (W.D. Ark. 1987).

200. *Id.* In another case, a publisher that planned to publish a collection of public-domain stories by the author Louis L'Amour was ordered to make clear on the book's cover and in its promotion that the author had nothing to do with the collections and that the stories were not new, and to redesign the proposed covers not to resemble the covers that appeared on the author's authorized books. The court stated that the publisher's proposed covers and promotion "have a tendency or capacity to deceive the relevant industry and the public into believing that [the author] either authored or participated in or authorized these two collections," which violated the author's rights under the federal Lanham Act and state unfair competition law. *L'Amour v. Carroll & Graf Publications, Inc.*, No. 83 Civ. 4658 (S.D.N.Y. 1983). *See also, Russell v. Turnbaugh*, 18 Med. L. Rptr 2189 (D. Colo. 1991).

201. *Preminger v. Columbia Pictures Corp.*, 49 Misc. 2d 363, 267 N.Y.S.2d 594 (S. Ct. N.Y. Co.) *aff'd*, 25 A.D.2d 830, 269 N.Y.S.2d 913 (1st Dept), *aff'd*, 18 N.Y.2d 659, 219 N.E.2d 436, 273 N.Y.S.2d

80 (1966); *Stevens v. NBC*, 148 U.S.P.Q. 755 (Super. Ct. L.A. Co. 1966).

202. *Gilliam v. ABC, Inc.*. 538 F.2d 14 (2d Cir. 1976).

203. *Id.* at 21.

204. *Id.* at 24.

205. *Id.*

206. *Id.*

207. *Id.*

208. *See Edison v. Viva International, Ltd.*, 421 N.Y.S.2d 203 (1st Dep't 1979). Although the moral right of an author, recognized in civil law countries but not in the United States, has an analogous right in the United States in judicial protection of the integrity and reputation of an author, when the parties have entered into a contract, that contract controls the so-called moral right and breach of the contract must be shown.

209. Cal. Civ. Code §987 (West 1979).

210. *Id.* 987(d).

211. *Jacobs v. Westoaks Realtors, Inc.*, *supra* note 186.

212. *Id.* at 644; 205 Cal. Rptr. at 624.

213. N.Y. Cult. Aff. L. §14.03 (McKinney Supp. 1990).

214. *Newman v. Delmar Realty Co.*, N.Y.L.J., June 11, 1984, at 12 (Sup. Ct., N.Y. Co.).

215. Connecticut Art Preservation and Artists' Rights Statute (C.G.S.A. §§42-116s, 116-t [1988]); Massachusetts Art Preservation Act (231 M.G.L.A. §85S [1985]); Pennsylvania Fine Arts Preservation Act (73 Pa. C.S.A. 161 §§2101-2105, 2108, 2121 [1986]).

216. Louisiana Artists' Authorship Rights Act (L.A.R.S. 51:2151 *et seq.* [1986]); Maine Moral Rights Statute (M.R.S.A. 27, §303 [1985]); Nevada (N.R.S. §598.970-976 [(1989]); New Jersey Artists' Rights Act (N.J.S.A. §2A:24A [1986]); Rhode Island Artist's Rights Act (1987 R.I.G.L. §§5-62-2–5-62-6). The statutes vary slightly concerning what works are covered, the standard for coverage, exclusions, and the interests protected.

217. *See, e.g.*, New Mexico Fine Art in Public Buildings, N.M. Stat. Ann. 13-4B-1–13-4B-3 (Michie 1990).

218. Pub. L. 101–650, Title VI, §603(a).

219. 17 U.S.C. §106A.

220. 17 U.S.C. §101.

221. *Wojnarowicz v. American Family Assn.*, 745 F. Supp. 131 (S.D.N.Y. 1990).

222. *Id.* at 147, *quoting Lerman v. Flynt Distrib. Co.*, 745 F.2d 123, 139 (2d Cir. 1984), *cert. denied*, 471 U.S. 1054 (1985).

223. The court's refusal to award damages because none were proved does not seem to be supported by the statute, which does not require a plaintiff to prove actual damage and provides for an award of "exemplary damages where appropriate."

224. *Id.* at 139.

225. *See* "France Gets 'Moral Right' Ruling," *Publishers Weekly*, July 25, 1991, p. 9.

226. *See generally* R. Callmann, *Unfair Competition Trademarks and Monopolies* (1982).

227. In fact, an attempt to secure trademark registration for *The Littles*, part of a title for a series of educational children's books, was refused because the term merely identified the main characters in the books and informed readers that that particular book was another one in a series about the Little family, and thus did not function as a trademark. *In re Scholastic Inc.*, 223 U.S.P.Q. 345 (T.T.A.B. 1983).

228. *Allen v. National Video, Inc.*, 610 F. Supp. 612 (S.D.N.Y. 1985).

229. *See generally* Nimmer ch. 16.

230. One theory of recovery in such cases might be for "unjust enrichment." *See Bevan v. Columbia Broadcasting System, Inc*, 175 U.S.P.Q. 475 (S.D.N.Y. 1972).

III

Contracts Involving Creative People

The author, artist, or other creative person who creates work solely for his own personal enjoyment or fulfillment and has no interest in selling or otherwise disseminating the work probably has no need to read this chapter. All others do, because almost any conceivable arrangement for the transfer, publication, or production of a work involves one or more contracts. Indeed, it is probably true that the contracts entered into by authors and artists will prove at least as important to them as the quality or popularity of their work.

We will first review some of the basic legal principles applicable to all contracts and then examine some of the most common contractual relationships involving creative people. Finally, we will deal with special legal problems and contractual concerns in such specific areas as publishing, screenwriting, theatrical production, rights acquisition, and the particular concerns of photographers and visual artists.

What is a contract?

A contract is a legally enforceable agreement or understanding reached between two or more parties about one or more subjects of interest to them. Contracts are often stated in writing, but many valid and enforceable contracts are not. In fact, many contracts are not even expressed orally; they are simply understood or "implied" by the conduct of the parties or the established customs of their business.

Not every agreement or understanding constitutes a binding contract. For example, an "agreement" between an author and a publisher that they do not desire to do business with each other would not be a contract. More significantly, a mere "agreement" or "understanding" between that author and publisher that they desire to do business together does not constitute a binding contract. An agreement or understanding must satisfy certain basic legal requirements before it will constitute a binding legal contract.

What are the legal requirements of a binding contract?

If you ask most lawyers, you will get a technically correct but largely incomprehensible response, including such terms as *offer, acceptance,* and *consideration.*[1] They will tell you that every contract requires them. However, in real life it is often impossible (and almost always irrelevant) to isolate these three factors.

It is probably more useful to see contracts as agreements in which each party commits itself to do something that it was not otherwise obligated to do, that commitment is acceptable to the other party, and in which the law will enforce the commitments or compensate for their breach.[2] The commitments or promises constitute the offer, acceptance, and consideration that the law requires.

For example, if an author agrees to allow publisher A to publish his book but the publisher remains noncommittal, no contract has been reached. If the publisher agrees to publish but the author remains noncommittal, there is still no contract. Only if they agree on publication does a contract exist. Moreover, the major components of the agreement must be discussed and agreed upon before the contract will be enforceable. If the sums to be paid the author are not included in the contract, the courts will almost certainly find it fatally incomplete and incapable of enforcement.

A recent case illustrates the point. John Cheever's widow entered into a formal written agreement with Academy Chicago Publishers for the publication of a book of some of her late husband's stories. The agreement, however, did not specify *which* stories; an editor was to help assemble and select the stories to be included, presumably with Mrs. Cheever. Mrs. Cheever subsequently wanted to terminate the relationship, and litigation ensued. The Illinois Supreme Court found that the agreement was too vague in too many critical respects to be enforceable:

> The agreement sheds no light on the minimum or maximum number of stories or pages necessary for publication of the collection, nor is there any implicit language from which we can glean the intentions of the parties with respect to this essential contract term. The publishing

agreement is similarly silent with respect to who will decide which stories will be included in the collection.[3]

This decision created considerable concern on the part of book publishers, who feared that it could jeopardize many of their existing contracts. At the same time, others proclaimed that the Academy-Cheever contract was not typical of most publishing agreements and that the decision posed no such threat.[4] Only future cases will establish which view is correct.

Who may enter into a contract?

Individuals and business entities such as corporations and partnerships can enter into binding contracts unless the law declares that they do not have the "capacity" to do so.[5] People who are insane or otherwise declared "incompetent" do not have this capacity, and in many states neither do children under a certain age (18 or 21); their contracts have to be approved by a legal guardian or parent. A loosely formed organization such as a local block association or ad hoc committee lacks the capacity to enter into contracts in its own name unless it establishes a more formal structure or members of the group join the contract as parties.

Is there a limit to how many parties can enter into a contract?

Except where the law decrees otherwise (as in the "contract" for marriage), the answer is no. Contracts involving authors and artists often have many parties, including several contributors to a work and several publishers. But most contracts are entered into between two parties. Note that the document of one "contract" can contain several contracts in the eyes of the law.

Are there contracts the law will refuse to enforce?

Yes. Contracts to commit crimes or otherwise violate the law will not be enforced.[6] Contracts that violate the prevailing "public policy," even though not technically illegal, may also be refused enforcement. For example, in one case an author had entered into a contract with a celebrity;[7] they agreed that the celebrity's name would appear as the author of the book.

When the celebrity changed his mind, the author sued to enforce the contract. But the court refused, holding that since the purpose of the contract was to perpetrate a fraud on the public, the contract was unenforceable. (The court was careful to distinguish this situation from the usual agreements among coauthors, collaborators, and even ghostwriters, the validity of which it did not question.)

Beginning in the late 1980s, some politically conservative politicians sought to require the National Endowment for the Arts (NEA), the federal agency established to help fund artistic projects, to include in its funding contracts provisions requiring the recipients not to create certain kinds of work with the grants. At the same time, other political voices sought to continue NEA funding without any restrictions (as was the case previously). For a brief period, recipients of NEA grants were required to sign agreements to the effect that none of works created or presented through the grants could be considered "obscene, including but not limited to depictions of sadomasochism, homoeroticism, the sexual exploitation of children, or individuals engaged in sex acts and which, when taken as a whole, do not have serious literary, artistic, political or scientific value."[8] But that requirement was challenged in court, and ultimately Congress rescinded it and replaced it with a directive that NEA's chairman "shall insure [*sic*] that artistic excellence and artistic merit are the criteria by which applications are judged, taking into consideration general standards of decency and respect for the diverse beliefs and values of the American public." That directive has also been challenged as a violation of the First Amendment.

Contracts that are entered into as a result of force or duress will not be enforced,[9] but mere "hard bargaining" will not free a contracting party. If a publisher told an author that if he did not sign the publisher's proposed contract, the publisher would destroy the author's only copy of the manuscript, that would be duress and would lead a court to declare the contract unenforceable. However, if the publisher knew it was the only firm interested in the book and offered the author a minuscule advance on a take-it-or-leave-it basis, such bargaining, however "unfair" or disadvantageous, would not be duress.

Otherwise, the parties to a contract are free to structure their agreement as they please, no matter how unorthodox, difficult, or "unfair" their agreements may seem. In general, the law will not protect or rescue parties from foolish contracts that meet the basic legal requirements.[10]

When must a contract be in writing to be enforceable?

Whenever the applicable law says so. For example, every state has enacted what is called a Statute of Frauds.[11] Under these statutes, contracts that cannot by their own terms be fully performed within a single year must be in writing to be enforceable. A contract to hire a collaborator to work on a project for two years or a contract to publish a book not sooner than a year after the contract is signed has to be in writing. Most states also provide that contracts involving at least some specified amount of money must be in writing. In addition, the U.S. Copyright Act,[12] as well as other state and federal laws, requires that specified agreements, such as the transfer of a copyright or the grant of an exclusive right in a copyrighted work,[13] be in writing.

Even if the law does not require a contract to be written, it is almost always advisable. Memories are unreliable, and it may often be difficult to reconstruct an agreement from the memories of the parties. More important, the exercise of reducing an agreement to writing usually forces the parties to focus on the terms of their agreement and deal with the contingencies that may arise. This can only enhance the effectiveness and enforceability of the contract. To be enforceable, the written contract should contain all the major rights and obligations that compose the agreement.

Is a lawyer necessary for a binding written contract?

Almost always, no. Binding contracts can be quite informal, as in a letter or an exchange of letters among the parties. It is rare that the law requires that a particular form or particular formalities be used. But the more complicated the contract and the more at stake, the more advisable it is to seek the assistance of a lawyer or similar person who is experienced in drafting such agreements. Such persons can usually anticipate potential problems and help ensure that the agreement is as clear and enforceable as possible.

Although many contracting parties (including most publishers, producers, and galleries), have standard forms that they insist be used in their agreements, the law does not require any particular form. Those parties almost invariably are prepared to modify at least some of the terms of their forms while negotiating an agreement. No one should assume that because a proposed contract is set forth on a printed form, it cannot or should not be challenged or changed. Sometimes each party has her own printed form, and the parties use neither and create a new form.

What happens if the parties to a contract disagree about what it provides or one party claims that the other has breached the contract?

Usually they try to resolve their differences by themselves, perhaps with the help of one or more third parties. This is almost always preferable to taking the matter to court because contract litigation is usually time-consuming and expensive, and often produces results unsatisfactory to all parties. Indeed, many agreements are providing for various forms of alternative dispute resolution (ADR, as it has come to be called in the legal profession), which can be as informal as the two parties' agreeing to meet with a third party mediator to facilitate the parties' reaching their own agreement or can involve the appointment of a neutral third party to render a binding or recommended decision. Critical to any ADR clause is a commitment by each of the parties to attempt to resolve any dispute before either party resorts to litigation or formal arbitration.

Arbitration is usually quicker and less expensive than in-court litigation. The parties present their dispute to one or more (often three) arbitrators (often experienced in the industry which is the subject of the contract) who have the power to render a full and final resolution to the dispute. Parties to arbitration may, but are not required to, have lawyers. The advantages of arbitration are economy and efficiency. Disadvantages are that arbitrators are not bound by legal precedents and can render almost any decision they consider appropriate and that a party unhappy with an arbitrator's decision cannot appeal it.

All the parties must agree before a dispute can be submitted to arbitration. As a general rule, the party who can least afford the costs of court litigation will desire arbitration; the party who is better able to afford to litigate will not. Arbitration clauses are especially appropriate (and most common) in collaboration agreements and the like where quickness and economy are important.

How do the courts deal with vague or incomplete contracts?

Often, especially with oral or very casual contracts, the parties fail to anticipate contingencies or leave a provision of the contract so vague that it is essentially meaningless. Suppose a collaborator gets sick and can't work for two months. The vague clause that refers to "incapacitation for a significant period of time" becomes important. If the parties cannot resolve their differences, the courts (or arbitrators) will resolve the differences for them.

The courts will first try to decipher the intentions of the parties.[14] They scour the terms of the agreement for clues. If possible, they resolve the dispute from the terms of the agreement. But if that doesn't work, the courts will examine the surrounding circumstances and if necessary consider the established "customs" or "practices" in the field and be inclined to assume that the parties intended to conform to these customs and practices.[15] Many oral or "handshake" contracts, where the parties don't bother even to express their agreement out loud, will be "construed" or "implied" by the courts using these techniques.

Not every contract can be salvaged this way. Sometimes a provision is so crucial to the agreement and yet so indecipherable that the courts will conclude that there never was an enforceable contract. For example, a publishing agreement that called upon the author to deliver the book "as soon as he was satisfied with it" would probably be found so vague as to be "illusory" and thus unenforceable. This shows how important it is for the parties to be as specific and objective as they can.

How do the courts enforce contracts?

In several ways. First, in appropriate cases, they can issue orders compelling parties to perform their obligations under the contract (*specific performance*), and they can issue injunctions prohibiting parties from engaging in conduct in breach of the contract.[16] Such orders are available, in general, only where the remedy of money damages would not adequately compensate for the breach and where the comparative fairness of the situation (the "equities") justifies the granting of extra-ordinary relief.[17]

Most of the time, however, the courts will require the breaching party to compensate the nonbreaching party for the consequences of the breach with money.[18] Not every breach causes injury; if it doesn't, the nonbreaching party is entitled only to a nominal award.[19] Even more important, not every breach causes provable injury. For example, if an author fails to deliver his manuscript as promised or if the publisher fails to publish it as promised, it is likely that the nonbreaching party will suffer some injury as a result, but before the courts allow recovery of money damages, the party claiming the injury will be required to prove (and not just speculate or surmise) that the injury was sustained and to offer a rational way to calculate the damages. In the absence of such proof, the nonbreaching party may not recover anything.[20]

Finally, depending on how serious the breach is, the courts can declare the contract terminated or keep it in effect and compensate for the breach. If a publisher is two weeks late in making royalty payments or underpays royalties by a small amount, it is unlikely that a court will terminate the contract. But if the publisher refuses to make any royalty payments or is found to have deliberately underpaid royalties by a substantial amount, the outcome may be different.[21]

THE AUTHOR-AGENT CONTRACT

People tend to be good at what they're good at and not so good at other things. Creative people are no exception. They may be very good at writing books but not very good at (and not very interested in) doing what is necessary to ensure that a book is published and otherwise disseminated on terms that are fair to the author. Or a screenwriter may have written a great script but have no idea how to get it to the attention of potential producers, so that it remains in the screenwriter's desk drawer. For this reason, many creative people enter into contracts with agents (or representatives).

What does an agent do?

Many things. First, the agent will "represent" (i.e., attempt to sell) the author's work to appropriate parties (publishers, producers, galleries, etc.). Second, when a sale is made, the agent will handle the negotiation of the terms of the contract. Third, the agent will oversee and collect all payments due the author or artist and attempt to ensure that the other party is complying fully with all contractual obligations. Fourth, the agent will explore, and often handle, other markets for the author's work, such as a motion-picture or television adaptation. And fifth, a good agent will give a client valuable advice and guidance about the client's work.[22]

What should the agency contract include?

As much of the parties' agreement as possible, preferably in writing. For example, does the relationship apply only to one work of the author or artist or all the work? Does it cover the world or only parts of it? Does it apply to the representation of the author-artist's work in all media or only some? Does the agent have the authority to commit the author-artist? Is the representation to be handled by one agent, or is any individual in the agency authorized to act for the author-artist? What compensation is the agent entitled to? What expenses should the agent be reimbursed for? What happens if the relationship is terminated?

All these questions, and many more, should be discussed and agreed upon before a creative person and an agent enter into a contract. Again, although it is not legally required that the agreement be in writing, simply considering these issues and setting down the parties' resolution of them will help ensure that there will be clarity and communication in the parties' relationship. And unfortunately questions that are not answered at the outset may have to be answered later, when one or both parties may be at a disadvantage.

What if a creative person works in more than one medium?

Then it's obviously important to have an agent that also works in more than one medium or at least has cooperating arrangements with other agents who work in those media the first agent doesn't. An author writing a novel for publication may be represented by a terrific agent in the publishing arena, but that agent may be less effective in handling a rights-acquisition agreement for a film based on the novel. In such cases, it would be important for that agent to have a cooperating arrangement with another agent who could properly represent the client's interests. Similarly, if the author wishes to write the screenplay, the agent has to be able to negotiate that arrangement. Authors wishing to write in more than one medium should ascertain a prospective agent's ability and contacts in those areas.

Does the law impose requirements on the author-agent relationship?

Yes. The law considers the agent a *fiduciary* of the author, a person who holds a special position of trust and therefore owes the author full loyalty and honesty.[23] In most contractual relationships, the parties are said to be at "arm's length," but an agent owes a much higher personal duty to an author. The courts will therefore scrutinize the agent's conduct closely.

Because the relationship is a fiduciary one, the law provides that either party can terminate the relationship at will.[24] However, even after termination, the agent may be entitled to compensation for services already performed. This can become particularly difficult if an author discharges his first agent and the new agent begins dealing with the publisher of that author's previously published books. Disputes can arise on the question of which agent is entitled to the commission on income from those books, the first agent arguing that she made the sale and the second arguing that he is doing the follow-up and maintaining communication with the publisher. If the parties are unable to agree about the aftermath of termination, the courts (or arbitrators) will resolve the question.

Many agents include in their contracts a clause that their relationship with their clients is an "agency coupled with an interest."[25] This gives the agent more rights; for example, the agency cannot be terminated at will. However, the mere declaration of "an agency coupled with an interest" does not suffice to make it one; the law requires that such an agent have an interest in the subject of the agency—for example, a financial investment in the project—other than the right to receive commissions or other compensation.[26] Creative people should discuss such a clause if it is proposed and agree on what it is supposed to mean.

COLLABORATION

Many creative efforts are collaborative. Sometimes the contributions are essentially equal (two people working together to research and write a historical novel or biography), while at other times the contributions may be very different, as where one person provides research or expertise to a playwright for the development of a play. All such collaborations require agreements.

What should a collaboration contract include?

As many specifics as possible, preferably in writing. For example, exactly what is each collaborator promising to do? Are there deadlines? How will disagreements be resolved? Who will have the authority to enter into contracts for the work? Who will own the copyright and other literary property rights in the work? Who will own the physical property? How will expenses be shared? How will earnings be divided? How will credit for the work be determined? What happens if a collaborator fails to fulfill his obligations or becomes incapacitated or dies? What about future works, especially works based on this one? Who will represent the work?

These important questions should be addressed and answered, in writing, at the beginning of the relationship. The entire project can be jeopardized (not to mention the emotional, professional, and financial well-being of the parties) if such questions are left to a time when it may be much harder to reach an amicable agreement.

Does the law impose any provisions on the collaboration relationship?

Some, but not many. Perhaps the most important are the provisions in the U.S. Copyright Act on "joint works."

Section 101 of the Act defines a *joint work* as "a work prepared by two or more authors with the intention that their contributions be merged into inseparable or interdependent parts of a unitary whole."[27] It is not necessary that the collaborators work together, work simultaneously, or even know each other. The crucial element is whether each contributor prepares her contribution with the knowledge and intention that it will be merged with the contribution of others as "inseparable or interdependent parts of a unitary whole."

Almost all collaborations on a written work, or collaborations between an author and an artist or photographer where the intention is to create a unitary whole, qualify as joint works for copyright purposes. The Copyright Act provides that "the authors [creators] of a joint work are co-owners of copyright in the work."[28] All the co-owners are presumed to own equal interests. Each co-owner is free to use or authorize others to use the work so long as he accounts to the other co-owners for the profits, and each is free to sell or otherwise convey his ownership interest and pass it on to heirs. The consent of all the owners is necessary to convey the entire copyright or grant any exclusive right related to the work.

In the absence of an agreement providing otherwise, the collaborators' rights in the work will be as set forth in the Copyright Act. Many collaboration relationships contemplate different arrangements, which makes it imperative that the collaborators agree on such issues and reduce their agreement to a written contract.

Are there form collaboration contracts?

In 1989, the Dramatists Guild, Inc., the professional organization for playwrights and dramatists, promulgated a draft form of collaboration agreement. Particularly because a musical play is often an effort involving more than one individual working in collaboration, the Guild determined that it would be advisable to have a draft for use by its members.

The Guild draft provides that copyright in the created work be jointly owned by all of the collaborators. Each collaborator under the Guild agreement could theoretically enter into agreements for the exploitation of the work, subject to accounting to the other parties.[29] However, it is unlikely that any producer would be willing to acquire rights in a play unless the grant was exclusive, and all the parties would have to agree to grant exclusivity.

THE AUTHOR-PUBLISHER CONTRACT

Except for the rare author who is self-published,[30] anyone who expects her work to be published must eventually enter into one or more contracts with publishers. These contracts can be extremely important to the author.

Unlike the situation in other media,[31] in the American book-publishing world there are no industrywide minimum terms for the author-publisher agreement.[32] Most major publishers of newspapers, magazines, and books have developed their own standard contract forms. However, as indicated above, authors should not assume that clauses in printed forms cannot be questioned or negotiated and should feel free to question any point in a form agreement they do not understand or agree with. Nevertheless, the use of such forms probably gives the publisher an advantage in negotiations since they put the author in the position of having to seek changes in the form rather than having both parties start negotiations on an equal footing. As in any field, the success an author has in negotiating a contract depends largely on his bargaining power; some authors inevitably have more power than others.

It is not our purpose to review in detail all of the usual provisions of author-publisher contracts. For guidance, an author should consult her literary agent or the comprehensive guides to author-publisher contracts prepared by the Author's Guild[33] and the P.E.N. American Center.[34] We will concentrate on the aspects of such contracts that have generated legal precedents or have the most direct legal significance for the author.

The provisions of a publishing contract depend in large part on the nature of the work and the publisher. Freelance articles written for newspapers or magazines involve significantly different considerations than books and can vary widely, from agreements for one-time use only to a blanket work-for-hire agreement. Textbooks are covered by contracts substantially different from contracts for "trade" books (the kind sold in bookstores), and trade book contracts vary, depending on the nature, size, and expense of producing the book. Most of our discussion is concerned with the typical trade book contract, but reference will also be made to other kinds of written work.

What is the essential component of every author-publisher contract?

What is sometimes called the *grant of rights*. As discussed in Chapter II, the author of an article, short story, or book begins as the owner of the copyright in the work.[35] As such, the author completely controls the destiny of the work. When an author and a publisher agree on publication, the author agrees to "grant" certain rights in the work to that publisher. The contract should set forth the nature and extent of these rights and the rights the author is not granting to the publisher but "reserving" to himself.

It is common for a publisher of magazine articles and stories to be granted very limited rights, usually the right to publish the work once in a magazine (and perhaps again in a collection or anthology drawn from the magazine).[36] But magazine publishers often seek much broader rights, even all the rights, and the author must negotiate about this.

Books are somewhat different. A publisher's standard contract usually states (before negotiation, anyway) that the author grants all, or almost all, her rights in the book to the publisher and that the publisher is obligated to pay the author specified royalties or other sums for those rights. Such an "all-rights" grant would include not only the right to publish the book in English in the United States but also the right to publish it in every language everywhere (and to authorize others to do so); the right to authorize others to base a movie, TV show or series, or stage play on the book; and the right to authorize others to manufacture and sell T-shirts, toys, and other commercial items based on the book or characters in the book. The rights in a book other than the right to publish it in book form are often called *subsidiary rights*.

The author (or agent) may not wish to grant all rights to the publisher; he may want to limit the grant to, say, the right to publish the book in the United States (and Canada) and limited subsidiary rights, including the right to authorize others to publish excerpts from the book and to sell the book through book clubs. In such instances, the author wishes to reserve such other rights as "foreign" rights; motion-picture, stage, and television rights; and "merchandising" rights, together with the right to dispose of such rights as the author sees fit.

Most trade-book authors today are particularly interested in the form in which their books will be published. Traditionally, trade books are published first in hardcover; then (usually a year later) a paperback edition might be published. In recent years, however, it has become increasingly common for books to be published only in paperback or in simultaneous hardcover and "trade paperback" editions. A few authors with rare bargaining power retain the paperback rights, granting only hardcover rights to their publishers. Other authors, who grant paperback rights to the hardcover publisher on the understanding that that publisher will license those rights to another publisher, will seek the right to approve the paperback publisher and the terms of the license that the hardcover publisher grants to the paperback publisher.

Also, many authors seek clauses that require the publisher to pay the author's share of major subsidiary-rights income immediately upon receipt, at least where advance payments to the author have been recovered by the publisher, instead of holding the money until the next scheduled royalty payment.

Authors should be as clear as possible about what is and is not being granted to the publisher in the publishing contract. Authors should also understand and be satisfied with the payments the publisher is agreeing to make, including royalty rates on book sales, the author's share of major subsidiary-rights income, and the "advance" (a payment trade publishers usually agree to pay before the book is written, much less published, that is "advanced" against royalties which will be due the author from sales of the work after it is published). An unclear contract can mean a messy court case later.

What are the author's obligations under a standard publishing contract?

The author's principal obligation in almost all book contracts and most magazine contracts is to deliver by a specified time a manuscript that the publisher finds "acceptable" or "satisfactory." The most common formulation is that the manuscript must be "satisfactory to the publisher in form and content."

The full legal significance of such clauses is far from clear, and they have recently been the subject of several important court cases.[37] Traditionally, such clauses have been interpreted to mean that the publisher had virtually unlimited discretion to decide whether the manuscript as delivered was acceptable. If it wasn't, the publisher had the right under the contract to declare the contract terminated and require the author to return any advance payments. And the publisher could base that determination solely on its own evaluation of the literary merits or financial prospects of the book. Under that traditional approach, the author was almost completely at the mercy of the publisher's discretion. The only limitation was that the publisher had to act in "good faith," a limitation one federal court found violated in an important 1982 case.[38]

The case involved a publishing agreement between (1) Senator Barry Goldwater and Stephen Shadegg, an experienced writer, who were to collaborate on a book of the senator's memoirs, and (2) Harcourt Brace Jovanovich, a major publisher. The contract had the standard "satisfactory to the publisher in form and content" requirement. After seeking but not getting editorial guidance from the publisher, the authors submitted their manuscript. The publisher found the manuscript unacceptable, formally rejected it, and then demanded that the authors return a $65,000 advance. When the authors refused to return that advance, the publisher sued.

After a full trial, the court rejected the publisher's claim in its entirety. With respect to the "satisfactory" clause, the court recognized the "very considerable discretion" the publisher had but then stated:

> It cannot be, however, that the publisher has absolutely unfettered license to act or not to act in any way it wishes and to accept or reject a book for any reason whatever. If this were the case, the publisher could simply make a contract and arbitrarily change its mind and that would be an illusory contract. It is no small thing for an author to enter into a contract with a publisher and be locked in with that publisher and prevented from marketing the book elsewhere.[39]

Before a book can be rejected as "unsatisfactory," the court held, the publisher must undertake certain editorial duties:

> some reasonable degree of communication with the authors, an interchange with the authors about the specifics of what the publisher desires; about what specific faults are found; what items should be omitted or eliminated; what items should be added; what organizational defects exist, and so forth. If faults are found in the writing style, it seems elementary that there should be discussion and illustrations of what those defects of style are. All of this is necessary in order to allow the author the reasonable

opportunity to perform to the satisfaction of the publisher. If this editorial work is not done by the publisher, the result is that the author is misled and, in fact, is virtually prevented from performing under the contract.[40]

Goldwater was an extreme case of the publisher's failure to perform. In a similar situation involving the rejection of a manuscript and dispute over the return of the advance but one where the publisher did provide editorial services, the publisher was found to have acted in good faith and well within its rights under the clause.[41] "A publisher may, in its discretion, terminate a standard publishing contract, provided that the termination is made in good faith, and that the failure of an author to submit a satisfactory manuscript was not caused by the publisher's bad faith."[42] In another situation, a publisher was held justified in rejecting a fiction manuscript when the agreement called for delivery of a nonfiction manuscript on the subject.[43] In other words, if the publisher renders at least some editorial guidance, its discretion is broad, and no author will want to litigate the validity of a publisher's rejection of a manuscript. It is preferable to deal with the possibility of rejection when the contract is made.

Several approaches can be explored. First, the contract can require the publisher to give the author a written statement of defects found in the manuscript and a period of time (e.g., 30 or 60 days) to correct the defects. Second, the contract can attach the outline, proposal, or sample materials the author had already shown the publisher, with a clause added that the book will be acceptable to the publisher if it is in substantial conformity with those materials. Third, the contract can incorporate a clause, proposed by the Authors Guild, stating that the manuscript must be "professionally competent and fit for publication," which the Guild considers an objective criterion compared to the subjectivity of the standard clause.[44] Fourth, the contract can include a provision for arbitration to determine whether the manuscript has been properly rejected. Fifth, the contract can provide that if the publisher rejects the book, the author is obligated only to repay the advance out of the first proceeds received from any other publisher for the book. (This is commonly called a *first-proceeds* clause.) Finally, if the author is relying on a particular editor at the publishing company and believes the book may be rejected if the editor leaves the company, a clause can state that the author may terminate the contract if the editor leaves the company before a decision is made on the book.

It may be difficult to get a publisher to agree to any of these clauses, but that does not mean the effort should not be made.

What are the publisher's obligations?

At least one court has ruled that a publisher is obliged to provide editorial assistance to an author, especially if the author requests it.[45]

A publisher who accepts a manuscript has the obligation to publish the book in good faith. Some publishers' form contracts do not contain such an affirmative obligation; however, the courts would probably construe the contract as requiring the publisher to proceed with publication in good faith since otherwise the contract would be "illusory." Authors should ensure that their contracts contain an affirmative duty to publish, preferably within a stated period (e.g., 1 year or 18 months after the book is accepted).

What is meant by the term *publish* is less than clear even in the publishing industry, as a recent case demonstrated. It is often customary for a hardcover publisher of a book to license another publisher to do a paperback edition. To make sure the hardcover publisher has enough time to sell as many hardcover copies as possible, these licenses often provide time limits on when the paperback publisher may start publishing its version of the book. In this case, the hardcover publisher of *The Hunt for Red October* claimed that Berkley Publishing Group, the licensee of the paperback publishing rights, had jumped the agreed-upon "not sooner than" October 1 date by shipping copies and having them available for sale in September.[46] The hardcover publisher claimed that as soon as the paperback edition became available, sales of the hardcover edition declined more than 80 percent. Berkley argued that the industry custom was to ship and make available a paperback edition before the "pub date" and thus it had not published the work in violation of the agreement.

The court found that the term *publication* was undefined in the agreement and that the parties' intentions on this issue were unclear. The hardcover publisher argued that the copy-

right law's definition of *publish*—"the distribution of copies
. . . of a work . . . [or t]he offering to distribute copies for
purposes of further distribution"[47]—should apply, and since
Berkley had shipped earlier than October 1, it had breached
the agreement. But Berkley convinced the trial judge that
shipment and sale prior to the agreed "pub date" was standard
in the industry and not a breach of the agreement.

The federal appeals court disagreed. Although the court held
that there were definitions of *publish* other than the one in the
copyright law, it also held that permitting substantial sales prior
to the agreed date would render meaningless the language that
the paperback edition would be published "not sooner than"
that date when that was included in the agreement to permit
a sufficient period to maximize hardcover sales. Thus the court
found that by shipping prior to October 1, Berkley had
breached the agreement and was liable to the hardcover publisher for damages.

Another federal decision has elaborated somewhat on the
publisher's duty to publish.[48] The author of an unflattering book
about the Du Pont family sued his publisher (and the Du Pont
company) because of the way the book was published and
promoted. The author claimed that as a result of pressure from
the company, the publisher significantly restricted its activities
on behalf of the book, thus breaching its contractual duty to
publish. The publisher contended that it acted fairly, reasonably, and responsibly in publishing and promoting the book
and that all of its actions were taken for legitimate business
reasons.

Although the federal appeals court disagreed with the lower
court's holding that the publisher had breached the publishing
contract, it nevertheless declared that a publisher has an implied contractual duty "to make certain efforts in publishing a
book it has accepted," including "a good faith effort to promote
the book including a first printing and advertising budget adequate to give the book a reasonable chance of achieving market
success in light of the subject matter and likely audience."[49]
But once such "reasonable initial promotion activities" are
made, "all that is required is a good faith business judgment"[50]
about how the book should be handled.

Thus authors have at least one legal precedent if they believe
their publishers have failed to publish their books in good faith.

But this does not mean that authors can tell their publishers how to publish their books or that the courts will second-guess the day-to-day decisions every publisher makes. Publishers still have (and probably must have) great discretion to decide how much energy and resources to put into each book they publish, and it seems likely that the courts will interfere only if they are persuaded that the publisher acted in bad faith or with no "sound business reason," something that is usually hard to prove.[51]

Authors can attempt to ensure that publishers publish their books vigorously. First, they should seek as large an advance payment of royalties as possible, since publishers often work harder to recoup a large investment, even with a book that disappoints them. Second, authors can try to impose specific obligations on their publishers; for example, to print a specified number of copies in the first printing of the book or to spend a specified sum of money on promoting the book, perhaps including a promotional tour by the author. Such clauses will usually be difficult to obtain, but the effort should be made.

Finally, a publisher is obligated to report sales and other exploitation of the book periodically to the author and to pay the sums due according to that report. Most publishers' form contracts permit the publisher to withhold some royalties as a reserve against returns of books shipped to bookstores; many authors and agents try to negotiate restrictions on these "reserves for returns." They also seek to require the publisher to report the number of copies printed, copies sold at particular discounts, copies returned, and so on, since many publishers provide only the sketchiest information about such matters. It is common for the author to have the right, at the author's expense, to review the publisher's financial records relating to the author's work. Such clauses usually provide that if errors to the author's detriment over a specified level (say, 5 percent) are found, the publisher must pay for the review. Authors should always try to have such clauses included in their publishing contracts.[52]

How are the author's royalties computed?

Generally, on the basis of the number of copies sold. Royalty amounts may be negotiated, although with hardcover trade editions there is not much room for maneuvering. The hardcover publishing standard is a royalty of 10 percent of the retail price on the first 5,000 books sold, 12.5 percent on the next 5,000 books, and 15 percent on all copies thereafter (i.e., all copies after 10,000). Some publishers will not grant a first-time author a royalty higher than 10 percent, and some established authors are able to insist on a 15 percent royalty from the first sale. With paperback sales, most publishers pay royalties as a percentage of the retail price, but the percentages differ— usually half the hardcover rate—and the increase levels differ, often in 100,000-copy increments. Where the royalty is based on the "retail price" of a work, the agreement may provide for the reduction of the stated cover price of the book to permit the publisher to deduct shipping costs.

Some trade-paperback publishers provide a royalty based on net amounts received by the publisher from sales of the work rather than a royalty based on the retail price, and in such cases the royalty percentage is likely to be the same as the hardcover percentages, although the step increases are likely to be after a larger number of sales than for hardcover books. In all cases, though, even if step increases in royalty are built in, publishers often seek to provide that for a small reprinting of the work, the author's royalty should not exceed the base amount, regardless of total number of copies sold.

Exploitation of other types of rights granted to the publisher (e.g., licenses to book clubs, licenses of rights to foreign publishers, sale of unbound copies or sheets outside of the United States, direct-mail circulation, and perhaps most important, paperback-rights licenses) are computed on a simpler basis, the author receiving a percentage of the income realized by the publisher for those rights, which percentage usually ranges from 50 percent to as high as 90 percent, depending on, among other things, the specific rights involved. Finally, the agreement will often provide for a reduction of the stated royalty in the event the publisher sells copies of the book at a larger than normal discount to distributors or for certain "special" sales (such as sales to a single buyer of a large number of copies, who will use them for gift or promotional purposes) and for retail sales directly from the publisher.

Obviously, how a publisher accounts for its sales can make a tremendous difference in income to an author, and although custom in the industry is fairly clear about what royalty category a particular sale should fall into, this is not without possible manipulation. In one case,[53] the court upheld an author's claim that his publisher improperly classified a sale as a "special sale" instead of a regular trade sale, with the result that the publisher made a much lower payment to the author than otherwise required, even though the contract provided that the publisher could sell books at such prices as it deemed appropriate.

An author's remedies if he successfully proves a publisher's failure to pay royalties or to pay those contractually provided depends on the extent of the publisher's failure to pay. Unless there has been an extreme case of nonpayment, an author is not likely to be awarded cancellation of the contract with the rights being returned to him.[54] In one case, there was a bona fide dispute concerning nonpayment of a portion of royalties, and thus the publisher's failure to pay fully did not establish a breach of contract entitling the author to cancellation.[55] However, where the publisher willfully and substantially failed to pay an author two-thirds of the total amount of royalties due from a best-selling book, the breach was held "material" and the author entitled to cancellation.[56]

What happens if a lawsuit is brought against an author because of something published?

First you cry. Then you quickly look up the provisions in your publishing agreement that deal with this contingency.

In most form contracts from publishers—indeed, as we shall see, in most agreements for the publication or production of any work—the author makes many "representations" and "warranties" to the publisher and agrees to "indemnify" the publisher against losses if certain contingencies occur. The author "represents" that nothing in the book is obscene, libelous, or otherwise illegal; invades anyone's right of privacy; infringes any copyright or other literary property right; causes any injury or violates anyone's legal rights. The author will reimburse, fully indemnify and "hold harmless" the publisher from—any expense (including its attorneys' fees and any damage award or settlement) incurred from any claim asserted against the book, even if the claim is without merit. Under such clauses, the author can be held responsible for the publisher's expenses even if the author did not breach any representations to the publisher, simply because a claim was asserted.

Understandably, many authors and agents consider these provisions grossly unfair, and more and more publishers have come to agree. This is especially true if the publisher has conducted, with the author's full cooperation, a legal review of the book and has declared the book legally suitable for publication. It seems difficult to justify requiring the author to serve as a backup insurer if the publisher's evaluation is wrong.

First, authors and agents can seek to restrict the author's representations to the publisher so that they are made "to the best of his or her knowledge." Second, they can seek to limit the author's obligation to indemnify the publisher to amounts paid pursuant to final court judgments. Third, they can ask the publisher to share equally the costs and payments before (and perhaps even including) a final judgment. Last and perhaps most important, they can demand that the publisher extend its insurance coverage to cover the author for such claims, so that except for a specified deductible, the author will be protected through the publisher's insurance.[57]

Such provisions, especially the insurance coverage, are becoming increasingly available. Authors should make every effort to secure this kind of protection.

What about other works by the author?

Most book publishers' form contracts contain two clauses dealing with other works by the author. First they provide in very broad terms that the author agrees not to publish any work that would "tend to compete with, or interfere with the sale of, the book" that is the subject of the contract. Second, they usually grant the publisher some form of "option" on the author's next book or books.

Many authors and agents are deeply troubled by standard "competitive-works" clauses because they are so vague that it is almost impossible to know what they mean. Courts have not interpreted them yet. It seems likely that if a case was brought, the courts would limit the clause to avoid constricting the author's ability to continue to write and publish. Nevertheless, it is important for authors to attempt to narrow the scope of such clauses when the contract is entered into, perhaps by the deletion of phrases such as *tend to* and the insertion of words such as *directly and significantly* before the word *compete*. It may also be appropriate to limit the duration of the clause to a year or two after the book is first published.[58]

Option clauses are equally troublesome. Sometimes they provide that the author is required to submit her next book-length work to the publisher before submitting it to any other publisher and that the publisher has the option to publish the work on the terms of the present contract. Although such a provision may be grossly unfair to the author, it is probably enforceable since it is specific on all of the necessary terms. It should be resisted as strongly as possible.

Some form contracts state that the publisher has the option to publish the author's next work on "terms to be agreed upon." Such clauses, however, have been held by several courts to be too vague (mere "agreements to agree") and thus unenforceable.[59] They should still be resisted.

Finally, under some form contracts the author agrees to give the publisher the first opportunity to consider and negotiate for the author's next book, and then perhaps the right to match any other publisher's offer. These clauses may well be enforceable. Although they are not as harsh as the option "on the same terms," they restrict the freedom of the author to control his future work and should be resisted. If the relationship between author and publisher has been good, no option clause should be necessary. If it has not been good, no option clause is appropriate.[60]

What about sequels and revisions?

Publishers of some kinds of books, notably textbooks, usually provide in their form contracts that they will have the right to decide whether sequels or revised editions of the book should be published and the right to have such editions prepared by others if the original author cannot or will not prepare them.[61] Textbook authors should be especially concerned about such provisions and should attempt to limit them. The contract can require the publisher to give the author the first opportunity to prepare further editions at a specified compensation, or at least the right to approve such editions if they are prepared by others. Also, textbook authors should seek compensation from future editions, even if they do not prepare them. They can also seek the right to have their names removed from future editions if they had nothing to do with them.

Some trade-book publishing contracts contain similar provisions, but they are less common and tend to be less important to trade-book publishers than textbook publishers. Trade-book authors should strongly resist any attempt by their publishers to have such control over subsequent editions. As long as the first contract remains in effect, a revised edition of the original book probably could not be issued by another publisher because it would probably infringe on the exclusive rights to the book granted to the first publisher. A sequel, however, could be published by another publisher unless the first contract forbids it or a "noncompete" clause is read *very* broadly.

How long do publishing contracts remain in effect?

Most book-publishing contracts remain in effect for the full term of the copyright in the book, the life of the author plus 50 years.[62] However, there are several ways the contract may be terminated earlier.

First, most book-publishing contracts contain "out-of-print" clauses that provide that if the book is out of print (which means there are few or no copies still available for sale), the author can demand that the publisher print additional copies within a specified time. If the publisher fails to do so, the author can terminate the contract and get back all rights previously granted to the publisher. Such clauses are often vague about when a book is out of print; frequently they provide that a book cannot be out of print if there are licenses in effect for the publication of the book by another publisher, even if no such books have been published. Authors and agents often seek to revise standard out-of-print clauses to be as specific and protective of the author's interests as possible.[63]

Many standard publishing contracts provide that if the publisher goes out of business, becomes insolvent, or files for bankruptcy, the contracts are terminated and all rights revert to the author. Although the legal validity of such provisions is open to question,[64] authors should seek to incorporate as much of this protection as they can.

Finally, publishing agreements often provide that the publisher's rights to the book can be "assigned" (i.e., given or sold) to another publisher. Particularly if the author has chosen the original publisher because of its reputation or special abilities, the author should seek to limit the publisher's right to assign, perhaps by making the assignment subject to the author's approval or limiting the assignments to a related company or to another company that is acquiring all of the first company's assets.

What is "vanity publishing"?

Vanity or subsidized publishing means that the author pays for the printing and publication of a book. Like the more traditional forms of book publishing in which the publisher bears the costs of publication and is obliged to pay royalties to the author, this kind of publishing depends on the contract between the author and publisher. An author who pays the costs of publication should have a full understanding about the number of copies to be printed, the manner and extent of distribution and promotion, and so on, all of which should be spelled out in a written agreement.[65] Otherwise, authors may find that their publishing contracts are more illusory than real and that they are the only customers for their books.

In one recent case, a "class action" in behalf of all the authors contracting with Vantage Press, the plaintiffs persuaded a jury that Vantage had fraudulently represented itself as a publisher.[66] Punitive damages were set at $3.5 million, and compensatory damages ranged between $4 million and $12 million. Although Vantage did print the books, it provided virtually no distribution or promotion. As the attorney for the plaintiffs put it, "The jury concluded that Vantage's real business was the selling of book production contracts, not books."[67] The outcome of Vantage's appeal from that verdict may shed more light on the permissible nature of so-called vanity publishing.

THE SCREENWRITER'S CONTRACT

As with our discussion of publishing contracts, we will not review in detail all of the terms of the typical screenwriter's agreement, especially since the industry standard—the Writers' Guild of America Theatrical and Television Basic Agreement—runs about four hundred pages. We will concentrate on those provisions that are the most significant in negotiations and legal disputes. And while there are some similarities between book-publishing and screenwriting contracts, particularly the requirement that the author make certain representations and warranties about the work and promise certain indemnities, for the most part screenwriting contracts are quite different from their publishing counterparts.

How do screenwriting agreements differ from book-publishing agreements?

The essence of a publishing agreement is the author's grant to the publisher of the right to publish the author's work, the publisher having relatively little control over the book's content. Not so with the screenwriter—usually, a screenwriter is hired by a producer to write a screenplay, and the producer's role during the writing and control over the final product is considerable. Thus, while a publishing contract is primarily a grant of rights, a screenwriting contract is usually both an agreement by which the producer hires the screenwriter to write a screenplay and a grant by the writer to the producer of rights in the screenplay.

What kinds of screenwriting contracts are used?

As with publishing, different contracts apply to different kinds of screenwriting work. A television writer's agreement is different from that for a feature-film writer.

There are many ways in which a screenwriting contract can arise. At one extreme, a writer might write an original screenplay entirely on his own, "on spec," after which the screenplay is acquired by a producer, and a film is produced directly from that screenplay. In this instance, the screenplay contract also has elements of the kind of "rights-acquisition" contract that is used when a producer acquires the right to produce a movie based on a book. This scenario, however, is quite rare.

At the other extreme, a writer might be hired to write a screenplay based on another work (say a previously published novel written by someone else) to which the producer has obtained the motion-picture rights. In this instance, the screenplay may be edited, rewritten, or modified by that writer and others, all at the discretion of the producer, and no movie may ever be made based on the screenplay. This is common. Somewhere in between is the contract for a screenplay based on an original "treatment"—a kind of proposal—written by the writer.

Whatever the circumstances, there is one critical element almost certain to be included in every screenwriting contract: The producer can do pretty much whatever she wants with the screenwriter's work. And that control, together with the fact that the screenwriter herself has virtually no say in what happens to that work, is the critical distinction between screenwriting and book-publishing contracts.

A screenwriting contract differs from its publishing counterpart in other ways. Because it is often a contract for material to be written in the future, a screenplay contract will specify what the writer is expected to do, giving particular attention to the types of services. Also, a "screenplay based on material from another medium" (to quote the Oscar category) is often written when the producer has a limited-time option to acquire the film rights to the underlying work and has not yet exercised that right (because that costs money). Thus the time frame for the performance of a screenwriter's services is critical. Further, screenwriters can often make much more money (at least in the short term) than their book counterparts because minimum payments for screenwriters are considerably higher than the typical advance paid to most book authors. This is due in large measure to an organization known as the WGA.

What is the WGA?

The Writers Guild of America, a labor union for screen, television, and radio writers, was first formed as the Screen Writers Guild in 1933, and it negotiated its first collective bargaining agreement in 1941. As technology advanced, radio and television writers also found protection in what eventually became the WGA. (Technically, there are two separate bodies—the Writers Guild of America East, whose members reside east of the Mississippi River, and the Writers Guild of America West.) The WGA performs many services for its members, including a registration service that establishes the date the written material was filed with it, which can be important in a controversy involving when the work in question was written.

Authors writing for the screen receive important contractual support from the WGA, something their counterparts writing for book publication do not have available from any source. The WGA has negotiated standard industrywide contracts, and an author's compensation on many deals will be described as

"WGA minimum" or some multiple of that minimum (i.e., "one and one-half times" the minimum). The WGA agreement also sets forth the terms for another critical contract provision, "credit," and a mechanism for resolving credit disputes. Although the WGA Basic Agreement is a lengthy document, authors interested in screenwriting should take the time to familiarize themselves with it so that they can more effectively evaluate a proposed deal. Copies of the WGA Basic Agreement can be obtained from the Guild.[68]

When is the WGA agreement applicable?

The WGA agreement applies if (1) a producer is a signatory to the agreement *or* the writer is a member *and* (2) the contract (a) is executed in the United States, regardless of where services are performed *or* (b) services are performed in the United States, regardless of where the contract is executed. This is how the WGA agreement works: A comprehensive contract is negotiated between representatives of the Motion Picture Association of America (MPAA), to which all studios and other major producers belong, and the networks on the one hand and representatives of the WGA on the other. Once a collective agreement is reached and ratified by the WGA, all MPAA member companies, the networks, and other interested parties sign the agreement, committing themselves to offer no less than its minimum terms in all their writers' contracts. Producers who sign this basic agreement often require a nonmember writer to join the WGA. If there is a conflict between the WGA agreement and a writer's separate agreement, the WGA agreement takes precedence to the extent that the other agreement's terms are less favorable to the writer. However, the WGA agreement is only a minimum agreement; the parties are free to negotiate terms more favorable to the writer.

How does the WGA agreement deal with credit?

Dealing with a writer's credit is one of the key components of the WGA Basic Agreement. Indeed, even though a contract may not be within the WGA's jurisdiction because it was executed outside the United States between a nonsignatory and a nonmember, the parties may still provide that credit will be determined in accordance with the WGA provisions. The WGA agreement provides for a credit arbitration if there is a dispute about a producer's proposed credit for the writer. Sometimes a writer will believe he is entitled to sole screenwriting credit (even though others may have worked on the script), and the producer believes the credit should be shared. Disputes can also arise about the order of names given credit.

This is how the system works: The producer sends notice of its proposed writing credits to all writing participants, together with copies of the final script. If there are no objections, the credits become final. A writer can lodge an objection with the WGA, and the credit determination will promptly be arbitrated by the WGA. There are no reported cases of a credit arbitration being challenged by a WGA member, probably because the agreement provides that no member will be entitled to damages or injunctive relief against the WGA or the production company as a result of the arbitration decision.[69]

How does the WGA agreement deal with the different stages of writing a screenplay?

The WGA discourages writers from writing scripts on speculation by specifying payment for work done at various stages, or steps, in the screenwriting process.

Although some experienced writers can obtain a "flat" agreement whereby they are paid a flat fee to complete the entire project, most screenwriters get a "stepdeal" that includes a series of options. Under those agreements, a producer can elect at certain stages of the project's development to terminate a writer's involvement in a project or to proceed with that writer. Payment at each stage is a portion of the total payment for services and the rights to be assigned. In recent years, however, some writers have begun to insist (with varying degrees of success) on the opportunity to see a project through a first draft and in some instances even a second draft, and to be paid through that stage.

Most of the writing of a screenplay has to be done in the development period, the period preceding the shooting of the film when critical elements of the production, including the final script, are assembled, budgeted, and scheduled. When the screenplay is based on a book, the development period is generally the term of the producer's option to acquire the rights. Without a finished screenplay, a film cannot be budgeted. Without an accurate budget, it's tough to get binding commitments for production funding.

On its way to becoming a finished screenplay, a script may go through some or all of the following stages, called *product forms*: The writer may first submit to a producer a first-draft treatment, basically a few pages containing a sketch of the plot and characters, as in the famous *Art Buchwald* case discussed below. The producer may give the writer specific comments and suggestions for changes, and the writer may then write a first revision of the treatment or, if the requested changes are more substantial, a second-draft treatment. This process may repeat itself, the producer again giving comments and the writer then submitting a second revision or third-draft treatment. At any point, the producer may elect to proceed to the next stage or terminate. The next step is to prepare a screenplay based on the treatment. As with the possible responses to the treatment, the producer will comment on the first-draft screenplay, and those comments will then be incorporated into a first revision or second-draft screenplay (depending again on the extent of the changes), and again the producer may make further comments that require still further revisions or drafts. A rewrite may be necessary. A "polish" is the last step, when the final changes in the screenplay are made.

In scheduling, the contract will likely provide for delivery by the writer of at least the first product form by a specific date or within a specified period after execution of the agreement. It will also provide for a specified period after delivery of each product form when the producer is to read and respond to it, the delivery date for the next product form measured from the conclusion of the preceding reading period. In most cases, a producer will have the right to terminate the agreement after any reading period (although writers are attempting with increasing frequency to insist on the right to write the first and second drafts of a script and be paid for them). Also, a producer often seeks the right to extend the agreement before proceeding to the next product form, giving the producer additional time to consider options or to arrange other aspects of the production before proceeding with the screenplay. But even if a producer obtains such a clause, this right to extend will usually be limited by time or subject to other obligations of the writer.

How is a screenwriter paid for these stages?

The agreement will probably provide for a total amount, to be paid in increments keyed to delivery of each product form. Although a part of that total amount is generally paid on execution of the agreement, most of the compensation is keyed to commencement or delivery of each product form, and any right of the producer to terminate or extend the agreement is contingent upon the producer's paying the sums due for services to date. The writer receives compensation for each product form completed. The WGA requires that 10 percent of the payment for each product form be paid on commencement of that form, although it is more common for a writer to be paid between 25 percent and 50 percent on commencement and the balance on delivery. Moreover, if a producer wishes to skip a form (e.g., omit the second-draft treatment and go directly to a first-draft screenplay) the writer must still be paid all amounts due before beginning that new form.

These payments are part of the fixed compensation to be paid to the writer. The amounts are certain, the only uncertainty being whether the project proceeds with the writer; as long as the writer does the work, she will get the prescribed payment. Again, the WGA fees are the minimum for each stage and for the entire process, those minimums keyed to a picture's budget, dependent in large part on whether the picture's budget is more or less than $2 million. These minimums can be increased in negotiations in light of various factors, key of which is the writer's track record.

What other forms of compensation are available?

In addition to the fixed-compensation approach, screenwriting agreements often provide for bonus, deferred, and contingent payments. The possibility and amount of a bonus often depends upon the credit (e.g., if the writer receives sole credit, a bonus may be paid). The bonus is often 25 percent to 50 percent of the fixed compensation. There may also be a bonus if the writer receives shared credit, although the amount of the bonus will be smaller.

Deferred payments are usually preferred by producers of low-budget, often independently financed projects. Let's say a producer can raise sufficient funding from private investors (i.e., not a studio) to produce a "bare-bones" film, but without the "right" talent for the project. To attract that talent to the project, the producer may promise specific percentages of the film's future earnings. If a writer is eager to be involved in a project, he may agree to participate for less money up front (i.e., on completion of the various product forms) for the possibility of more later, after the project starts earning money (although not necessarily profits).

Any such provisions should be specified with care in the contract. For example, although a deferred payment is often made after repayment to investors of their investments and before a distribution of net profits, such payments are sometimes made, at one extreme, prior to repayment to investors and, at the other extreme, after investors (or other participants) have not only been repaid their investments but also received some profits. Also, since deferred payments are often paid pro rata with other participants (which means that all deferred payments are totaled and each participant gets his proportionate share of each payment made), it is important to put limits on deferred payments to others or at least be aware of them. Otherwise the amount paid to the writer in comparison with what's paid to other recipients of deferred-payment may not be adequate. The ultimate risk with the deferred payment approach is that the production won't be distributed or that not enough income will come in to reach the point where deferred payments are to be made.

What are contingent payments?

The contingent payment is a participation in profits. The most successful writers can sometimes negotiate a small participation, usually no more than 1 or 2 percent, of the film's gross profits, the amounts received from distribution of the picture, less only certain limited deductions. If a writer is fortunate enough to obtain a gross participation, she may actually see some payments.

This is not the case for most of their less renowned colleagues, who are unable to command a gross-profits participation. Many writers will receive some participation, usually between 2.5 percent and 5 percent, of *net* profits, although it is a rare film that generates any net profits. To calculate net profits, there must be deducted from the gross (i.e., the total income received from the distribution and exploitation of a film) all deferred payments for talent, production recoupment, distribution fees, distribution expenses, and assorted other items. There are then two principal types of net profits that may be distributed. Writers prefer a participation based on "100 percent of net profits"; producers prefer to offer a participation in "producer's net profits" because the producer's net is what's left after participants in 100 percent of net profits have been paid. But even with 100 percent of net profits most writers should not expect to see any real participation; *net profit* definitions generally are exceptionally long, confusing, complicated, and seemingly designed by the producer to make sure there are none.

A good example is the *Art Buchwald* case, which received international attention in the late 1980s.[70] The author and columnist Art Buchwald sold to Paramount Pictures an eight-page treatment entitled "King for a Day" about an African king, stranded penniless in the United States, who falls in love with a young woman. Although Paramount told Buchwald that it had no interest in producing a movie based on that treatment, Buchwald claimed that Paramount's subsequent hit film *Coming to America* starring Eddie Murphy was based on his work. Buchwald sued Paramount, claiming breach of the provision in his treatment contract that he would be paid if Paramount produced a motion picture "based upon [his] work." The trial court agreed that *Coming to America* was "based upon" Buchwald's treatment and found that under his contract with Paramount, Buchwald was entitled to a percentage of the film's "net profits," if any.[71] Even though the film earned almost $300 million at the box office, Paramount contended that *no* net profits had been earned under the applicable *net profits* definition. In fact, Paramount claimed, the film was still millions in the red. As noted in a contemporary article, "The most important thing to know about 'net profit' participation definitions and formulas in the motion picture industry is that they have little to do with profits."[72]

Profit participations in the motion picture industry are best characterized as supplemental contingent compensation based upon cash actually "received" by the studio ("gross receipts" as defined in the particular participation agreement) less certain deductions for certain fees that are typically calculated as a percentage of gross receipts and the direct and indirect cost of making the motion picture.[73]

Given that a typical *net profits* definition, like Buchwald's, can go on for more than twenty-five pages of that kind of double-talk, it's small wonder that producers rarely declare that net profits have been realized, even for the most successful films.

What Buchwald ultimately receives is to be determined by the court in the third stage of the litigation, the determination of damages. Of enormous significance for both Buchwald and the film industry, the court held in the case's second stage that several parts of Paramount's *net profits* definition—which was similar to that of much of the industry—were "unconscionable" (i.e., so unfair that the court would refuse to enforce them.) It seems clear that the outcome of the case will have a major impact on the motion-picture industry.

What does the producer get for his payments to the screenwriter?

Plenty. In fact, with one important exception, noted below, the producer gets the right to do whatever the producer wants with the material created. The writer often has to sign a certificate confirming and conveying ownership to the producer. The producer has the right to modify the writer's work without the writer's permission. The producer can even merge the writer's work with material written by others. The producer can generally use the work in any and all media (now known or hereafter created) throughout the universe. The writer specifically waives any rights of *droit moral*.

The sole limitation on the rights conveyed to the producer is a screenplay written from scratch, from an independent creative idea not based on material from another source. In such cases, the WGA Basic Agreement provides that the writer may be entitled to "Separation of Rights," which means that writer may be entitled to certain publication, dramatic, and sequel rights in the original material. Under the WGA agreement, the producer can acquire the separated rights from the writer for additional payment, although such an acquisition should be specifically discussed and included in the agreement; it is not deemed included in the grant of rights to the producer, even if the payment for the writer's services exceeded WGA minimums. However, most producers include a separate grant of separated rights in their form agreements, and in such cases the writer will be deemed to have granted those rights unless the clause is removed or modified.

Does the original writer benefit if there's a sequel or a television series based on the film?

Yes. A typical screenwriter's agreement provides that for a sequel (such as *Jaws 30* or *Friday the 13th Part 700*), the original writer is entitled to receive stated payments.[74] The WGA minimum payment is 25 percent of the original compensation, although 33⅓ percent to 50 percent is more typical. The same is true of a remake of the original film, even if it has a different title. The writer may also want to provide in the agreement that he will have the right to write the sequel or remake. If agreeable to any such provision, the producer will usually try to limit it to a right of *first negotiation* (which means the producer has to negotiate in good faith with the writer before approaching another writer) and to limit the provision to a specified period, often between 7 and 10 years from first release of the initial picture. The original writer will also receive a royalty for each episode of a television series based on an original screenplay. Again, the writer may also seek a right to participate in the creation of the series, although that effort is usually unsuccessful.

THE PLAYWRIGHT'S AGREEMENT

A playwright's agreement with a producer resembles the author-publisher agreement and the screenwriter's agreement, and in other ways is unique to the theatre. The playwright, like the author, often conceives and writes the play independently, rarely writing for hire as the screenwriter often does. Also, like the author, the playwright generally retains a good deal of control over what happens to the play; indeed, the playwright generally influences the selection of the director, cast, designers, and other creative personnel associated with a production, so much so that she probably has more to do with the ultimate outcome of her work than the book author.

Conversely, the fact that the playwright has a permanent

organization, the Dramatists Guild, Inc., to represent her interests vis-à-vis those who acquire rights to her work is more reminiscent of the screenwriter's situation, although the Dramatists Guild's influence is rather less pervasive than the WGA's. Ultimately, however, the theatre has unique customs and practices that are reflected in the typical playwright's agreement.

When is the typical playwright agreement made?

Occasionally a producer has an idea for a play and hires people to write it. This occurs most frequently with musicals where the producer assembles in advance the necessary creative contributors, including bookwriter, composer, and lyricist. Even in these situations, however, the producer will rarely own the finished product, as the producer of a film does. Rather, the writers of the play will usually own the finished product, subject to the specific production rights granted to the original producer.

But in most instances the negotiations for the typical playwright's agreement begin only after the playwright has written the play, or at least a draft of the play that may be revised during production. The dramatist's agreement, called a *production agreement*, generally gives the producer (one or more individuals or companies) the right to produce the play in a particular venue (i.e., a city, state, country, or territory) or in a particular theatre or size of theatre, provided that the producer presents the first performance of the play before a paying audience by an outside date specified in the contract.

For example, a typical off-Broadway production contract would provide that the producer must present the first paid public performance in an off-Broadway theatre in New York City within a stated period (perhaps 6 months or a year) from the date of the agreement. *Off-Broadway theatre* must be defined, and the location of the theatre is not necessarily determinative. According to commonly used definitions, the size of the house controls, so that an off-Broadway theatre would be any theatre in New York City with 499 or fewer seats, including certain houses ("middle houses") in the Broadway theatre district that have 499 seats. The producer may also have the right to extend the outside date of the first performance by the payment of additional sums to the author.

What does the producer get?

The producer's right to produce the play is an "option." Staying with the above example, during the producer's option period, the producer will try to raise the necessary funds to produce the play, usually from private sources. The customary investment structure is the "limited partnership," where investors purchase limited interests in the entity that will produce the play and the producer acts as general partner. At the same time, the producer will try to assemble the best team for the project—the general manager (responsible for the day-to-day management of the production) and the creative team: director, designers, and perhaps key cast members who will best bring to life the playwright's vision.

The option is exercised by the producer's presentation of the play in accordance with the contract with the playwright—that is, within the time and at the type of theatre specified in the agreement. When that happens, the producer has the right to continue thus to present the play indefinitely until the production closes. In addition, if the necessary number of performances are presented (discussed below), the producer also becomes entitled to acquire additional production rights in the play; for example, the right to present the play in other countries, on tour, or other ways.

What payments are made to the playwright for the producer's option?

When an option contract is made (or extended), a payment is usually made to the playwright—by screenwriter (or even publishing) standards, rather modest. One possible reason playwrights have more control over their plays is that they generally share more of the risk. The playwright's hope of realizing real money from the play depends on its presentation. Also, although the sums paid on execution or extension of the option are nonreturnable and nonrefundable, they are treated as an advance against the royalties the playwright may earn in the future.

What kinds of productions are there?

There are several kinds of productions a playwright may authorize, including nonprofit and commercial productions. Frequently, particularly in the early life of a play, it may first be produced at one of the many regional theatres throughout the country or at a "subscription" theatre in New York. These theatres, usually operated on a nonprofit basis, present initial limited-run productions. This gives the playwright an opportunity to revise the play in a production setting prior to its presentation on a more commercial basis.

The agreement with the regional or subscription theatre usually includes an option to produce a subsequent commercial production. If a regional or subscription production is particularly successful, that production may be moved to a commercial theatre and reorganized as a commercial production by the regional or subscription producer, alone or with others. For example, *A Chorus Line*, the longest running musical on Broadway, began as a limited engagement at the New York Shakespeare Festival, and *Steel Magnolias* began at WPA in New York before moving off-Broadway and then to the screen.

If the regional or subscription theatre does not wish to move its production immediately to a commercial setting, it will still probably have the right to produce a commercial production of that play for a certain period following the close of its limited run. It may produce a subsequent commercial production itself or more likely assign its option to an independent commercial producer in exchange for a flat fee or a royalty. An off-Broadway production is a commercial production, as is a "first-class" production, which includes any production presented in a Broadway theatre. A commercial production is one that has the potential of an unlimited run (as opposed to the limited engagement of a nonprofit production) and gets its production funding from investors seeking a profit. The standard terms of the playwright's contract—indeed, in some instances what is required by the Dramatists Guild—depend on the kinds of productions included in the producer's option.

What options are covered by the Dramatists Guild contract?
The Dramatists Guild has promulgated form contracts for virtually every type of production—first-class, off-Broadway, regional. However, it does not follow that these agreements are actually used. For example, although the Guild's Approved Production Contract (APC) is almost always used for Broadway and other first-class productions, the Guild's off-Broadway agreement is almost never used. This is because the Approved

Production Contract was intensely negotiated between the League of New York Theatres and Producers and the Dramatists Guild before it was issued, while negotiations between off-Broadway producers and the Guild over the off-Broadway contract broke down, and the Guild decided to promulgate its own agreement anyway, hoping it would be used. But it almost never is: "It has never been accepted as a viable contract by knowledgeable attorneys and agents working in theatre, although some agents representing authors of plays have tried to impose it on producers. . . . The contract is so 'pro-Author' that it would be difficult to find financing for any play acquired by a producer pursuant to its terms."[75]

Recently the Guild issued an Approved LORT Production Contract for plays "to be presented at theatres that are members of the League of Regional Theatres (LORT) or other resident or regional not-for-profit theatres." However, this agreement also was not the result of producer-Guild negotiations. The Guild has stated that it will insist upon its members using the agreement, on penalty of expulsion, but the response of LORT theatres to it has been quite hostile, and they have stated their intention to continue using their own agreements. Time will tell.[76]

Once the option agreement is signed, what happens next?

If the option is for a commercial production, the producer has to raise the necessary production funds. If it's for a nonprofit regional or subscription production, the producer will already have the funding and will proceed directly to production.

Once production funding is secured, the rehearsal period can begin. The playwright always has the right to attend rehearsals. Usually the playwright has the right to approve the director, designers, and perhaps most important, the cast. The playwright will also generally promise to work with the director and producer in rewriting that may be necessary from a production standpoint. If rehearsals are away from the playwright's city of residence, the agreement will generally require the producer to provide the playwright round-trip transportation and a per diem for expenses. Whether the transportation is to be first class and the amount of the per diem are often hotly negotiated.

Assuming all goes reasonably well, the play will first be presented to the public in "preview performances" where the producer and director can assess the production with live audiences. Additional rewrites and revisions may be necessary, and the industry routinely buzzes with gossip about changes being made at this point. After the previews, there is generally an official "opening" to which critics are invited. The playwright has the right, by contract, to purchase a given number of "house seats" (seats in the front center section of the house) for each performance and in most cases a few more for the opening. Once the play opens, everyone involved hopes it runs for a long time, because if it doesn't, no one—the producer, the director, the investor, and certainly not the playwright—will make any money from it.

How does the playwright make money?

With a regional or subscription production, the playwright shouldn't expect to make much money. Such productions don't pay well and generally are not presented in large theatres. Since payment is most often based on the gross, and since the gross is directly related to the size of the house, a small house means a small gross, which means little money for the author. But the key reason there isn't much money here is that the productions are generally for limited runs, so there isn't an opportunity for extended ticket sales.

It's only when a run is potentially unlimited that there are real possibilities for financial gain for a playwright. How that gain is computed requires some explanation since nearly every agreement contains one traditional method of payment and an alternate method, which today is almost always used, at least until a production has earned its production costs.

The custom in the theatre for decades was that the playwright's compensation was a royalty computed as a percentage of the "gross weekly box-office receipts"; thus, by definition, the more weeks the play runs, the more gross there will be for the author's royalties. And unlike the screenwriter's net profits, the definition of *gross* is short and uniformly accepted: all income from the sale of tickets, less commissions for theatre parties, discount and cut-rate sales, admission taxes, charge-card expenses, amounts equal to New York City's former amusement tax (which are now sent to union pension and welfare funds), subscription fees, and actors' fund benefits. Often, the royalty percentage increases when the production has recouped all of its production costs (i.e., the production has generated sufficient income to "reimburse" the producer for the costs of producing and keeping the play running).

In straight (i.e., nonmusical) plays, the playwright's royalty for a first-class production under the Dramatists Guild APC is 5 percent of the gross, which increases to 10 percent on recoupment of production costs. For an off-Broadway or second-class production, the prerecoupment royalty is generally 5 percent or 6 percent, which may increase to 6 percent or 7 percent after recoupment. For musicals, the off-Broadway or second-class royalty is almost always 6 percent and increases after recoupment are less frequent. For a Broadway or first-class musical production, the authors are paid 4.5 percent, increasing to 6 percent after recoupment. This percentage is shared by the bookwriter, composer, and lyricist as they may agree in their collaboration agreement (the most common agreement is for equal shares). Of course, musicals generally are in larger theatres, so even 1.5 percent of the gross can be represent a good deal of money on a weekly basis, especially when the price for a ticket to a Broadway musical can now exceed $50.

Typically, not only the authors but also the director, producer, theatre owner, and perhaps even the designers and stars will be entitled to a percentage of the gross. Under such a "financial food chain," the royalty participants eat first; the fixed costs of running the production are then taken from what's left of the gross; any advertising and promotional costs follow; a reserve for emergencies is set aside; and finally the investors share what little of the gross may be left. As a result, even with seemingly successful productions, investors do not receive profit participations very quickly or (comparatively speaking) in especially large amounts.

Since investment in a commercial theatrical production is at best an extremely speculative venture, investors understandably do not want to be at the end of the "food chain." To attract investors, producers have created a way for everyone to participate in whatever funds come in: the "royalty pool," the alternative method of payment mentioned above. Nearly all playwright agreements now provide for a pool from which a production's weekly fixed costs are paid first. Whatever is left ("operating profits") is distributed to investors and royalty recipients, from 30 percent to as high as 50 percent being allocated to the royalty recipients.[77] Thus, if all of the royalty participants (e.g., authors, producer, director, theatre owner, etc.) are collectively entitled to 12 percent of the gross and the playwright to 6 percent under the pool approach, the playwright would get half of the operating profits allocated to royalty participants, reflecting the playwright's share of the total royalty participation. To ensure that the playwright's payments do not fall below a specified level, royalty-pool provisions guarantee that a minimum payment per royalty point will be made weekly. That minimum can be as low as $150 for off-Broadway or second-class productions, and as high (for some well-established playwrights) as $1,000 per point in first-class or Broadway productions.

What does the producer get for producing the play?

It depends on the kind of producer. A commercial producer generally receives a share of the gross as a "producer's management fee" and will continue to participate in gross distributions, or in the pool if one is in effect. If the production runs long enough to recoup production costs and repay investors, the limited partnership formed to produce the play will typically be earning partnership profits, and these profits are shared by the limited partners (investors) and the producer as general partner. In addition, if enough performances are presented, the producer may also earn the right to present the play elsewhere (with the same income opportunities available)—on tour, in foreign countries—and, perhaps most important, to participate in subsidiary-rights income.

The *subsidiary rights* ("sub rights") of a play refer to its future exploitation, including other productions of the play—for example, in foreign languages or stock or amateur versions (which rights can be quite lucrative with plays that had successful commercial runs)—and the right to base a motion-picture or television production on the play. Because a "motion-picture rights sale" will likely generate more income than any other single sub-rights sale, it often gets the most attention. Such sales are discussed further below.

The justification for a producer's participation in sub-rights income is that by presenting the play and introducing it to the public, the producer has contributed to the value of the play and should thus participate in the fruits of its future exploitation. There can be no question that the longer a play runs, the more attention the public has paid to it; that recognition alone can be said to increase its value. Accordingly, at least in theory, the longer a play runs, the greater the producer's participation in sub rights should be. For example, a typical off-Broadway agreement might give the producer the following percentages of the playwright's income from subsidiary-rights deals made within a given period (say 10 years) after the close of the producer's run of the play:

> Ten percent (10%) if the Play shall run for at least twenty-one (21) consecutive paid performances; twenty percent (20%) if the Play shall run for at least forty-two consecutive paid performances; thirty percent (30%) if the Play shall run for at least fifty-six paid performances; forty percent (40%) if the Play shall run for sixty five (65) consecutive paid performances or more. For the purposes of computing the number of performances, provided the Play officially opens in New York City, the first paid performance shall be deemed to be the first performance, however only eight paid previews will be counted in this computation.[78]

A commercial producer of a second-class production rarely receives more than 40 percent of the playwright's sub-rights income, but the producer of a first-class or Broadway production under the APC may receive up to 50 percent of certain types of sub-rights income.

What does a nonprofit regional or subscription producer get?

A regional or subscription-theatre producer generally gets, at most, whatever may be left of ticket income after everyone else involved with the production is paid. And since most such producers can rarely pay their production costs from ticket-sale income and rely heavily on charitable contributions, they generally don't get anything from their productions.

However, if the play is produced in a subsequent production within a given period after the close of its production, the playwright's agreement with the regional-subscription producer usually provides for a royalty percentage of 1 percent or 2 percent of gross or a pro rata share of the royalty pool, whichever is applicable. The agreement might also require the playwright to secure for that producer a share in the net profits of a subsequent commercial company's rendition of the play. Also, the agreement usually provides for that producer to receive a percentage of sub-rights income since these theatres present new and untested works that continue to be developed during the production and are thus entitled to share in some of the play's future success. Rarely, however, will this percentage be as high as 10 percent, and it is often as low as 5 percent, although such sub-rights participations are in addition to the royalty or pool participation mentioned above. As a result, when a play meets with commercial success, the playwright is only one of the beneficiaries.

What happens when a producer commissions a play?

A producer may have an idea for a play and, like a film producer, seek the right person (or persons if it's a musical, as commissioned plays often are) to write it. Often, the producer bases his idea for a play on a work in another medium, such as a book or movie. For example, one of the producers of the hit musical *La Cage aux Folles* first secured the stage rights to the property, originally a nonmusical movie, and then assembled the team that wrote the book, music, and lyrics for the musical.

An agreement like this usually provides that the writers must contribute material satisfactory to the producer, but the producer generally does not have the sweeping rights of a film producer to do pretty much whatever she wants to with the material submitted. The agreement may also provide that the producer has the right to replace the writers, subject to payment for material used. The agreement will also give the producer the right to present the play for a limited period. The producer may also have a limited continuing participation (similar to a nonprofit theatre's participation as described above) in future productions and subsidiary rights. Of course, it's possible that the writers may decide to write a play based on other material; if so, they will have to negotiate a rights-acquisition agreement directly.

THE RIGHTS-ACQUISITION AGREEMENT

All of the contracts discussed so far involve the initial exploi
tation of an author's work. But what happens when someone
wants to create a work in one medium, say a movie or a play
that is based on something written for another medium, such
as a novel, a biography, or even a song? The contract is called a
rights-acquisition agreement. From the author's point of view
such agreements can be depressing and burdensome. They are
usually lengthy, involve assigning away most of the author'
rights in the work, and in the short term do not involve much
money. In the long term, however, a rights-acquisition agree
ment can be extremely lucrative for the author, and in some
cases can offer a new world of opportunity for the fortunate
writer willing and able to make the transition to writing fo
another medium.

Almost always, the original author will have to give up contro
over the fate of his work. As a well-known literary agent special
izing in rights acquisition agreements has put it, "If the mos
important thing to the writer is that the film be faithful to the
book, don't sell the rights; if that's not so important, sell the
rights for as much as you can, and don't see the movie!"

What does the purchaser acquire?

Virtually all the available rights in the work—and some tha
don't yet exist! In the first place, the *property* (the play or book
or whatever) is invariably defined very broadly; it may include
all "plots, themes, narrative, dialogue, titles, characters and
copyright thereof."[79] So even though the purchaser is ostensibl
acquiring only rights to this one work, by so defining the prop
erty, the exclusive grant of rights to this purchaser may preven
the author from selling movie rights to another work that in
volves the same character or theme.

Entire paragraphs (indeed pages) of the agreement are ofter
devoted to describing in exquisite detail the rights being
granted by the author to the purchaser. A motion-pictur
rights-acquisition agreement usually includes all exclusiv
rights in the property, including the right to create films and
taped productions based on the property, in any language, with
music synchronized or otherwise; to record such films and
productions, using any processes now known or hereafter in

vented; to exhibit, distribute, and otherwise exploit the created productions in any manner whatsoever, including but not limited to theatrically, nontheatrically, on free or pay television, broadcast or cable, in home video, and so on; to produce and present remakes and sequels; to exploit certain limited publication rights; to release a soundtrack; to exploit merchandising rights (such as *Teenage Mutant Ninja Turtles* sheets, clothing, lunch boxes, ad infinitum) and commercial rights (using the property to sell toothpaste, for example).

If the purchaser is acquiring theatrical dramatization or musicalization rights (as the creators of *Cabaret* did in acquiring Christopher Isherwood's *I Am a Camera*), the agreement usually includes all the rights mentioned above and others. Most plays are not likely to be produced commercially unless the movie rights in the play are also available, so the adapters will want the right to have their new creation adapted to yet another medium.

In any case, the acquisition agreement invariably includes the right to make changes of any kind in the property. The author specifically waives any right of *droit moral* (discussed in Chapter II). The purchaser can change any character, add to or delete from the story, and even combine the property with a completely different property. In most instances, the author will have no rights of approval unless he has tremendous bargaining power. Even in those rare cases, however, the author's rights of approval are usually quite limited.

What does the author keep?

Book-publication rights (in the case of a published work acquired for adaptation to another medium) and in other instances the right to continue to exploit the work in its original medium. Motion-picture and television-rights acquisition agreements usually do not include live dramatic or musical rights, which are usually reserved to the granting party along with the right to release a cast album. However, the fact that an author may still grant a third party the right to create a dramatic production based on the property does not mean that a film could be based on that play, since all film rights to the property go to the original purchaser.

Book authors generally retain certain rights to write sequels for publication ("author-written sequels"), although this would not diminish the rights the producer acquires in the characters. As a result, an author can write a written sequel using a particular character while the producer can produce a filmed sequel using the same character, and they can be entirely different stories. The author also usually retains radio rights as well a the right to do recordings, both nondramatic and dramatic (with sound effects, etc.), derived directly from the original work (as distinguished from film sound-track recordings.)

Usually, however, the author will not be able to exploit any of these reserved rights immediately, except for the right to continue to exploit the property in its original format. There is generally a stated period during which the author is required to "hold back" from exercising or permitting others to exercise those rights. The hold-back period is often 5 years from the release of the first motion picture based on the work or 7 years from the date of the agreement, whichever occurs first. The author's rights for an author-written sequel may be even more restricted since the purchaser often insists on a right of "first negotiation" (the author has to negotiate with the purchaser before approaching a third party), "last refusal" (the purchaser has the right to meet the terms a third party has offered for the rights), or even an option to acquire the movie or television to the author-written sequel.

How is a typical acquisition agreement set up?

On rare occasions a purchaser will acquire all the rights outright and will pay the full purchase price immediately. But far more often the purchaser wants to make sure that she *can* acquire the rights and that she really *wants* to. The preliminary work can be extensive; for motion pictures, for example, it can include actually causing a screenplay to be written. What is usually most critical to a potential purchaser deciding whether to acquire the rights is whether he can obtain a commitment for funding or the actual funding necessary to see the project through.

The acquisition contract is premised on this two-stage process and results in two separate but interconnected legal agreements whereby the purchaser acquires an option (the first agreement) to activate the actual rights acquisition (the second agreement). In the option agreement, the purchaser pays the author for the right for a limited period to acquire the property under the terms and conditions set forth in the rights-acquisi tion agreement, which is prepared and attached to the option agreement. The option agreement often provides that the option period can be extended one, two, or even three times beyond the original period, provided timely notice and additional payments are given to the author.

A typical option in a movie or television rights-acquisition agreement will provide for an initial period of 1 year, renewable for 1 or 2 additional years. When the purchaser is acquiring the right to create a theatrical play based on the property, he may want even more time since he must first have the play written and then get the production financed. The option period is almost always extendable for reasons of *force majeure* (i.e., acts of God, war, catastrophe, and perhaps most significantly, strikes, although there is often a requirement that to extend the option term, the *force majeure* must directly and materially affect the agreement). Such clauses offered significant consolation to the various producers affected by the 1988 WGA writers' strike since they meant that as long as the writers couldn't write, the option clock was not ticking.

The acquisition agreement provides for payments to the author for the purchase of the property. The purchaser can exercise the option at any time by sending the author written notice together with that part of the purchase price due on exercise. However, many agreements also provide that the option is deemed exercised by taking certain actions, with payment then due for that exercise. For a movie or television production, the acquisition agreement often provides that the commencement of principal photography constitutes the exercise of the option. In the theatre, an option is deemed exercised by the production of a play in the type of theatre contemplated by the agreement.

What kind of money are we talking about?

Prices for an option can vary widely, from a nominal payment (say, $1,000) to six figures, depending on a variety of factors, including how hungry the market is for property, the form the property is in, its popularity, when (and if) it's been published, the author's track record, and how sure the purchaser is of being able to proceed with it. The first option payment is almost always applicable (treated as an advance) against the ultimate purchase price. Payments made for extensions of the option term are usually not (or only partially) applied against the purchase price. A rule of thumb is that the price of an option represents 10 percent of the purchase price.

Like the option price, the ultimate purchase price can vary widely, depending upon many of the factors listed above as well as the work's age, scope, story, name recognition, potential cast, and the number of other offers at hand. The parties may include "escalators" in the purchase price to reward a property that does well in its initial medium; for example, the acquisition price for a novel may increase depending on the number of weeks it appears on the best-seller list or the sale of book-club rights. The purchase price may be made adjustable during the production of the film, so that the price could be set as a percentage of the final approved production budget but not less than a stated minimum or more than a stated maximum. In television, the purchase price may be one figure for a two-hour movie, with increases for any film longer than that.

As with the bonus, deferred, and contingent forms of compensation paid to screenwriters, there are additional forms of compensation customarily paid to the rights owner. For example, as in the screenwriter's contract, the author-owner will often be entitled to contingent compensation of a participation in net profits of from 2.5 to 5 percent, but such participations will be subject to the same limitations presented by the definition of *net profits* discussed above. If the first production is intended for initial release on television and the film is subsequently released theatrically in the United States or abroad, additional payments to the owner are customary, usually half the purchase price on domestic release and half on foreign release. The owner often receives additional compensation in the form of royalties if a television series is based on the production based on the property.

If the acquisition agreement is for theatrical dramatization rights, in addition to the purchase price (which will usually be modest when compared to the price for film rights) the agreement will provide for a royalty (of between 1 percent and 2 percent, based on the play's gross receipts, with a possible increase after the producer has recouped production costs), and/or participation in a royalty pool. Finally, if there is a sale of subsidiary rights in a play based on the property that is the subject of the acquisition agreement, the owner will often participate in the playwright's share of subsidiary-rights income n the same proportion that the rights seller's royalty from a heatrical production bears to the total royalty of the rights holder combined with that of all parties who wrote the play.

For example, the musical *Les Miserables* was based on Victor Hugo's novel of the same name. Since Hugo (1802–1885) was long dead, that property was in the public domain, and no rights payment was necessary. Suppose, however, that it was still protected and that the theatrical producers of the play had to pay Hugo a royalty from theatrical productions, which they agreed would be 1.5 percent of the gross. Suppose further that the composer, bookwriter, and lyricist of that musical collectively received 6 percent of the gross. Finally, suppose the film rights in the play were sold to a film producer for $100,000. Hugo would be entitled to $20,000. His 1.5 percent royalty was 20 percent of 7.5 percent, which is the total royalty of all of the authors plus the rights holder, so he's entitled to 20 percent of the film subsidiary-rights payment. However, if the play's authors also wrote the screenplay for the film version and received additional compensation (over and above the rights payment) for those services, Hugo would not be entitled to any participation in that payment.

Does the original author receive credit in a subsequent production?

Yes, although in the theatre the credit is often smaller than (usually half) the size of the credit given to the authors of the new material. The credit to the original author is generally to appear wherever and whenever those authors' names appear. In film and television, the credit to the original author generally appears on a "single card" (no other credits appear at the same time) and in paid advertising in which any other writer is credited. Unlike the theatre, in film and television the original author's credit is the same size as that of the screenwriter.

What other rights might the original author obtain?

Some fortunate authors are able secure the opportunity to write at least the first draft of the adapted work. This can provide not only additional income to the author (above the rights-acquisition price) but also exposure and experience in writing in a different medium. Unfortunately, it is relatively rare for the original author to get this opportunity.

If the purchaser does nothing with the rights, can the owner get them back?

Until recently, the answer was almost always yes. If a production based on the property was not begun within a stated period from the date of the agreement (say, 7 years), the acquisition agreement provided that the rights would revert to the owner, although sometimes the owner had to repay the producer what she had received from the producer and sometimes the owner also had to repay the producer for costs incurred in connection with the development of the property (e.g., payments made to screenwriters, etc., to develop the property). Since the owner would usually exercise this right only if another producer was interested in acquiring the rights, such payments would normally be made by that second producer.

These days, however, producers increasingly insist that the rights to a property cannot revert under any circumstances. Although producers argue that the cost of a rights acquisition justifies their continued ownership of the rights whether or not they do anything with them, that view seems unpersuasive in light of the importance to the author's career of a film based on his book (not simply having sold the movie rights). The producers' argument also seems to ignore the tremendous income potential that a production has for the author. For these reasons, many authors and their agents are insisting on a right of reversion, even if it means losing a rights sale.

CONTRACTS INVOLVING PHOTOGRAPHERS

There are two principal ways photographers can make a living as such: as salaried employees of an entity (a newspaper or magazine, advertising agency, government body, or business corporation) or as freelance self-employed professionals hired by others for assignments. In almost every relevant way, the contracts and legal rights applicable to the employee-photographer are different from those applicable to the freelancer. For the most part, this section will discuss the customary contract made by freelance photographers.[80]

What rights do employee-photographers have vis-à-vis their employers?

Only those rights set forth in their employment contracts. The law, including in particular the U.S. Copyright Act, assumes that all legal rights, including all copyrights, in the photographs they take for their employers belong automatically and for all purposes to the employer. The applicable legal doctrine is "work made for hire," which simply means that the work product of the photographer is created by her as the employer's representative and for its benefit, and the employer is considered the creator of the work and the owner of all legal rights in it.[81]

As a result, unless the parties agree otherwise, the employee has no individual right to use or exploit work created for his employer, and the employee could violate the legal rights of (and jeopardize his or her employment with) the employer by attempting to do so. Of course, the employer might permit the employee to make certain uses of, and perhaps even sell, such work, but such permission would have to be specifically sought and obtained. On the other hand, unlike their freelance counterparts, employee-photographers do not have any separate overhead expenses (for studios, cameras, lighting, etc.) and can count on a regular paycheck (and other benefits).

What kinds of assignments do freelance photographers receive?

There is probably no limit to the kinds of assignments freelance photographers receive, and the specific aspects of those assignments (including the method of payment, working conditions, and rights to the work) can vary as widely as the assignments themselves. For example, there are enormous differences between an assignment from the local newspaper to cover a press conference at city hall and an assignment from a major corporation to take the photographs for its annual report; an assignment to photograph a wedding and an assignment to take photographs for a national advertising campaign for an exotic perfume (or fast-food chain); and taking publicity photographs for an entertainer and shooting an elaborate layout for a fashion magazine. These kinds of assignments require different talents and temperaments. They also inevitably involve different kinds of contracts and legal relationships.

Although there are any number of assignments a freelance photographer might receive, all probably fall into one of two major categories: "editorial" (photographs designed for use in the editorial as distinct from advertising or promotional parts of a newspaper, magazine, or book) and "commercial" (all other assignments, including advertising, corporate, promotional, and other internal business uses, such as resources for lawyers, doctors, designers, builders, etc.). Where appropriate, the differences between editorial and commercial assignments will be discussed below.

What is the significance of who owns the copyright in the photographs?

The owner of the copyright in a photograph, as with any other created work, is the person who controls how that work can be used and exploited, not just in the immediate present but in the future. In the case of "work made for hire," that person is the employer, and the employee-photographer has no say in that control. In contrast, with freelance assignment, it is the photographer and not the employer who is the owner of the copyright, at least until the parties agree otherwise.[8] Thus, subject to the contract with the party who assigns work to the photographer (the "client"), the photographer controls and can exploit all uses of the work not specifically granted ("licensed") to the client. The ownership of the copyright in the work can be of enormous importance to the freelance photographer.[83]

How do contracts deal with the ownership of copyrights in the assigned work?

Although under the law the freelance photographer is presumed to be the owner of all her photographs, it is not uncommon in both editorial and commercial assignments for the client to claim and/or seek to acquire from the freelance all those copyright rights.

Essentially, those clients seek to accomplish this in two ways. First, those contracts (in both editorial and commercial assignments) may provide that the work shall be considered "work made for hire" and thus the copyright property of the client and not the photographer. Under current law, if the work fits within one of the categories where such contracts are permitted (including in newspapers or magazines) and the work is "specially ordered and commissioned" for that use, such contracts will generally be upheld.[84] Most freelance photographers who find such "work-for-hire" provisions in contracts try to have those provisions deleted so that they can retain at least some rights to their work, but often the clients insist that those provisions remain in the agreement. Even where such provisions remain, however, it may be possible for the photographer to be permitted some limited rights to use and exploit the work, such as use in the photographer's promotional materials and display in any show of the photographer's work. And photographers who are asked to sign such "work-for-hire" contracts can try to negotiate additional compensation because all rights in the work are being granted to the client.

Second, the photographer is asked to transfer (in effect, sell) his copyrights in the work to the client in the contract confirming the assignment. Here too, most freelance photographers confronted with such provisions will try to resist them or at least obtain greater compensation and some limited rights in those contracts.

In practice, most clients (including publications, advertising agencies, corporations, etc.) will have well-established policies, and experienced photographers will know what to expect when offered assignments from them. If a photographer does not know a client's policies and wants to know as soon as possible, she should raise the issue immediately upon being offered the assignment to avoid confusion and misunderstanding later. And photographers can always refuse any assignments that contain provisions they consider unfair or inappropriate.

The most difficult situations arise when the photographer does not know that the client expects to own the copyrights in the work until the assignment has been completed and the photographer requests payment. Such situations can create serious tensions between the parties and lead to litigation. However, such situations are increasingly rare, partly because reputable clients disclose in advance their copyright expectations and partly because photographers have learned that they should be clear about those expectations before they accept the assignment.

It is far more common in commercial photography than in editorial photography for the client to expect the photographer to transfer copyrights in the work to the client. In fact, in most editorial assignments for newspapers and magazines, where the need for the work is immediate and short-lived, the client usually expects only "one-time use" in the work and is willing to let the photographer own and control all other rights in it. Such clients will generally pay less for those assignments than if greater rights were transferred to the client. Also, some magazines, particularly those for whom photographs represent an important part of their publications and who tend to use them more than once, expect to acquire the copyrights (sometimes referred to as "all-rights" assignments) and are prepared to pay for those greater rights.[85]

What else do most photography contracts include?

Unlike the contracts that are commonly used to reflect book-publishing, screenwriting, and theatre agreements, which often can run for dozens of excruciating pages, the contracts generally used for freelance photography assignments are often little more than one or two pages. Most clients, especially those who make such assignments on a regular basis, develop their own relatively simple forms, often called work or purchase orders. Those forms generally identify the assignment, the completion or delivery date, the compensation (or method of computing it), the photographer's expenses, the copyright ownership (including any rights the photographer will have), and various representations, warranties, and indemnities running from the photographer to the client. Such contracts may also require the photographer to deliver to the client signed releases from any people (occasionally for places and things) appearing in the photographs. Some of these issues are discussed more fully below.

Many photographers also develop their own form contracts, often denominated confirmations or invoices, which they submit to their clients. Those contracts often contain provisions that flatly contradict provisions in the client's form contract, such as providing that the photographer owns the copyright in the work and narrowly limiting the rights being acquired by the client, and both sides may think that their contracts govern the assignment. In the end, however, it is the client who will probably have the last word if the photographer wants to get paid for the assignment and receive future assignments from that client.

It is possible that the parties' agreement will not be in writing but will be an oral agreement or entirely (or almost entirely) unspoken. Thus, an editor of a newspaper or magazine might simply telephone a freelance photographer and ask her to cover an event without saying more about the assignment. In such circumstances, the contract of the parties will be deemed consistent with their prior relationship or be inferred from the established customs and practices that generally apply to such assignments. Importantly, neither a "work-for-hire" relationship nor a transfer of copyright can be accomplished in such an oral or unspoken contract since the law requires a written agreement for those purposes.[86]

One further point should be made: Sometimes it may not be clear exactly who the client is, especially where an advertising agency is hiring the photographer to take photographs for a client of the agency.[87] Who is responsible to the photographer for payment and honoring the other terms of the contract? If there is any doubt on this issue, the photographer should attempt to make clear in the contract who the real client is.

How are freelance photographers paid?

In a variety of ways, depending on the nature of the assignment and the policies and practices of both parties. Many assignments provide that the photographer will be paid at an hourly, daily, or weekly rate, regardless of the number of photographs taken or ultimately used. Other assignments provide for payment based on the number of photographs taken, which might be appropriate for elaborate and complicated shots. Still other assignments provide for payment based on the use the client makes of the photographs (usually referred to as the *page* or *space* rate), commonly used when a magazine assigns a photographer to shoot a whole feature for it but won't know until it sees the results how much of it will actually be published, although in such cases there will usually be a minimum payment to the photographer.

In most cases, regardless of the form of compensation, the client will also reimburse the photographer for at least some of his expenses on the assignment, although those expenses may have to be approved in advance. Also, particularly where the photographer has doubts about the reliability (or solvency) of the client, it would be prudent to add to the contract the time of payment and a provision that the client will not be authorized to use the work until full payment has been made.

The photographer should always feel free to negotiate the best compensation for the assignment, and it can happen, especially if the client wants the special talents (or availability) of the photographer, that the photographer will be able to negotiate terms more favorable than originally offered.

As a general proposition, commercial photography pays better than editorial, at least in monetary compensation.[88] However, editorial photography, especially when it appears in the most "sophisticated" publications, can provide greater exposure and prestige, and, if the photographer retains rights in the work after the assignment, the potential for future exploitation of the work. Contracts for editorial assignments usually provide that if the client makes use of the work beyond the one-time use originally contemplated, additional payments will be made.

What kinds of representations, warranties, and indemnities do photography contracts contain?

Photography agreements are similar to the agreements book authors, screenwriters, and playwrights are often asked to sign. They usually provide that the photographer "represents" and "warrants" to the client that the work does not violate any copyrights or other property rights of third parties, does not contain anything that is libelous, invade anyone's right of privacy or publicity, or otherwise present any legal risk to the client. Such provisions also usually provide that the photographer will indemnify and hold the client harmless from any expenses or damages incurred as a result of any breach or alleged breach of any of those representations or warranties. In many respects (including in particular the obligation to indemnify for an "alleged breach," where the photographer may not have done anything wrong), such provisions seem especially harsh and unfair. However, as in the other media where similar requirements are common, it will often be difficult to persuade the client to delete or modify these provisions, but this does not mean the effort should not be made.

Especially when the client requests the photographer to

make such representations, the photographer should at least consider requesting corresponding representations from the client. Through such provisions, the client would "cover" the photographer if claims are made against the photographer based on the use of the work by the client, anything added to or removed from the work by the client, or anything else done by the client over which the photographer had no control.[89]

What about credit to the photographer?

An important component of the contract for freelance photography is the credit to be given the photographer when the work is used by the client. If the contract does not deal with credit, it is likely that the client will have no obligation to credit the photographer. The photographer should insist that the work be credited to her, along with (if appropriate) a copyright notice in the name of the photographer.[90] This is particularly important if the photographer expects a particular form of byline and copyright notice in a book. Under the Copyright Act, the omission of a separate copyright notice in the photographer's name will normally not jeopardize that copyright since the copyright notice covering the work as a whole will be deemed to protect the separately owned components of the work.[91]

When is it necessary to obtain releases from the subjects of photographs?

Whenever the contract says you must. Beyond that, the answer depends on a variety of factors, including the circumstances of the shooting and the intended use of the photographs. Photographs of public events or everyday street scenes that are used for editorial purposes normally do not require any permission or release from the subjects, at least where there is a "reasonable" editorial basis for their use.

In a recent case, a magazine used a photograph of a large family to illustrate an article about how injections of caffeine supposedly increased the fertility of a man's sperm. The family did not consent, was not even aware that its photograph was to be used in this way, and did not use caffeine or any other fertility enhancements. In 1990 the highest court of New York rejected the family's claim of invasion of privacy, finding that the photograph had a "reasonable relationship" to the article and that the magazine therefore had the legal right to use it in that way.[92]

Similarly, in an earlier case, the *New York Times Magazine* published an article on the "black middle class" and used a photograph of a well-dressed black man on a New York street to illustrate the article. That man did not consent to that use, wasn't aware of it until it was published, and did not agree with the thesis of the article. But the same New York court rejected his privacy suit, holding that as long as the photograph was reasonably related to the article, it was immune from legal liability.[93] While the court absolved the magazine of liability for that reason, it also held that the photographer could be sued for selling the photograph to the magazine. However, the New York legislature soon thereafter amended the New York "Right of Privacy" statute to make it clear that where the publication can't be sued for any such use, neither can the photographer.[94]

Generally, photographs of people that are to be used in advertisements or for other commercial purposes, even if taken at public events or street scenes, do require written releases or permission from those people. This is because the law in most states protects individuals (whether or not they're well known or have any publicity value) from the commercial (as distinct from editorial) use of their likenesses.[95]

In some cases, even photographs destined for editorial use may require releases. This is especially true where the shooting involves professional models, celebrities, or others who have been asked and agree to be photographed by the photographer. In such cases, the relationship between the photographer and the subject can be seen as a contractual one, and it's always possible that the terms of that "contract" will be disputed later. For example, the subject of the photos might claim that she was promised approval rights over the photos to be used or that they could be used only one time in one specified publication or that the ownership rights in them would belong to the subject.[96] To avoid future confrontations, it is desirable to get a release or other contract from the subject confirming the terms applicable to the shooting.[97]

What happens when a photographer wants to exploit rights to preexisting work?

In addition to work created pursuant to an assignment, most photographers create work on their own, for pleasure, for future exploitation, or both. Also, photographers who do not convey to the client all rights to work created on an assignment will own and control rights to that work. As a result, most freelance photographers own rights to a large stock of their photographs.

There are two principal ways photographers can exploit that work. First, they can attempt to exploit those rights themselves by letting potential users (e.g., newspapers, magazines, advertising agencies) know of the availability of the work and by entering into agreements for the use of such work. The ways to do this include preparing and sending promotional material describing the work and its availability, running appropriate advertisements in trade publications and the like, and visiting potential users face-to-face. In most cases, the license fees payable for limited ("one-time") use of preexisting work are fairly modest, ranging from as little as $25 to several hundred and (infrequently) many thousands of dollars.[98] Photographers will obviously have to devote considerable time and energy exploiting their preexisting work if they expect to realize significant income in this way.

Which leads to the other way photographers can exploit that work—the "stock house." A stock house is a business that handles the preexisting work of photographers. It gathers such work from the photographers it represents, including negatives and transparencies, and then licenses (in effect, as agent for the photographers) rights to that work to potential users. Most stock houses develop a reputation for the kind of photographs they have available (celebrities, sports action, travel, etc.), and potential users who need a particular kind of photograph will call one or more of those houses to see what they have.[99] The stock house will send selected photographs to the potential client, and if the client chooses to use one or more, the client and the stock house will quickly enter into a contract covering that use.

Such dealings tend to be quite informal, many based on oral understandings and assumptions. When a stock house sends photographs to a potential client, it is essentially trusting that client not to use the work until an agreement for that use has been reached, to return the work, and not to lose or damage it. If the client violates that trust, the stock house and the photographer will feel the consequences—through the loss of income from the use, the loss of control over the work, and perhaps the loss of the work itself.

Photographers should be careful in selecting the stock house that will handle their work. They should always try to discuss and agree upon the terms governing the relationship, including the scope of the stock house's authority to deal with the work (e.g., minimum acceptable fees, unacceptable uses or users, special limits on certain photographs); the house's compensation for its services (usually at least 50 percent of the generated income); what happens if the work is lost or damaged; credits to be given the photographer when work is used; and the nature and extent of the house's reporting and payment obligations to the photographer. And whenever possible, the parties should reduce their agreement to a written contract.

What happens when a photographer's work is lost or damaged?

Unfortunately, this seems to happen with some regularity, and more and more photographers (and stock houses) have brought suit in recent years to recover damages for such losses. Many photographers, encouraged by the American Society of Magazine Photographers, the leading organization representing freelance photographers,[100] attempt to put into their contracts a provision that each photograph lost or damaged is worth at least $1,500 or a similar amount. Most clients, however, will refuse to agree to such provisions, and most courts will not enforce them.[101] Instead, the courts will try to ascertain the true value of the lost or damaged photographs by looking to such factors as their uniqueness, prior income-producing history, and cost of replacing them.

The photographer or stock house will first have to prove which photographs were lost or damaged by the client. For this reason, it is crucially important that they keep complete records on all deliveries of their work to others.

What is the role of the photographer's representative?

Many freelance photographers use the services of a photographer's representative ("rep"). In such cases, the terms of the parties' agreement should be discussed and reduced to writing at the beginning of the relationship. Issues such as the rep's responsibilities and authority to speak for and commit the photographer, compensation to be paid the rep and reimbursement of the rep's expenses, the rep's reporting and payment obligations, and the circumstances and consequences of a termination of the relationship, should all be clearly spelled out in that contract. If any potential users of the photographer's work are to be excluded from the rep's role (sometimes called *house accounts*), this should also be made clear in the contract.[102]

What happens when the photographer's work is considered fine art?

In addition to the use of photographs in publications and advertising and other commercial uses referred to above, photographs are often sold in galleries and otherwise treated as fine art. For the most part, the applicable contracts are essentially the same as those used in connection with original works of visual art, discussed in the following section.

CONTRACTS INVOLVING VISUAL ARTISTS

Although legally speaking the works of authors and artists have much in common, the differences in work product have led to different legal problems and solutions. Writings of authors are intended to be reproduced and disseminated to as large an audience as possible, and original manuscripts usually have little value. The opposite is true of visual artists: The original often has the most value, and the right to own and control the original may be more important than the right to own and control reproductions. This helps explain the existence of the theories of *droit moral* and *droit de suite* discussed in Chapter II. This may also explain the differences between the contracts involving visual artists and some of the others we've discussed thus far.

What is the standard contractual relationship between an artist and a gallery?[103]

There are two principal kinds of artist-gallery relationships.[104] In the first the gallery purchases the work of the artist outright and sells it for its own benefit. This happens most often when an artist dies and the estate does not wish to continue to own the artist's works.

In the relationship most common for living artists, the gallery accepts an artist's work on consignment and acts as the artist's agent or representative in seeking to sell it. Laws have been passed in New York[105] and California[106] governing consignment of artworks to art dealers for exhibition and sale. They provide that unless artwork has been sold outright to a gallery or the artist has received full compensation, the work is deemed on consignment.

How does consignment operate?

Under the statutes, the dealer is "deemed to be the agent of such artist," the work of fine art "is trust property in the hands of the consignee [dealer] for the benefit of the consignor [artist]," and "any proceeds from the sale of such work of fine art are trust funds in the hands of the consignee for the benefit of the consignor."[107] The New York statute provides that

> whenever an artist . . . delivers or causes to be delivered a work of fine art . . . to an art merchant for the purposes of exhibition and/or sale on a commission, fee or other basis of compensation, the delivery to and acceptance thereof by the art merchant establishes a consignor/consignee relationship . . . and such work shall remain trust property notwithstanding its purchase by the consignee for his own account until the price is paid in full to the consignor. If such work is thereafter resold to a bona fide third party before the consignor has been paid in full, the proceeds of the resale are trust funds in the hands of the consignee for the benefit of the consignor to the extent necessary to pay any balance still due to the consignor and such trusteeship shall continue until the fiduciary obligation of the consignee with respect to such transaction is discharged in full.[108]

The statute also provides that "any provision of a contract or agreement whereby the consignor waives [most of the major provisions of the statute] is absolutely void."[109]

In states where no statute like New York's has been enacted, the consignment relationship is governed by the law of consigned goods generally.[110] The "fiduciary" and "trust" protections of the New York and California laws are not available, although it is generally believed that the artist-dealer relationship is always one of principal and agent, the agent assuming fiduciary responsibilities to the artist, especially where there is a significant disparity in business acumen.[111] In those states where no special protection is available, an artist's work in the custody of a gallery can be subject to the claims of the gallery's creditors[112] unless (1) certain notices to the contrary are properly posted, (2) it can be established that the dealer is known by creditors to be engaged in the business of selling the goods of others, and (3) a financial statement has been filed in a governmental office. Artists who want the kind of protection afforded by the New York law will have to obtain it in their contracts with their galleries.

If a gallery is acting as an artist's agent, what should their agreement include?

A gallery will usually insist on the exclusive right to represent the artist's work in a geographic territory. The artist should seek to exclude from exclusive coverage his studio sales, gifts, or barter of his work. The borders of the territory should be carefully spelled out. The agreement should be clear about what works are covered: For example, does it apply only to existing work, or does it include works created after the agreement is entered into? Is the agreement limited to a specific number of works per year, to all of the artist's output in a particular year, or perhaps to the artist's work in one medium? Who chooses from the artist's work, the gallery or the artist? The agreement should always confirm the artist's ownership of the work and that the works are not subject to creditors' claims. It is most important that such questions be fully agreed upon when the contract is made.

The agreement should have a time limit. Any period longer than 3 years is probably unwise from the artist's point of view. Many artists seek to impose an annual minimum-sales requirement on the gallery as a condition of keeping the agreement in effect.

If the gallery has branches, the agreement should specify where the work will be displayed. Also, if the artist is relying on a particular person in the gallery to handle the work, the agreement should so specify.

The artist may seek the right to approve, or at least be consulted on, how and where in the gallery her works may be shown and whether some will be on permanent exhibition. The agreement can require a minimum number of exhibitions devoted to the artist during the term of the agreement and can specify the location, opening date, duration, and space for the exhibitions. It can give the artist the right to be present and participate in the hanging, arranging, and lighting of exhibitions. It can specify whether the exhibition will be exclusive or other artists' work will also be shown. The artist may desire the right to withdraw from a group show if she does not approve of the other artists. It is important that the agreement specify who will bear the cost of exhibitions; otherwise, the artist may assume that the gallery will pay while the gallery assumes that the costs will be deducted from the artist's return on sales. The cost and content of promotional and advertising material should also be dealt with in the agreement.

How does the gallery get paid?

Two methods are common. In the "net-price" method the gallery's compensation is the difference between a price agreed between gallery and artist and the price received by the gallery.[113] In the "commission" method, the gallery gets a percentage of the sales price.[114] The problem with the net-price method is that the gallery may profit unconscionably if the artist's work substantially increases in value after the contract price is fixed. Problems with the commission method include the allocation of prices if there are bulk sales and the risk that the gallery may conduct internal sales (i.e., sales to itself). Many artists seek to combine the two methods of payment or seek other remedies to these problems.[115]

How does the gallery price the artist's work?

The agreement should provide for consultation with the artist, if not the artist's prior approval. If prices have been agreed upon, the gallery may request discretionary authority to vary them by a certain percentage. The prices should be reviewed periodically. The agreement may also deal with rental prices. If the gallery extends credit to purchasers, the agreement should specify whether the payment to the artist is to be based on the amount of the sale or on the money actually received by the gallery, the issue being whether the artist is to participate in the risks and delays inherent in the gallery's decision to grant credit.

What other provisions may the agreement include?

The agreement should contain provisions about record keeping. The artist should insist that records about his works be kept in a separate ledger and that the gallery keep separate receipts for each piece. Payment schedules should also be listed in the book. The artist should have the right to inspect the gallery's books and records periodically, and the agreement should provide for monthly or quarterly payments to the artist, accompanied by a statement. The agreement may grant the artist the right to recapture the work from time to time, without payment to the gallery, to exhibit or renovate it.

Every contract, especially a contract that excludes the artist's sales from her studio, should include a specific description of the work consigned and terms of payment and should specify whether the artist or the gallery bears the risk of loss before delivery to the gallery and the time and method of delivery. Moreover, if the eventual purchaser will acquire the right to reproduce the work, the contract must expressly so provide; otherwise, the provisions of the Copyright Act[116] and the laws of several states[117] provide that reproduction rights do not go with the work but remain with the artist.

What about commissioned works?

Again, it is important to agree in writing. The subject matter of the work should be clearly described. Schedules for completion and payment should be spelled out; usually payments are made at the beginning, on delivery of sketches, and on delivery of the final work. Since such a contract requires the artist's personal services, it is terminated by the artist's death or disability.[118] The agreement should make clear which rights in the unfinished work go to the commissioning party and which to the artist if the contract is terminated before completion. If the agreement provides that the work is to be completed to the "satisfaction" of the commissioning party, a matter that has been a continuing source of controversy,[119] it should state how such satisfaction will be determined.

In one recent case, a large work of sculpture that was commissioned by the U.S. government for placement in a plaza in front of a federal office building in New York became the subject of controversy when the government decided to move it to another location in response to complaints from pedestrians whose passage through the plaza was obstructed by the work. Despite the sculptor's claim that his contractual and First Amendment rights would be violated if the work was removed from the place for which it was created, the federal courts approved the move.[120] The case highlights the importance (in dealing with all commissioned work, but perhaps especially when the commissioning party is the government) of including in the contract protections against the commissioning party's taking unilateral actions the artist might find objectionable.[121]

What if an artist is fortunate enough to have a showing at a museum?

There should be a written contract that spells out all the rights and responsibilities of the museum and the artist. (Most museums will have their own forms for these purposes.) Matters to be considered include the museum's receipt of the work, the condition and description of the work, whether the contract constitutes a loan of the work to the museum, how long the museum is entitled to keep the work, special precautions for the preservation and safety of the work, who bears the responsibility for loss of the work, and who pays for insuring the work. The museum may seek an option to purchase; if so, the terms should be clearly stated. If the method of installation is important, it should be specified, along with any requirements the artist considers important about framing or exhibiting the work. If prints are to be included in the museum's catalog, the artist can seek the right to approve the reproductions. Many museums now seek the right to reproduce for commercial purposes works of art they have on exhibition; such a request should be considered carefully by the artist.

What about an agreement between an artist and a publisher?

An artist enters into an agreement with a publisher when a work is to be reproduced in a book or magazine, when the artist creates graphic work for reproduction and distribution as an edition, and when the artist is asked to illustrate a book.

Many of the considerations discussed in the section on author-publisher contracts apply to artists: the grant of rights, the manner of payment and accounting for them, representations and warranties, and so on.

If the artist is doing graphic work for reproduction and distribution as an edition, the agreement should specify the method of reproduction, the materials to be used (color, ink, paper, etc.), the size of the image, the size of the edition, perhaps even the printer. If only one or a few works are to be reproduced, the agreement can specify method of reproduction, size of publication, and time and place of publication.

For illustrated books, it may be important to state whether the publisher or the artist has the right to the original work and who can exploit subsidiary rights such as using the work commercially or as a graphic design. The agreement should spell out how many illustrations are necessary, their size, when they are due, and what colors will be used.

Regardless of the type of publication, the artist should always seek the right to examine and approve proofs of the work before printing. The contract should make clear who owns the copyright in the artist's work and whether the artist is working as an "employee for hire" of the publisher.

How have artists attempted to secure a continuing interest in increasing values of their work?

Although only California has a law giving artists the right to receive resale royalties,[122] many artists have attempted to include such a right in contracts.

Artists have attempted to use the Artist's Reserved Rights to Transfer and Sale Agreement, a proposed form contract drafted in 1970 by Robert Projansky, a New York lawyer, and Seth Siegelaub, an art dealer.[123] The "Projansky agreement" provides that when a work is resold, the artist is entitled to 15 percent of any increase in sales price. The agreement also provides the artist with

1. a record of who owns each work at all times
2. the right to be notified when the work is to be exhibited so that the artist can advise upon or veto the proposed exhibition
3. the right to borrow the work for exhibition for 2 months every 5 years without payment to the owner
4. the right to be consulted if repairs are necessary
5. half of any rental income paid to the owner for the use of the work at exhibitions

6.   all reproduction rights

Financial participation in future sales continues for the life of the artist and the artist's spouse, and for 21 years thereafter. The agreement also provides that if the work is destroyed by fire, the artist is to receive 15 percent of the insurance proceeds.

How is the Projansky agreement designed to be used?

An artist is generally a party only to the first sale contract. To be binding on future purchasers, the agreement must be in the first sale, gift, or barter by the artist, and each owner must be required to incorporate it in every following transfer of the work. It is not designed for use when works are lent for exhibition or left with a dealer on consignment. To ensure that successive owners use the agreement or at least are aware of it, it is necessary to affix a notice of the existence of the agreement somewhere on the work itself.

Since each owner uses the agreement in transferring the work to a successor, the agreement provides a ready record of the work's authenticity and chain of title, providing a benefit to the owners. It has been said that owners also benefit when a continuing relationship is created between owner and artist, providing assurance to each owner that the work is being used in harmony with the artist's intentions and recognizing that the artist maintains a moral relationship to the work, even though the owner has possession and control of it.

Has the agreement been widely used?

Unfortunately, from the artist's point of view, the answer is no. It has generated the same heated controversy that has engulfed most proposed legislation in this area; it has encountered tremendous resistance from galleries and owners;[124] and doubts have been raised about its enforceability.[125]

An introduction to the agreement by coauthor Siegelaub acknowledged the radical changes the agreement would cause in the art world. It nonetheless exhorted the artists to whom the agreement is addressed to be steadfast in their determination to use it. The introduction recognizes that to be effective, the agreement must be used systematically by artists and that its acceptance depends upon the strength of the artists' will. The authors of the agreement have emphasized the importance of that effort: "We realize that this Agreement is essentially unprecedented in the art world and that it just may cause a little rumbling and trembling; on the other hand, the ills it remedies are universally acknowledged to exist and no other practical way has ever been devised to cure them."[126]

Have there been attempts to devise similar contracts?

Yes. Several years after the Projansky agreement was introduced, another New York attorney, Charles Jurrist, developed a variation that in some respects is simpler and more practical.[127] The artist receives a more modest package of rights, and collectors receive safeguards designed to make the contract more palatable to them. Perhaps most significantly, the 15 percent royalty to the artist is payable only on the first resale of the work. This eliminates the requirement of ongoing contracts and consequently does not restrict the market for the work as much as the Projansky agreement does. However, it also denies the artist the right to participate in what may be the largest increases in the value of his work.

The Jurrist agreement has not been widely adopted either.[128] It is still true that artists who want to participate in increased resale value and to enjoy the other benefits of the Projansky and Jurrist agreements will have to continue to fight for their rights every time they enter into a contract for their work.[129]

NOTES

1. *See, e.g.*, J. Calamari & J. Perillo, *The Law of Contracts* (1970) (hereinafter, Calamari & Perillo); 17 *Am. Jur.* 2d Contracts §10 (1964) (hereinafter, *Am. Jur.*).

2. For example, a contract is defined in *Restatement (Second) Contracts* §1 (1979) (hereinafter, *Restatement*) as "a promise or set of promises for the breach of which the law gives a remedy, or the performance of which the law in some way recognizes as a duty."

3. *Academy Chicago Publishers v. Cheever*, 18 Med. L. Rep. 2327, at 2329 (Ill. 1991).

4. *See, e.g.*, "AAP, AAUP Support Academy on Contract Issue," *Publishers Weekly*, July 25, 1991, p.7; "Authors Guild 'Appalled' by AAP Letter Criticizing Cheever Ruling," *Publishers Weekly*, August 23, 1991, p.10; Garbus & Smith, "Will the 'Cheever' Case Affect Other

Author/Publisher Relationships?," *N.Y. Law Journal*, Aug. 6, 1991, p.1.

5. *See generally Am. Jur.* §16; *Restatement* §§12–16.
6. Calamari & Perillo at 10; *Restatement* §§178–85.
7. *Roddy-Eden v. Berle*, 108 N.Y.S.2d 597, 600, 202 Misc. 261, 264 (Sup. Ct. N.Y. Co. 1951).
8. *See* "Congress Kills Helms Effort to Censor NEA Grants," *Publishers Weekly*, Nov. 22, 1991, p.15.
9. *See generally, Am. Jur.* §§151–54; *Restatement* §§174–77.
10. However, in a proposal that was somewhat controversial at the time it was first announced, Section 208 of the Restatement provides: "If a contract or term thereof is unconscionable at the time the contract is made a court may refuse to enforce the contract, or may enforce the remainder of the contract without the unconscionable term, or may so limit the application of any unconscionable term as to avoid any unconscionable result." Obviously, insofar as this proposal is concerned, the definition of "unconscionable" becomes crucial. In this connection, the drafters of the Restatement have commented as follows: "A bargain is not unconscionable merely because the parties to it are unequal in bargaining position, not even because the inequality results in an allocation of risks to the weaker party. But gross inequality of bargaining power, together with terms unreasonably favorable to the stronger party, may confirm indications that the transaction involved elements of deception or compulsion, or may show that the weaker party had no meaningful choice, no real alterative, or did not in fact assent or appear to assent to the unfair terms."
11. *See generally Restatement* ch. 5.
12. 17 U.S.C. §§101 *et seq.*
13. *Id.* §204.
14. *See. e.g., Am. Jur.* §§244–45; *Restatement* ch. 9.
15. *See, e.g., Restatement* §§219–23; Calamari & Perillo §52.
16. *See generally, Restatement* §§357–69.
17. *Id.* §§359–60.
18. *Id.* §§346–56.
19. *See* Calamari & Perillo §203.
20. For example, in *Freund v. Washington Sq. Press, Inc.*, 34 N.Y.2d 379 (1974), the plaintiff had delivered a manuscript in accordance with his agreement with the defendant publisher, which then failed to publish the work. The author sued for lost royalties. The court refused to permit any award for the claimed lost royalties, saying that unless there was a "stable foundation for a reasonable estimate of what a book might earn," royalties could not be approximated. *See also Demaris L. G. P. Putnam's Sons*, 379 F. Supp. 294 (C.D. Cal. 1973); *Gilroy v.*

American Broadcasting Co., 58 A.D.2d 533, 395 N.Y.S.2d 658 (1st Dept. 1977) ("The proper measure of damages flowing from defendants' wrongful appropriation of plaintiff's literary property is the reasonable value thereof and opinion evidence of the value of the property is admissible.")

21. In *Frankel v. Stein & Day, Inc.*, 470 F. Supp. 209 (S.D.N.Y. 1979), the authors successfully sued for reversion of rights due to the publisher's failure to pay royalties. *See also Nolen v. Sam Fox Pub. Co.*, 499 F.2d 1394 (2d Cir. 1974); *Septembertide Pub., B.V. v. Stein and Day, Inc.*, 884 F.2d 675 (2d Cir. 1989).

22. In 1991, the two major organizations of literary agents, the Independent Literary Agents Association (ILAA) and the Society of Authors' Representatives (SAR), which was divided into a literary branch and a dramatic branch, merged into a new organization called the Associatic of Authors' Representatives. Authors interested in learning more about how agents function, or in obtaining lists of the agent members of that organizations should contact it at 10 Astor Place, Third Floor, New York, NY 10003. In addition, agency contracts are discussed in Crawford, *The Writer's Legal Guide* ch. 6, (1977).

23. *See* 3 *Am. Jur.*, 2d Agency §199 (1964).

24. *Id.* §§37–50.

25. *Id.* §§62–67.

26. *See Bernstein v. G. Schirmer, Inc.*, N.Y.L.J., May 2, 1986, p. 7 (Sup. Ct., N.Y. County).

27. 17 U.S.C. §101.

28. *Id.* §201(a).

29. The agreement is discussed—and criticized—in 3 Farber, *Entertainment Industry Contracts* at 124–25, 124–32 (1990) (hereinafter, Farber).

30. The legal aspects of self-publication are beyond the scope of this chapter. Interested authors should consult Henderson, ed., *The Publish-It-Yourself Handbook*, (1973), and Appelbaum, *How to Get Happily Published*, 4th ed. (1992). The latter provides a wealth of pertinent and practical information.

31. *See* the sections on playwrights and screenwriters below.

32. In Great Britain, the two writers associations, the Society of Authors and Writers Guild, had prepared a Minimum Terms Agreement. Recently, the Penguin Group, a major house, signed the minimum agreement. One significant term is that the grant is not for the life of the copyright; rather, it is for a limited 10 year term, and either party has the right to review the agreement after that term. "Penguin Signs Authors' Minimum Terms Agreement," *Publishers Weekly*, August 3, 1990, at 14. Attempts in the United States by groups representing

authors to negotiate similar "minimum terms" agreements with American publishers have been largely unavailing.

33. The Authors Guild makes available a form contract prepared from the author's perspective, a guide for use along with it, and another earlier guide containing excellent explanations and comparisons of various clauses (hereinafter, A.G. Guide). It is available at the Guild's office, 234 W. 44th St., New York, NY 10036.

34. P.E.N. Standards for Author's Access to Information from Book Publishers (hereinafter, P.E.N. Standards) was published in the December 1980 issue of the P.E.N. newsletter. Reprints are available from P.E.N. at 568 Broadway, New York, NY 10012.

35. The provision of the Copyright Act that establishes the author's ownership is 17 U.S.C. §102.

36. The U.S. Copyright Act provides that in the absence of an express agreement providing otherwise, a magazine that acquires a freelance article or work of visual art "is presumed to have acquired only the privilege of reproducing and distributing the contribution as part of that particular [issue of the magazine], any revision of that [issue], and any later [issue] in the same series." 17 U.S.C. §201(c).

37. *E.g., Harcourt Brace Jovanovich, Inc. v. Goldwater*, 532 F. Supp. 619 (S.D.N.Y. 1982); *Random House, Inc. v. Gold*, 464 F. Supp. 1306 (S.D.N.Y.), *aff'd*, 607 F.2d 998 (2d Cir. 1979); *Stein and Day, Inc. v. Morgan*, 5 Med. L. Rptr. 1831 (Sup. Ct. N.Y. Co. 1979).

38. *Harcourt Brace Jovanovich, Inc. v. Goldwater, supra* note 37.

39. *Id.* at 624.

40. *Id.*

41. *Doubleday & Co., Inc. v. Curtis*, 763 F.2d 495 (2d Cir. 1985).

42. *Id.* at 501.

43. *Prentice-Hall v. Kamen*, (Civil Ct., N.Y. Co., 1984) (Index No. 40742-82).

44. *See* Supplement No. 3 of Recommended Trade Book Contract, published by the Authors Guild, *supra* note 33, which also appeared in the Jan.–Feb. 1981 issue of the Authors Guild Bulletin.

45. *Harcourt Brace Jovanovich, Inc. v. Goldwater, supra* note 35. *See also, Dell Publishing Co. v. Whedon*, 577 F. Supp. 1459 (S.D.N.Y. 1984).

46. *United States Naval Institute, v. Charter Communications, Inc.*, 875 F.2d 1044 (2d Cir. 1989), *rev'g* 867 F. Supp. 114 (S.D.N.Y. 1989).

47. 17. U.S.C. §101.

48. *Zilg v. Prentice-Hall, Inc.*, 717 F.2d 671 (2d Cir. 1983).

49. *Id.* at 680.

50. *Id.*

51. For example, in *Prentice Hall, Inc. v. Bregman*, (Civ. Ct., NY County,

1985) (Index No. 57741-82), the court granted summary judgment to a publisher seeking return of the advance after determining the author's manuscript to be unacceptable, rejecting the argument that the publisher had a duty to provide suggestions and guidance after reading the author's first draft.

52. An extensive discussion of publishers' royalty statements may be found in a three-part 1981 article by Richard Curtis in *Locus, The Newspaper of the Science Fiction Field*, reprinted in Curtis, *How to be Your Own Literary Agent* (1983). *See also Supplement No. 4 of Recommended Trade Book Contract*, published by the Authors Guild, *supra* n. 33, which also appeared in the Sept.–Oct. 1981 issue of the Authors Guild Bulletin; and P.E.N. Standards, *supra* note 34.

53. *Levering v. Addison-Wesley*, 12 Med. L. Rep. 1807 (N.D. Cal. 1986).

54. *Nolan v. Sam Fox Pub. Co.*, 499 F.2d 1394 (2d Cir. 1974) (cancellation is granted only where breach is material and substantial, as where fraud exists or there has been a total failure to pay royalties; it was denied here where 26 percent of the royalties due were paid).

55. *Arthur Guinness & Sons v. Sterling Pub. Co.*, 732 F.2d 1095 (2d Cir. 1984).

56. *Sperber v. Lawrence Freundlich Publishers*, 14 Med. L. Rep. 18798 (Sup. Ct., N.Y. County, 1987). *But see Septembertide Pub., B.V. v. Stein and Day, Inc.*, 884 F.2d 675 (2d Cir. 1989).

57. *See generally*, Speiser, "Insuring Authors: A New Proposal," *Publishers Weekly*, May 7, 1982; Speiser, "Writing a New Page for Authors on Indemnification of Publishers," *National Law Journal*, Feb. 1, 1982; Pell, "Insuring Free Speech," *Nation*, Mar. 13, 1982.

58. *See, e.g., Supplement No. 1 of Recommended Trade Book Contract*, published by the Authors Guild, *supra* n. 33, which states in part: "Non-compete clauses should be deleted. If the publisher refuses, the clause should be tightened. There should be a reasonably short time period, after which it expires. The types of books to which it applies should be stated, specifically. Authors of textbooks should be particularly careful that they limit the effect of the clause, so that the contract for one book on a subject does not prevent them from writing other texts on the subject for other age groups, or for different types of classes or schools." *See also, Wolf v. Illustrated World Encyclopedia. Inc.*, 34 N.Y.2d 838 (1974), *aff'g* 41 A.D.2d 191 (1st Dept. 1973); "Author Charges Non-Compete Clause in Restraint of Trade," *Publishers Weekly*, Aug. 10, 1990, p.320.

59. *See e.g., Harcourt Brace Jovanovich, Inc. v. Farrar, Straus & Giroux, Inc.*, 4 Med. L. Rptr. 2625 (Sup. Ct. N.Y. Co. 1979).

60. *See Supplement No. 1, supra* note 33, which states in part: "The best way to deal with an option clause is to delete it from the publisher's

contract form. Many authors (even newcomers) and agents insist on this, and publishers do delete the clause. Some publishers accede because they recognize the clause is unfair; and that a harmonious relationship, and an author's continuing loyalty, cannot he coerced by this one-way provision."

61. *See Arneson v. TSR Hobbies, Inc.*, 225 U.S.P.Q. 1252 (D. Minn. 1985), where the plaintiff author was awarded summary judgment in a contract dispute with the publisher as to whether an expanded manual for "Dungeons and Dragons" was a "revised edition" warranting additional royalties under the agreement.

62. 17 U.S.C. §302.

63. *See Authors Guild Recommended Trade Book Contract, supra* note 33, at 20.

64. Although such a clause was upheld in *In re Little & Ives Co.*, 262 F. Supp. 719 (S.D.N.Y. 1966), it may well run afoul of the provisions of the revised Bankruptcy Act, which invalidates such clauses under certain circumstances. *See* 11 U.S.C. §365(e).

65. For further discussion of this kind of publishing, with conflicting points of view, *see* Appelbaum, *supra* note 30, at 74–76; Crawford, *supra* note 22 at ch. 8; and McDowell, "More Authors Turn to Vanity Presses," *New York Times*, May 26, 1982.

66. "$3.5 Million Verdict Against Vanity Publisher," *N.Y.L.J.*, April 9, 1990, at 1; "Jury Awards $3.5 Million in Damages Against Vantage Press," *Publisher's Weekly*, April 20, 1990, at 18.

67. *Publisher's Weekly, supra* note 66.

68. There are actually two separate Writers Guilds—the Writers Guild of America, West, Inc., at 8955 Beverly Blvd., West Hollywood, CA 90048-2456, ((213) 550-1000), and the Writers Guild of America, East, Inc., 555 West 57th St., New York, NY 10019, (212) 245-6180).

69. *See, e.g.*, Para. 19, Theatrical Schedule A, Basic Agreement, Writers Guild of America 261 (1985). However, the *Los Angeles Times* reported in 1987 the filing of an action in Los Angeles Superior Court by Gore Vidal to challenge a WGA determination to give to Steve Shagan sole writing credit for the screenplay entitled *The Sicilian*. Farber at 8–86 n.1 (1990).

70. *Buchwald v. Paramount Pictures Corp.*, Sup. Ct. L.A. County, No. C 706083 (Dec. 21, 1990).

71. *Buchwald v. Paramount Pictures Corp.*, 1990 Cal. App. LEXIS 634 (Sup. Ct. 1990).

72. "Hit Picture Still Shows No Profit: Buchwald Suit," *National Law Journal*, April 30, 1990, at 1.

73. *Id.*

74. In a sequel, the principal characters of one story are presented in an entirely new and different story; it depends on the new work's content, not it's title. *See Trust Co. Bank v. MGM/UA Entertainment Co.*, 593 F. Supp. 580 (N.D. Ga. 1984), *aff'd*, 772 F.2d 740 (11th Cir. 1985); *Rossner v. CBS*, 612 F. Supp. 334 (S.D.N.Y. 1985).

75. Farber at 125–6.

76. Every playwright should know about the Dramatists Guild, Inc., and its various agreements. The Guild's address is 234 West 44th St., New York, NY 10036; its telephone number is (212) 398-9366.

77. *See generally*, Farber, ch. 128.

78. Farber at 125–67.

79. Farber at 123-1.

80. The principal organization representing the interests of professional photographers is the American Society of Magazine Photographers (ASMP), 419 Park Avenue South, New York, NY 10016, (212) 889-9144. The ASMP publishes a variety of materials relating to the business practices and legal rights of professional photographers, including its *Professional Business Practices in Photography* (1986), which contains valuable background information and sample form documents designed for use by its members. Another useful resource for the legal rights of photographers is Cavallo & Kahan, *Photography: What's the Law* (1976).

81. The "work made for hire" doctrine is discussed in Chapter II. Section 201(6) of the U.S. Copyright Act provides that "in the case of a work made for hire, the employer or other person for whom the work was prepared is considered the author [of the work]. . . ." Section 101 sets forth the two different ways by which a work will be considered a work made for hire. In an important 1989 case, the Supreme Court made clear that a person need not be a full-time salaried employee for "work for hire" purposes, so long as the relationship between the employer and that person satisfies a well-established set of legal guidelines that are used to determine when the employer would otherwise be legally responsible for the "independent contractor." *Community for Creative Non-Violence v. Reid*, 490 U.S. 730, 109 S. Ct. 2166 (1989).

82. That the photographer is generally the copyright owner of photographs taken by her was established by a 1884 decision of the Supreme Court, *Burrow-Giles Lithographic Co. v. Sarony*, 111 U.S. 53, 57–61, 4 S. Ct. 279, 280–82 (1884).

83. In *Malinowski v. Playboy Enterprises, Inc.*, 706 F. Supp. 611 (N.D. Ill. 1989), a freelance photographer sued the publisher of *Playboy* magazine claiming that he and not the publisher was the copyright owner of photographs taken on assignment from the magazine and

that the magazine had infringed those copyrights. The case was dismissed on the ground that it only involved a contractual dispute between the parties. The photographer subsequently acknowledged that the photographs in question constituted work made for hire and that the magazine was therefore the owner of the copyrights in them.

84. 17 U.S.C. §101. In *Community for Creative Non-Violence v. Reid, supra* note 81, the Supreme Court noted that an attempt during the drafting of the current Copyright Act to include "photographic or other portrait(s)" to the list of commissioned works eligible for work for hire status failed. 109 S. Ct. at 2176, n. 13.

85. Sometimes such contracts refer to a "buyout" of the photographer's rights, which the ASMP considers "a complete transfer of rights from the photographer to the purchaser." In contrast, the ASMP believes a contract that provides for an "all-rights" transfer may have somewhat different consequences: "The all-rights transfer is different from a buyout, in that a buy-out is a general transfer of everything in and to the work whereas an all-rights transfer could be either general or limited. Often the words are used interchangeably, and it is, therefore, important that the contract, invoice, or purchase order specify whether the photographer is reserving any rights." *Professional Business Practices in Photography, supra* note 80, at 12. It is far from clear that a court would agree with the ASMP's distinction between a "buyout" and an "all-rights" transfer, especially if the parties' agreement does not limit or qualify in any way the reference to "all-rights."

86. 17 U.S.C. §101.

87. An annual publication that contains comprehensive listings of potential purchasers of photographers' services is *Photographer's Market: Where to Sell Your Photographs*, published by Writer's Digest Books, Cincinnati, Ohio.

88. In 1985 the ASMP sponsored a nationwide survey of photographers' pay scales. The survey ascertained that the typical "day rate" for a photographer engaged to work on a corporation's annual report was between $800 and $1,600 for two-thirds of the photographers who responded. In contrast, more than two-thirds of the responding photographers who did editorial work reported earning less than $750 per day. *Professional Business Practices in Photography, supra* note 80, at 26.

89. The ASMP strongly recommends that photographers seek such "reciprocal indemnities." As an example of the kind of problem that would be covered by such a provision, it cites the situation where a model signed a release to the photographer authorizing use of the photographs in automobile advertisements, but the advertising agency that

commissioned the shooting used the work instead in cigarette ads. If the model sues the photographer, the "reciprocal indemnity" would require the agency to protect the photographer from liability and expense resulting from that suit. *Professional Business Practices in Photography*, supra note 80, at 16.

90. The ASMP suggests that photographers include in their contracts, and/or stamp on the back of their photographs, a provision to the effect that the client's failure to provide the appropriate credit will result in "triple billing." *Id.* at 23. Although it is not clear that such provisions would be legally enforceable, they might serve to induce the client to exercise greater care in handling its credit obligations.

91. 17 U.S.C. §401.

92. *Finger v. Omni Pub. Int. Ltd.*, 77 N.Y.2d 138, 564 N.Y.S.2d 1014 (1990).

93. *Arrington v. New York Times Co.*, 55 N.Y.2d 433, 449 N.Y.S.2d 941, *cert. denied*, 103 S. Ct 787 (1982).

94. New York Civil Rights Law, §§50–51.

95. The applicable law relating to such uses will vary from state to state. Typical of such laws in the New York "Right of Privacy" statute, *supra* note 94.

96. *See, e.g.,, Brinkley v. Casablancas*, 80 A.D.2d 428, 438, 1004 (1st Dept. 1981).

97. The ASMP recommends that photographers get such releases at the time of the shooting, and specify on the releases the date and subject matter, etc., of the shooting. *Professional Business Practices in Photography*, supra note 80, at 69–74.

98. *Photographer's Market*, supra note 87, sets forth the range of fees normally paid by publications and others for the use of preexisting photographs.

99. *Photographer's Market* divides stock houses into five subcategories: (1) archival (old, often historical photographs); (2) editorial (photojournalist photographs); (3) specialty (for example, sports photographs); (4) boutique (representing the work of a small group of recognized photographers); and (5) generalist (large, all-purpose stock houses).

00. *See* note 80, *supra*.

01. In *Miller v. Newsweek, Inc.*, 675 F. Supp. 872 (D. Del. 1987), a photohrapher sued *Newsweek* magazine for the loss of 72 of his photographs. Relying on an ASMP survey that concluded that the appropriate value of a lost photograph was $1,500, the photographer sought damages of $108,000 for the lost work. The court rejected that survey and the "arbitrary" value of $1,500 per lost photo, stating

that the survey was "not necessarily an accurate reflection of the market value of each . . . photograph." *Id.* at 874. The court held that where there was no clear market value for lost photographs, "courts in cases of lost pictures . . . have looked to the cost of replacement or the value of the lost property to the owner." *Id.* at 878. The court considered the uniqueness of the lost photos, the photographer's prestige, established use prices, and the technical quality of the photographer's work, and then awarded him a total of $16,250 as compensation for all the lost photographs.

102. The ASMP provides a detailed description of the kinds of issues that can arise between a photographer and his representative, as well as a sample contract for use by photographers and their reps. *Professional Business Practices in Photography, supra* note 80, at 27–34.

103. *See also* the discussion in Associated Councils of the Arts, *The Visual Artist and the Law*, Praeger Publishers, 2d ed., 1974 (hereinafter Praeger). Furthermore, there are excellent (and seemingly exhaustive) checklists of items that can be included in an artist-gallery contract in R. Lerner and J. Bresler, *Art Law: The Guide for Collectors, Investors, Dealers and Artists*, 11–26 (Practicing Law Institute 1989) and F. Feldman & S. Weil, *Art Works: Law, Policy, Practice* 499–504 (1974). The Lerner and Bresler work is especially recommended as a thorough and current resource for legal issues that affect visual artists.

104. Praeger at 20–21; Duffy, *Art Law: Representing Artists, Dealers and Collectors*, at 380.

105. N.Y. Gen. Bus. L. §§11.01, 12.01 (McKinney Supp. 1991).

106. Cal. Civ. Code §§1738, 1738.5–9 (West Supp. 1977).

107. N.Y. Gen. Bus L. §12.01(1)(a)(i, ii, iii) (McKinney Supp. 1991); Cal. Civ. Code §§1738.6, 1738.7 (West Supp. 1977).

108. N.Y. Gen. Bus. L. §12.01(1)(a)(iv) (McKinney Supp. 1991).

109. *Id.* at §12.01(b).

110. *See* R. Duffy, *supra* note 104, at 380-84 (1977).

111. *Id.*

112. *See* U.C.C. §2-306(2).

113. *See* Duffy, *supra* note 104, at 389–90.

114. *Id.*

115. *See* Praeger, *supra* note 103, at 20–21.

116. 17 U.S.C. §202.

117. *See, e.g.*, N.Y. Gen.Bus L. §14.01 (McKinney Supp. 1991).

118. *See, e.g.*, Calamari & Perillo at 307.

119. *See e.g.*, the discussion in Calamari & Perillo at 240.

120. *Serra v. United States General Services Admin.*, 667 F. Supp. 1042 (S.D.N.Y. 1987), *aff'd*, 847 F.2d 1045 (2d Cir. 1988).

121. *See generally*, R. Lerner & J. Bresler, *supra* note 103.
122. Cal. Civ. Code §986 (1988).
123. The agreement is reprinted in Feldman & Weil, *supra* note 103, at 81.
124. *Cf.* Duffy, *supra* note 104, at 288–89.
125. *Id.* at 284–88.
126. Feldman & Weil, *supra* note 103, at 90.
127. *See* Duffy, *supra* note 104, at 282.
128. Lerner and Bresler state that the Jurrist agreement, like the Projansky agreement, suffers from the legal infirmity that there is a lack of "privity," or legal continuity, between the artist and subsequent purchasers of the work. As a result, the courts would probably find the agreements unenforceable against subsequent purchasers because "there is no manner of giving notice to a bona fide purchaser in good faith." Lerner & Bresler, *supra* note 103, at 485.
129. A new law took effect in New York in 1991 to protect buyers of sculpture: N.Y. Arts and Cultural Affairs Law, §§14.05–14.08, (McKinney Supp. 1991). The law makes it illegal to produce or sell unauthorized casts of fine art sculpture, or to sell such sculpture without the disclosure of certain information, including the name of the artist, the title of the work, its dimensions, the material from which it is made and the number of casts already produced. It applies to all works of sculpture—except those made of glass—selling for more than $1,500 and produced after the law took effect. The seller's disclosure documents must also carry such information as whether and how the sculpture is numbered, the size of the proposed or previous editions of the same sculpture, and whether the artist intends to produce additional casts. Recordkeeping relating to the production and sale of sculptures is required on the part of both foundries and dealers. Fines of up to $5,000 a work can be levied on foundries that mislabel or fail to identify their products with a mark and a date. Violations by sellers can bring fines of $500 for each violation.

IV

Libel, Privacy, and Other Claims of Injury

Most nonfiction writers, and an increasing number of fiction writers, are directly affected by the law of libel and privacy. Even photographers and other visual artists can be confronted by claims in these areas. In addition, especially in recent years, creative people have been accused of causing injury to plaintiffs in other ways by the publication of their works. It is important that authors, artists, and other creative people understand the nature and extent of these claims and how to deal with them.

What is the purpose of the law of libel?

As the Supreme Court has put it, "The legitimate state interest underlying the law of libel is the compensation of individuals for the harm inflicted on them by defamatory falsehoods. The individual's right to the protection of his good name 'reflects no more than our basic concept of the essential dignity and worth of every human being—a concept at the root of any decent system of ordered liberty.'"[1]

Nevertheless, it has been argued, by no less than late Supreme Court Justices Hugo Black and William O. Douglas among others, that any law of libel violates the freedoms of speech and press guaranteed by the First Amendment.[2] This view has not been accepted by any American court or legislature and is not likely to be in the foreseeable future.

But this is not to say that the First Amendment is irrelevant to the law of libel and privacy. In 1964 the U.S. Supreme Court ruled for the first time that libel cases directly implicate the essential freedoms of speech and the press that are protected by the First Amendment;[3] since then, the Court has substantially rewritten much of libel law to reconcile it with those precious First Amendment freedoms. The major changes imposed by the Supreme Court on the law of libel and privacy will be discussed later in this chapter.[4]

When can a statement give rise to a successful libel claim?

The answer varies with the nature of the statement, the speaker, the subject, the claimed injury, and other factors including the particular law that will apply.[5] In short, there is no short answer.

However, it is possible to list six requirements that must almost always be established before a statement can result in a successful libel suit: (1) The statement must be libelous (or defamatory). (2) It must be false. (3) It must be about ("of and concerning") the living person claiming to be libeled. (4) It must be "published." (5) It must be published with "fault." (6) It must cause actual injury to the plaintiff.

What is meant by libel?

Libel and *slander* together compose what the law calls *defamation*. Libelous statements are in writing or otherwise set down in concrete nonephemeral form; slanderous statements are generally oral and lack concreteness. It is unlikely that authors and artists will be confronted by claims of slander, so this chapter will be primarily concerned with libel.[6]

A libelous statement must tend "to harm the reputation of another as to lower him in the estimation of the community or to deter third persons from associating or dealing with him."[7] Expanded and formalized somewhat, it must be an

> accusation against the character of a person . . . which affects his reputation, in that it tends to hold him up to ridicule, contempt, shame, disgrace or obloquy, to degrade him in the estimation of the community, to induce an evil opinion of him in the minds of right thinking persons, to make him an object of reproach, to diminish his respectability or abridge his comforts, to change his position in society for the worse, to dishonor or discredit him in the estimation of the public, or his friends and acquaintances, or to deprive him of friendly intercourse in society, or cause him to be shunned or avoided.[8]

In short, a libelous statement is one that tends to injure a person's reputation. However, a great many statements that appear to provide the basis for a libel suit (as lawyers say, to be "actionable") are protected by the law.

What kinds of statements may be found libelous?

There is no legal boundary since the libelousness of a statement depends on its relation to the reputation of its subject.

As further discussed below, it is conceivable that any statement about another, even one that appears to be laudatory, can be libelous.

The law has historically recognized four major categories of potentially defamatory statements, and although those categories are not conclusive or all-encompassing, they are useful examples of the imputations that are most often alleged to be libelous: (1) crime,[9] (2) loathsome diseases,[10] (3) incompetence or dishonesty in one's business or profession,[11] and (4) unchastity in a woman.[12] On the face of it, the false charge that a woman is "an AIDS-laden prostitute who regularly cheats her clients" could give rise to a claim of libel. However, as we shall see, even this statement might not result in a libel judgment. (A list of "red-flag" words that frequently lead to libel claims is set forth in Appendix B.)

If the libelous nature of a statement is apparent from the statement itself, it is considered *libelous per se,* and the law does not require further proof of the defamatory nature of the statement.[13] (Injury and damages, among other issues, would still have to be established; those issues are discussed more fully later in this chapter.)

Can a statement that seems innocent be libelous?

Sometimes, if it is false, even a seemingly innocent statement can injure its subject's reputation. For example, the false statement that a woman was the guest of honor at a lavish dinner at a Steak and Brew restaurant could be found libelous if it turned out that she is the president of the local branch of Vegetarian Teetotalers. Similarly, the false statement that John Smith is "distinguished war hero" could be found libelous if Mr. Smith is an avowed lifelong pacifist.[14]

When, as here, the libelous nature of the statement must be established by extrinsic facts, sometimes referred to as *libel per quod,* it is obviously much more difficult to guard against than libel per se. For this reason, among others, the law in most states requires a plaintiff claiming to have been libeled by extrinsic facts to prove that he has sustained specific (*special*) damages as a result of the statement, not merely injury to his general reputation.[15] The issue of special damages is discussed more fully later in this chapter.

Can a true statement be libelous?

Probably not, although the law in some states, predating recent Supreme Court rulings, may suggest the contrary.[16] Under libel law as it existed before the Supreme Court revolutionized large parts of it during the last three decades, defamatory statements were "presumed" false. The burden was on the libel defendant to prove that they were true, which was not always easy.

In the years since 1964, however, the law has become clear (at least where the alleged libel arose out of publication through the "media") that the person claiming libel (the plaintiff) must prove that the statement is false.[17] Moreover, it has long been the law that substantially true statements cannot give rise to successful claims of libel. The plaintiff must prove not merely that the statement is not completely true in every particular but that it is substantially false in its material elements.[18]

Can a person be libeled by implication?

Yes, at least under certain circumstances. In an important 1990 libel case, *Milkovich v. Lorain Journal Co.*,[19] discussed further below, the Supreme Court stated in what may turn out to be an extremely important aside: "Even if the speaker states the facts upon which he bases his opinion, if those facts are either incorrect or incomplete, or if his assessment of them is erroneous, the statement may still imply a false assertion of fact."[20] Also in 1990, the federal court of appeals in Washington, D.C., squarely addressed the issue of libel by implication and declared the rule thus:

> If a communication, viewed in its entire context, merely conveys materially true facts from which a defamatory inference can reasonably be drawn, the libel is not established. But if the communication, by the particular manner or language in which the true facts are conveyed, supplies additional, affirmative evidence suggesting that the defendant *intends* or *endorses* the defamatory inference, the communication will be deemed capable of bearing that meaning.[21]

It seems likely, especially after *Milkovich*, that more and more cases claiming libel by implication will be brought even if the facts that are reported are essentially accurate, and authors

and publishers should be especially sensitive to the libelous
implications in the material they propose to publish.

Can a statement of opinion be libelous?

Yes and no. Although the Supreme Court has reiterated in
several cases that only a false statement of "fact" can give rise
to a successful libel claim, it also made it clear in an important
1990 decision that statements of "opinion" under certain circumstances can result in legal liability.

In a 1974 libel case, *Gertz v. Robert Welch, Inc.*,[22] the Court
grandly stated: "Under the First Amendment there is no such
thing as a false idea. However pernicious an opinion may seem,
we depend for its correction not on the conscience of judges
and juries but on the competition of other ideas."[23] Applying
what they believed to be the mandate of that passage, many
lower courts held that if a statement was one of opinion, as
distinct from a statement of fact, it could not be found libelous.[2]
Following the lead of an influential decision from the federal
court of appeals in Washington, D.C.,[25] courts considered four
factors in deciding whether a statement was one of fact or
opinion: (1) the specific language, (2) whether the statement
was verifiable, (3) the general context of the statement, (4)
the broader context in which the statement appeared. If after
analyzing and weighing those factors the court found the statement to be one of opinion, it would dismiss the libel suit for
that reason alone.

Although that approach had become widely accepted
throughout the United States in the 16 years following *Gertz*,
the Supreme Court in *Milkovich* dramatically changed the
rules. In that case, a high school wrestling coach sued for libel
because a sportswriter in the local newspaper, writing about a
court hearing looking into the coach's role in a brawl at a
wrestling meet, said: "Anyone who attended the meet . .
knows in his heart that [the coach] lied at the hearing." The
lower courts found that the statement was immune from the
coach's suit as an expression of opinion.

The Supreme Court, by a 7–2 vote, disagreed and ordered
the case revived. The Court stated that the "opinion" passage
in *Gertz* was not "intended to create a wholesale defamation
exemption for anything that might be labeled 'opinion'"[26] and
observed that "expressions of 'opinion' may often imply an

assertion of objective fact."[27] The issue, the Court indicated, is whether the allegedly libelous statement contains "a provably false factual connotation,"[28] not whether the statement is called fact or opinion. However, in so ruling, the Court did not provide the kind of guidance that will enable authors, publishers, and their lawyers to determine whether a statement contains such a "connotation." The Court also made it clear that the individual states could still adopt the pre-*Milkovich* opinion doctrine under their state laws, and it may be anticipated that several states will do just that.

How will the fact-opinion distinction be made after *Milkovich*?

Because the Court in *Milkovich* was not particularly illuminating in this regard, it will remain unclear just how the fact-opinion dichotomy will be interpreted and invoked, at least until the courts have had a chance to apply the new *Milkovich* holding to future libel cases. It may be wondered how the statement "From reading his decisions, it is clear that Chief Justice Rehnquist is an idealogue who is determined to destroy free speech in America" or that a named senator is "a corrupt liar and post-crypto Nazi" will be treated under the Court's new formulation.[29] In the meantime, prudent authors and publishers will examine potentially libelous utterances with special care to ensure that statements intended as opinion do not contain "a provably false factual connotation."

The courts (including the Supreme Court in *Milkovich*) have made it clear that the mere use of such phrases as "in my opinion" or "I believe" will not convert a statement of fact into one of opinion and that purported statements of opinion will be treated as statements of fact if they suggest criminal activity.[30] Thus, on both scores, a statement like "In my opinion, Jack Brown is a thief" will ordinarily be treated as a statement of fact and not as a protected statement of opinion. However, it is still true that a statement that on its face seems to charge another with a crime will not be treated as a libelous statement of fact if the context makes it clear that the charge could not have been taken literally (such statements are discussed below). Even before *Milkovich*, a leading authority on libel set forth what may still be the best guidance available:

The determination of what is fact and what is opinion (or "comment") is made on the basis of the effect which the communication may reasonably be expected to have on its recipient. Although difficult to state in abstract terms, as a practical matter, the crucial differences between a statement of fact and opinion depends upon whether ordinary persons hearing or reading the matter complained of would be likely to understand it as an expression of the speaker's or writer's opinion, or as a statement of existing fact. The opinion may ostensibly be in the form of a factual statement if it is clear from the context that the maker did not intend to assert another objective fact but only his personal comment upon the facts he had stated—and vice versa.[31]

Can epithets and hyperbole be libelous?

Generally, no—unless they can reasonably be taken as literal statements of fact.

A few cases will illustrate the point. In *Curtis Publishing Co. v. Birdsong*,[32] the plaintiff had been referred to as one of "those bastards." A federal court of appeals rejected his claim of libel, declaring:

> It is perfectly apparent that these words were used as mere epithets, as terms of abuse and opprobrium. As such they had no real meaning except to indicate that the individual who used them was under a strong emotional feeling of dislike toward those about whom he used them. Not being intended or understood as statements of fact they are impossible of proof or disproof. Indeed, such words of vituperation and abuse reflect more on the character of the user than they do on that of the individual to whom they are intended to refer. It has long been settled that such words are not of themselves actionable as libelous.[33]

In *Greenbelt Cooperative Pub. Assn., Inc. v. Bresler*,[34] the plaintiff's bargaining position in a dispute with the local government was characterized as "blackmail." The Supreme Court rejected the claim of libel, stating:

> It is simply impossible to believe that a reader who reached the word "blackmail" in either article would not have un-

derstood exactly what was meant: it was Bresler's public and wholly legal negotiating proposals that were being criticized. No reader could have thought that either the speakers at the meetings or the newspaper articles reporting their words were charging Bresler with the commission of a criminal offense. On the contrary, even the most careless reader must have perceived that the word was no more than rhetorical hyperbole, a vigorous epithet used by those who considered Bresler's negotiating position extremely unreasonable. Indeed, the record is completely devoid of evidence that anyone in the city of Greenbelt or anywhere else thought Bresler had been charged with a crime.[35]

Similarly, in 1988 the Supreme Court unanimously found that an ad parody in *Hustler* magazine that portrayed the Reverend Jerry Falwell as having had sex with his mother in an outhouse "could not reasonably have been interpreted as stating actual facts about the public figure involved."[36]

The Supreme Court in *Milkovich* emphasized that those holdings were still good law. But not every epithet is immune from a claim of libel. In one (pre-*Milkovich*) case, a federal court of appeals stated that calling a scientist a "liar" because of his perceived misuse of statistics would be a statement of opinion and hence not libelous but that reference to him as a "paid liar" would not be similarly protected because of its greater factual nature.[37]

Under *Milkovich*, the test will be whether the statement contains "a provably false factual connotation," or, put another way, whether the statement could "reasonably be interpreted as stating actual facts" about its subject.

Who can sue for libel?

Only people who are alive at publication can sue for libel. The law considers that the interest in one's reputation the law of libel is designed to protect no longer applies when a person dies; as a result, it is generally impossible to libel the dead.[38]

Corporations, partnerships, associations, and the like also have protectable interests in their reputations, but usually to a more limited extent than those of living people. Such entities can sue for libels that affect their financial credit or standing in their fields or that cast aspersions on their honesty or on the quality or integrity of their products.[39]

Must a person be named to sue for libel?

No, but the plaintiff must prove that the alleged libel refers to her—in the words of the law, that the words are "of and concerning" her. Obviously, a named person meets this requirement. Several persons may have the same name as the person named in an alleged libel, and it has happened that a person other than the one intended has successfully sued.[40]

Without being named, a person can sometimes prove that the libel is "of and concerning" him. For example, a libelous reference to "the only dentist in town" will be found to apply to the person who meets that description; a reference to "a Main Street dentist" will be found to apply to the dentist who can prove that he is the only dentist on Main Street.[41]

Can members of groups sue for libelous statements about their groups?

Generally, no. The courts have consistently held that a libelous statement about a large group (e.g., "All Lithuanians are child molesters" or "All Republicans cheat on their taxes") does not refer to each member of that group.

Nevertheless, it may be possible for a group member to sue successfully for libel. If the context of the statement indicates that the plaintiff was its intended target (e.g., if the statement "All lawyers are thieves" is made in an article about one lawyer), the plaintiff may be found to have been libeled by the general statement.[42] Similarly, the courts have been willing to find group members libeled if the group is small enough to justify the conclusion that the members were effectively referred to.[43] As a leading authority has concluded, "While it is not possible to set definite limits as to the size of the group or class . . . the cases in which recovery has been allowed usually have involved numbers of 25 or fewer."[44]

Must a statement be published to give rise to a successful libel claim?

Yes. The most libelous statement imaginable cannot give rise to a successful libel claim if it remains in the author's manuscript (or diary) and is not *published* to anybody else. The traditional rule is that a statement is published if it is shown to a person *other than* the subject of the libel. A letter from A to B in which B is seriously libeled does not enable B to sue A for libel, unless, for example, A dictated the letter to her secretary.[45]

What about someone (not the originator) who repeats or reports a libelous statement?

The traditional rule is that anyone who repeats, republishes, or distributes a libelous statement made by another can be held legally responsible,[46] which technically means that the printer and seller of an allegedly libelous work can be sued. But this rule has been significantly modified in recent years.

First, the law now requires that a plaintiff prove that a libelous statement was published with some degree of "fault," which means at least that it was published negligently. It is conceivable, and in some cases probable, that the repeater of a libelous statement will be found to have acted reasonably, even if the original speaker has not, and thus cannot be held liable. This would almost always be the case with respect to printers, sellers, and others who did not participate in the origination of the libel.

Second, a few courts have extended a special protection from liability to those who repeat libelous statements in the course of reporting on newsworthy subjects, even if the writer knows the statement is false or has serious doubts about its truth. As one federal court of appeals put it:

> At stake in this case is a fundamental principle. Succinctly stated, when a responsible, prominent organization like the National Audubon Society makes serious charges against a public figure, the First Amendment protects the accurate and disinterested reporting of those charges, regardless of their reporter's private view regarding their validity. What is newsworthy about such accusations is that they were made. We do not believe that the press may be required under the First Amendment to suppress newsworthy statements merely because it has serious doubts regarding their truth. Nor must the press take up cudgels against dubious charges in order to publish them without fear of liability for defamation. The public interest in being fully informed about controversies that often rage

around sensitive issues demands that the press be afforded the freedom to report such charges without assuming responsibility for them.[47]

It should be emphasized that other courts have refused to adopt this "neutral reporting" privilege and that the Supreme Court has not yet addressed it.[48]

Third, legal protection has been established for the accurate (or "fair") repetition of libelous statements made during official governmental proceedings such as trials, legislative hearings, or debates. This "qualified privilege" is discussed more fully below.

When is a libelous statement insulated from legal liability?

Whenever the law (the courts and the legislative branch of government) decides that the public interest requires that certain otherwise libelous statements be protected. Then the libelous statements are "cloaked with a privilege."

How many kinds of privilege does the law provide?

Two. An *absolute privilege* completely protects a libelous statement from legal action, regardless of circumstances, motive, or injury caused. A *qualified privilege* cloaks a libelous statement with a legal immunity that can be overcome by showing that the maker of the statement "abused" the privilege. The burden is generally on the plaintiff to prove this.

What kinds of statements are protected by an absolute privilege?

Statements made in the course of official governmental activities may be so protected. This includes statements made in judicial proceedings, including those by judges, attorneys, parties, witnesses, and jurors.[49] In general, statements by federal and state legislators are also protected if made in connection with their official duties, although this is not as clearly true of lesser legislative bodies.[50] In the executive branch, statements made by high federal and state officials are generally protected. Again, this is less clear for lower-level officials and units of government.[51]

Outside the government, otherwise libelous statements made by one spouse to the other are generally protected by an absolute privilege, as are statements that are made with the consent of their subjects.[52]

It is important to remember, however, that absolute privilege applies only to a statement made in a privileged setting and is generally not available if the statement is repeated outside the setting, whether the repetition is by the original speaker or someone else.[53] Such repetitions may, however, be protected by a qualified (conditional) privilege.

When are statements protected by a qualified privilege?

Basically, when it is considered more important to encourage (and protect) the making of statements that may be false and libelous than to allow victims of such statements to recover damages for libel. A qualified privilege generally applies only if the statement is made in good faith, consistent with the purposes that gave rise to the privilege.[54] Examples include statements to proper authorities accusing another person of a crime or other improper conduct (unethical conduct by a doctor or lawyer, physical abuse by a policeman) and statements made by credit-reporting agencies and private detectives to clients.[55]

Of special interest to writers is the qualified privilege that protects "fair" reports of governmental statements (which themselves are protected by an absolute privilege).[56] As one legal authority has summarized it, "The publication of defamatory matter concerning another in a report of an official action or proceeding or of a meeting open to the public that deals with a matter of public concern is privileged if the report is accurate and complete or a fair abridgement of the occurrence reported."[57] A fair report in a book or newspaper article that Tom Brown testified during the trial of his lawsuit against his partner Bill Jackson that Jackson embezzled money from the firm, cheated clients, and was always drunk is privileged even if the testimony is false and Brown and the writer knew or suspected it was false. But if the report is not "fair"—if the charges are taken out of context, are erroneously reported, or are reported to be true—then the author and publisher can be successfully sued for libel.[58]

How has the Supreme Court changed the law of libel?

Dramatically. Before 1964, a libelous statement was presumed to be false. The plaintiff was virtually assured of victory once he established that a libelous statement had been published about him unless the defendant maker of the statement could prove that the statement was true, protected by a privilege, or caused the plaintiff no injury.

Against that background, one L. B. Sullivan, an elected commissioner of Montgomery, Alabama, sued the *New York Times* and four black Alabama clergymen because of what he considered libelous references to him (even though he wasn't named) in a full-page advertisement signed by a number of civil-rights leaders (including the four Alabama defendants) that sought support for the civil-rights movement in the South. Applying the traditional law of libel, a Montgomery jury awarded Sullivan $500,000 in damages (the full amount requested), and the award was upheld by the Alabama appellate courts.

A unanimous Supreme Court found that the traditional libel rules that gave rise to that result violate the protections for speech and press in the First Amendment. The Court set aside the jury's award and declared that a public official like Sullivan could not recover for allegedly libelous criticisms of his official conduct such those in the *Times* ad.[59]

In reaching that conclusion the Court, speaking through Justice William J. Brennan, Jr., observed that "freedom of expression upon public questions is secured by the First Amendment" and that this constitutional safeguard "was fashioned to assure unfettered interchange of ideas for the bringing about of political and social changes desired by the people."[60] As a result, Brennan wrote, "we consider this case against the background of a profound national commitment to the principle that debate on public issues should be uninhibited, robust, and wide-open, and that it may well include vehement, caustic, and sometimes unpleasantly sharp attacks on government and public officials."[61] He continued: "The present advertisement, as an expression of grievance and protest on one of the major public issues of our time, would seem clearly to qualify for the constitutional protection. The question is whether it forfeits that protection by the falsity of some of its factual statements and by its alleged defamation of respondent."[62]

The Court stated that some factual error is "inevitable in free debate" and that such error "must be protected if the freedoms of expression are to have the 'breathing space' that they 'need

. . . to survive.'"[63] It added that the defamatory nature of such criticism of public officials does not alter this: "Criticism of official conduct does not lose its constitutional protection merely because it is effective criticism and hence diminishes their official reputations."[64] It was not enough that the Alabama libel law allowed the defense of truth:

> A rule compelling the critic of official conduct to guarantee the truth of all his factual assertions—and to do so on pain of libel judgments virtually unlimited in amount—leads to . . . "self-censorship." Allowance of the defense of truth, with the burden of proving it on the defendant, does not mean that only false speech will be deterred. . . . Under such a rule, would-be critics of official conduct may be deterred from voicing their criticism, even though it is believed to be true and even though it is in fact true, because of doubt whether it can be proved in court or fear of the expense of having to do so. . . . The rule thus dampens the vigor and limits the variety of public debate. It is inconsistent with the First and Fourteenth Amendments.[65]

In what may be the most important sentence in the law of libel, the Court rewrote a significant part of that law: *"The constitutional guarantees require, we think, a federal rule that prohibits a public official from recovering damages for a defamatory falsehood relating to his official conduct unless he proves that the statement was made with 'actual malice'—that is, with knowledge that it was false or with reckless disregard of whether it was false or not."*[66] From then on, at least as far as public official libel plaintiffs were concerned, the rules of the game were different indeed.

What does "actual malice" mean?

The term *actual malice* as used by the Supreme Court is confusing and does not mean what most people think it means. As one federal judge put it, "'Actual malice' is . . . a term of art having nothing to do with actual malice."[67]

In the *New York Times* case, the Court indicated that actual malice means that a statement alleged to be libelous was made "with knowledge that it was false or with reckless disregard of whether it was false or not." Later, the Court elaborated,

indicating that actual malice required a "high degree of awareness of [the statement's] probable falsity";[68] "either deliberate
falsification or reckless publication 'despite the publisher's
awareness of probable falsity";[69] "sufficient evidence to permit
the conclusion that the defendant *in fact* entertained serious
doubts as to the truth of his publication";[70] and "subjective
awareness of probable falsity."[71] (Emphasis added.)

It is clear that negligence (which simply means acting in an
"unreasonable" or careless way) is not actual malice. Misre-
membering the facts underlying an event, failing to confirm
the substance of a story, or relying on a source that turns out
to be unreliable, which may constitute negligence, does not
qualify as actual malice in the absence of proof that the author
"entertained serious doubts as to the truth of his publication."
In an important 1990 decision in which the federal court of
appeals in California overturned a $5 million judgment in favor
of entertainer Wayne Newton against NBC, the court stated:
"Even an extreme departure from accepted professional standards of journalism will not suffice to establish actual malice;
nor will any other departure from reasonably prudent conduct,
including the failure to investigate before publishing."[72] Further, proof of malice in its commonsense (and common-law)
meaning—"hatred, ill will or enmity or a wanton desire to
injure"—does not in itself prove actual malice.[73]

How has *reckless disregard* been defined under Times v. Sullivan?

Besides "knowledge of falsity," the *New York Times* standard
provides for recovery in case of "reckless disregard of the truth
or falsity" of a defamatory statement.[74] Obviously, reckless disregard is a looser concept than actual knowledge of falsity. It
means that the publisher entertained serious doubts and then
without further checking or adequate verification, published
the material while continuing to harbor those doubts.

Under the Supreme Court's decisions, a finding of "recklessness" depends on the publisher's subjective state of mind and
not an objective determination of whether a reasonably prudent
person would have published the material. However, mere
"professions of good faith" will not necessarily defeat liability
"when the publisher's allegations are so inherently improbable
that only a reckless man would have put them in circulation.

Likewise, recklessness may be found where there are obvious reasons to doubt the veracity of the informant or the accuracy of his reports."[75] In 1989 the Supreme Court reaffirmed the subjective nature of the "recklessness" requirement, stating: "Although the concept of 'reckless disregard' cannot be fully encompassed in one infallible definition, . . . we have made clear that the defendant must have made the false publication with a 'high degree of awareness of . . . probable falsity,' . . . or must have 'entertained serious doubts as to the truth of his publication.'"[76] In the same case, the Court also said: "Although courts must be careful not to place too much reliance on such factors, a plaintiff is entitled to prove the defendant's state of mind through circumstantial evidence, . . . and it cannot be said that evidence concerning motive or care never bears any relation to the actual malice inquiry."[77]

How has actual malice been established in libel actions?

It is difficult to establish that an author or publisher published a statement whose truth she seriously doubted. The threshold of proof is high to protect freedom of expression.

Still, libel plaintiffs have been able to establish actual malice; for example, a widely publicized action brought by Carol Burnett against the *National Enquirer* resulted in a $1.6-million jury verdict against the *Enquirer*,[78] which verdict was subsequently reduced to $200,000. The falsity of the article, which strongly implied that Carol Burnett was drunk, rowdy, and caused a disturbance with Henry Kissinger in a Washington, D.C., restaurant, was not in dispute. And there was, according to the trial and appeals courts, sufficient proof that the *Enquirer*'s gossip columnist had serious doubts about the truth of the publication. Indeed, according to the trial court, "There is a high degree of probability that [the editor] fabricated part of the publication [relating to Henry Kissinger]."[79] Moreover, in attempting to verify the story received from a "free-lance tipster," there was uncontradicted evidence that the editor was warned of the tipster's unreliability and that witnesses at the scene gave the editor information that substantially contradicted the tipster's story. The story was nonetheless published without removing the defamatory information.

In 1989, the Supreme Court affirmed a finding that a newspaper was guilty of actual malice in an article about a candidate in a local election.[80] Among the factors emphasized by the Court were the paper's failure to listen to tape recordings supplied by the candidate that he said would support his position and the paper's failure to make any attempt to interview a key witness in the underlying dispute. As the Court put it: "Although failure to investigate will not alone support a finding of actual malice, . . . the purposeful avoidance of the truth is in a different category."[81]

In a much-discussed case,[82] the Supreme Court in 1991 held that a writer's alteration of statements directly attributed in quotation marks to the plaintiff can constitute actual malice, at least under certain circumstances. The case involved a profile of Jeffrey Masson, an outspoken critic of the institutions of psychoanalysis, written by Janet Malcolm and published first in the *New Yorker* magazine and then in a book published by Alfred A. Knopf, Inc. In a suit for libel, Masson claimed that Malcolm had fabricated numerous statements that were set forth as spoken by him and that as attributed to him, the statements were libelous. The defendants denied that any quotations were fabricated, and that issue had not been resolved. The lower courts held that actual malice could not be found *even if* the quotations were fabricated since they were "rational interpretations" of things Masson might have said.

The issue before the Supreme Court was the extent to which the deliberate alteration or fabrication of quotes attributed to the plaintiff can constitute actual malice. To the relief of many in the publishing community, the Court acknowledged that quotations are frequently altered in the publishing process and that the fact of alteration alone could not establish actual malice. Instead, the Court held that "a deliberate alteration of the words uttered by a plaintiff does not equate with knowledge of falsity . . . unless the alteration results in a material change in the meaning conveyed by the statement." The Court returned Masson's suit to the lower courts for a determination whether that new test had been met and whether the magazine and book publishers of the profile could be found liable under it.

In what situations has actual malice failed to be established?

Plaintiffs have failed in many cases to meet this demanding standard. Among allegations that have failed to prove actual malice are these:

- Publication of "emotionally tinged" documents[83]
- Insufficient checking or verification of the details of a news story[84]
- Negligence combined with hostility toward the plaintiff[85]
- Mere ill will toward the plaintiff[86] and
- Political or editorial bias[87]

Who qualifies as a "public official"?

In the *Times* case, an elected city commissioner was held to be a public official. Subsequently, the courts have found a mayor, a former public recreation area supervisor, a county attorney, an elected clerk of a county court, a police chief, a deputy sheriff, and a candidate for public office public officials.[88] However, the Supreme Court has emphasized that while it has "not provided precise boundaries for the category of 'public official,' it cannot be thought to include all public employees."[89]

In the important *Gertz* case (discussed below), the Court had no difficulty finding that being a lawyer (hence an "officer of the court") and membership on committees appointed by a big-city mayor do not make a libel plaintiff a public official. A California case held that a public-school teacher was not a public official.[90] However, other cases have found teachers to be public officials.

For whatever guidance it provides, the Supreme Court has said, "The 'public official' designation applies at the very least to those among the hierarchy of government employees who have, or appear to the public to have, substantial responsibility for or control over the conduct of government affairs."[91]

The Court has ruled that the protection of allegedly libelous statements about public officials applies to statements made after the official has left office. But the Court added, without further elaboration, that there may be cases where the plaintiff is so far removed from a former position of authority that comment on the way in which he performed his responsibilities no longer has the interest necessary to justify the *Times* rule.[92]

Are all statements about public officials protected by the actual-malice standard?

Not necessarily. The Court has held that the protection of the *Times* case only applies to statements about *official conduct*. However, the Court has also stated: "The New York Times rule is not rendered inapplicable merely because an official's private reputation, as well as his public reputation, is harmed. The public-official rule protects the paramount public interest in a free flow of information to the people concerning public officials, their servants. To this end, anything which might touch on an official's fitness for office is relevant."[93] Moreover, the Court has declared that a charge of criminal conduct, no matter how remote in time or place, can never be irrelevant to an official's or a candidate's fitness for office when one is applying the actual-malice requirement.[94]

What about libel plaintiffs who are not public officials?

We knew you'd ask. In 1967, three years after the *Times* case was decided, the Court extended the protection of its new rule to allegedly libelous statements made about people who were not public officials but were "public figures": a college football coach and an outspoken retired army general.[95] In 1971 the Court also seemed to extend the new rule to libelous statements about people who were neither public officials nor public figures (i.e., "private figures") where the statements concerned matters "of public or general interest."[96] However, in the *Gertz* case (1974) the Court withdrew this protection and rewrote further most of our law of libel.

What happened in *Gertz?*

In *Gertz v. Robert Welch, Inc.*,[97] the Court declared that libel plaintiffs who were not public officials or public figures should not be required to meet the stringent *Times* test to recover for libelous statements made about them—even if the statements concerned matters of public or general interest. However, the Court also ruled that the First Amendment would not tolerate a return to the pre-1964 law where a defamatory statement was presumed to be false and to have caused injury to the subject's reputation. Instead, the Court created a new set of groundrules for libel cases brought by private persons while leaving intact its rules for public officials and public figures.

What was *Gertz* about?

The plaintiff, a practicing lawyer in Chicago, was active in community and professional affairs, had served as an officer of local civic groups and various professional organizations, and had written several books and articles. As a private lawyer, he was retained by the family of a youth killed by a Chicago policeman for the family's lawsuit against the policeman for damages. The defendant was the publisher of *American Opinion*, a publication of the John Birch Society. In an article that purported to demonstrate that the prosecution of the policeman was a "frame-up" and part of a Communist campaign to discredit local law-enforcement agencies, Gertz was portrayed as an architect of the frame-up (whose police file took "a big, Irish cop to lift"), a former official of the "Marxist League for Industrial Democracy, originally known as the Intercollegiate Socialist Society, which has advocated the violent seizure of our government," a "Leninist," and a "Communist-fronter," among other charges.

The trial and appellate courts dismissed Gertz's libel suit, concluding that although he was neither a public official nor a public figure, the actual-malice test still applied because the defendant's statements about him involved a matter of public interest. They found that the plaintiff could not show that the defendant published the statements with actual malice, and thus he could not recover for libel.[98]

What did the Supreme Court do?

A lot. It reversed the lower court rulings and ordered a new trial with new rules.

The Court agreed that Gertz was not a public official or a public figure but did not agree that the actual-malice standard applies to statements about private figures that involve matters of public interest. The Court declined to go back to the pre-1964 libel law, however. It made important rulings on the definition of a *public figure*, the law governing private-figure libel suits, and what kinds of damages a libel plaintiff can recover.

If not actual malice, then what standard applies to private-figure libel suits?

The Supreme Court held that the First Amendment does not require the stringent actual-malice test applicable to public officials and public figures when private figures like Gertz sue because such "private individuals are not only more vulnerable to injury than public officials and public figures; they are also more deserving of recovery."[99]

The Court adopted what it considered a middle ground between pre-1964 law and recent rulings, that "so long as they do not impose liability without fault, the States may define for themselves the appropriate standard of liability for a publisher or broadcaster of defamatory falsehood injurious to a private individual."[100] The Court ruled that a private figure must prove at least that the defendant was negligent in making a statement and that the states were free to impose more stringent requirements, including the actual-malice test.[101]

How did the Court deal with the public-figure issue?

On whether Gertz was a public figure, the Court stated:

That designation may rest on either of two alternative bases. In some instances an individual may achieve such pervasive fame or notoriety that he becomes a public figure for all purposes and in all contexts. More commonly, an individual voluntarily injects himself or is drawn into a particular public controversy and thereby becomes a public figure for a limited range of issues. In either case such persons assume special prominence in the resolution of public questions.[102]

The Court continued:

Although [Gertz] was consequently well known in some circles, he had achieved no general fame or notoriety in the community. None of the prospective jurors called at the trial had ever heard of [Gertz] prior to this litigation, and respondent offered no proof that this response was atypical of the local population. We would not lightly assume that a citizen's participation in community and professional affairs rendered him a public figure for all purposes. Absent clear evidence of general fame or notoriety in the community, and pervasive involvement in the affairs of society, an individual should not be deemed a public personality for all aspects of his life. It is preferable to reduce the public figure question to a more meaningful context by looking to the nature and extent of an individual's participation in the particular controversy giving rise to the defamation.[103]

After applying that analysis, the Court concluded: "In this context it is plain that [Gertz] was not a public figure. He plainly did not thrust himself into the vortex of this public issue, nor did he engage the public's attention in an attempt to influence its outcome."[104]

The law now recognizes two kinds of public figures: (1) the person who is a "public figure for all purposes and in all contexts" and (2) "more commonly," the person who "voluntarily injects himself or is drawn into a particular public controversy and thereby becomes a public figure for a limited range of issues."[105]

What became of the *Gertz* case?

A new trial was finally held in 1981. The jury found for Gertz and awarded him $100,000 in compensatory damages and $300,000 in punitive damages. In 1982 the verdict was affirmed by the federal appellate court in Chicago. Ironically, even at the second trial, Gertz was required by the trial judge to prove actual malice on the part of the defendant since the judge found that such proof was necessary to defeat the defendant's qualified "fair-report" privilege.[106]

Who qualifies as an "all-purpose" public figure?

Although the Supreme Court indicated in *Gertz* that all-purpose public figures were relatively rare, the lower courts have found a wide variety of individuals and entities who so qualify, including Clint Eastwood,[107] Johnny Carson,[108] the Holy Spirit Association,[109] Ralph Nader,[110] William F. Buckley,[111] and the Reverend Jerry Falwell.[112] In a number of other libel cases, plaintiffs who are less famous nationally but prominent in their localities have been found to be pervasive public figures.[113] Nevertheless, most libel plaintiffs will not qualify as all-purpose public figures.

Who qualifies as a "vortex" public figure?

Besides those who "thrust" themselves "into the vortex" of public issues, the Court in *Gertz* acknowledged that people could become public figures through no choice of their own.

As the Court put it: "Hypothetically, it may be possible for someone to become a public figure through no purposeful action of his own, but the instances of truly involuntary public figures must be exceedingly rare."[114]

In a number of cases since *Gertz* the Supreme Court has proved reluctant to find libel plaintiffs vortex public figures. In *Time, Inc. v. Firestone*,[115] a socialite sued *Time* magazine for its account of her divorce litigation. Although the woman had given a number of press conferences, felt it necessary to employ a clipping service, had her divorce reported in over one hundred Florida publications, and was involved in a trial that according to the judge included evidence of sexual escapades "which would have made Dr. Freud's hair curl,"[116] the Supreme Court said she did not qualify as a public figure: Since she had no choice but to use the courts in connection with her divorce, such use did not make her a vortex public figure in accounts of the divorce.[117]

The Court reached similar results in two 1979 cases. In *Hutchinson v. Proxmire*,[118] a scientist who received public funds to conduct research on monkeys and behavior patterns found himself the recipient of Senator William Proxmire's "golden fleece" award. When the scientist sued for libel, the defendants claimed he was a public figure. Not so, said the Court. The receipt of public funds, the publication of scholarly articles, and limited access to the media was not enough.[119]

The plaintiff in *Wolston v. Reader's Digest Assn*[120] had failed to appear at grand-jury proceedings investigating Soviet intelligence activities in the United States in 1958, although he had been subpoenaed. He later pleaded guilty to contempt, largely because his pregnant wife became hysterical on the witness stand during his contempt trial. At the time, he was mentioned or discussed in at least fifteen news stories. Some 13 years later he was listed in a book as "a Soviet agent convicted of contempt charges following espionage indictments." The Court said that he was not a public figure even in 1958, since he "was dragged unwillingly into the controversy."[121] His failure to respond to the grand-jury subpoena, the Court found, resulted not from a desire to draw attention to himself or influence the public on an issue but from his ill health.

Summarizing the gist of the Court's ruling, and casting serious doubt on the likelihood of a person's ever being found a involuntary public figure, Justice Harry Blackmun observed: "The Court seems to hold . . . that a person becomes a limited-issue public figure only if he literally or figuratively 'mounts a rostrum' to advocate a particular view."[122] Justice Blackmun would have limited the inquiry to whether the plaintiff was a public figure when the book was published, which he would have answered in the negative, but the Court as a whole did not address the "passage of time" issue in determining the plaintiff's public-figure status.[123] In a 1981 case,[124] a federal appeals court held that a key witness in a notorious rape prosecution in the 1930s remained a public figure for purposes of comment on that controversy 40 years later.

In spite of these rulings, lower courts have not hesitated to find a wide variety of libel plaintiffs vortex public figures, including a worldwide religious movement claiming 5 million adherents,[125] a high school senate president,[126] a former secretary in an urban-renewal agency,[127] the president of a major oil company,[128] a prisoner spokesman for other inmates,[129] a law school dean,[130] an author of a self-help book,[131] antinuclear protestors,[132] and a grand-jury foreman.[133] However, Miss Wyoming of the Miss America pageant,[134] the son of the president of a major oil company,[135] an apartment-house manager interviewed in a television documentary,[136] an unsalaried police informant,[137] and a country-club tennis pro[138] were all found not to be vortex public figures.

In dealing with this issue, many courts have adopted a two-pronged inquiry: (1) Does the alleged libel arise out of a public controversy (i.e., a "dispute which must, when resolved, affect some segment of the general public other than its immediate participants;" a dispute that "must be more than merely newsworthy . . . must not be an essentially private concern such as a divorce"). (2) What was the plaintiff's role in that controversy, including the extent to which the plaintiff's involvement was voluntary, the extent to which the plaintiff had access to the channels of communication to counteract false statements, and the prominence of the plaintiff's role in the controversy.[139]

Can fiction and satire be libelous?

Yes. Some of the most controversial libel judgments in recent years have involved works of fiction and satire, which because of the difference in their nature will be discussed separately.

In most fiction, by definition, the characters and events are "fictitious"; they are created by their author and are not supposed to be accurate portrayals of actual people and events. Nevertheless, the courts have held that a person who believes he is depicted and libeled in a work of fiction can sue.[140] A person claiming to have been libeled by a work of fiction (or any other work) must establish that the alleged libel was "of and concerning" her. Although the characters in most works of fiction have names and appearances different from their models in real life, if any, it is possible for a plaintiff to persuade judge and jury that the fictional portrayal is of and concerning her and is libelous.

A controversial California case provides a good example. A principal character in the defendant's novel *Touching* was a psychologist named Simon Herford who among other things conducted nude marathon therapy groups. The author had attended a nude therapy session conducted by a real Dr. Paul Bindrim. Although the novel's therapist had a different name, physical description, and professional background, Dr. Bindrim claimed to recognize himself in the book and (supported by a few colleagues who testified that they recognized Bindrim in the novel) sued for libel. Although the court ruled that Dr. Bindrim was a public figure and had to prove actual malice, the California appellate court upheld a substantial libel judgment in Bindrim's favor.[141]

The court's use in *Bindrim* of the actual-malice test, which looks to the author's knowledge of falsity, seems anomalous since fiction by definition is "false." Also dubious was the court's reliance on the testimony of a few of Bindrim's colleagues in concluding that the fictional portrayal was "of and concerning" Bindrim. Several courts since *Bindrim* have grappled with the problem and in so doing have alleviated much of the concern among authors and publishers about the implications of *Bindrim*.

In *Lyons v. New American Library, Inc.*, a novel based upon the notorious "Son of Sam" murders referred in passing to an unnamed sheriff in a manner suggesting incompetence and perverted sexual proclivities. A sheriff from the same county sued, but an appellate court held that he could not prove the statements referred to him because the book was clearly labeled

fiction and described incidents in which he had never participated.[142]

In *Springer v. The Viking Press*, a female character in a novel
dealing with the Vatican was portrayed as a prostitute who
engaged in abnormal sexual activity. A former friend of the
author's whose first name was the same as the character's sued
for libel. An appellate court ruled that a person who knew
the plaintiff and who had read the book could not reasonably
conclude that the plaintiff was the fictional character since
the similarities between the two were "superficial" while the
dissimilarities in both manner of living and outlook were "profound." For a plaintiff to recover in such cases, the court declared, "statements made about a character in a fictional work
. . . must be so closely akin to the real person claiming to be
defamed that a reader of the book, knowing the real person,
would have no difficulty linking the two. Superficial similarities
are insufficient, as is a common first name."[143]

In *Pring v. Penthouse International, Ltd.*, a multimillion-
dollar libel judgment arising out of a satire of the Miss America
pageant was overturned by a federal appeals court because the
plaintiff failed to prove that the publication contained statements of fact about her. Several similarities between the article's Miss Wyoming and the plaintiff, a former Miss Wyoming,
claimed by the author to be coincidental, persuaded the court
that the story was "of and concerning" the plaintiff. However,
the court further held that "the story must be reasonably understood as describing actual facts about the plaintiff or her actual
conduct." And because the allegedly defamatory events about
the plaintiff were physically impossible and could not reasonably be believed, the court held that those descriptions must
be considered statements of opinion, not fact, and therefore
incapable of being libelous.[144]

Whether the author (and publisher) intended the fictional
references to be taken as a reference to the real-life plaintiff or
acted in reckless disregard of whether they could reasonably
be so taken appears to provide an appropriate test that balances
the interests of plaintiffs and the rights of authors and publishers, but this test has not yet become the law.[145] The traditional
rules of libel, designed to deal with nonfiction, continue to be
applied to fiction, and until special rules for fiction are adopted,

writers and publishers of fiction are advised to recognize their
potential liabilities and take steps before publication to avoid
these problems. Disclaimers, changes in details that might
suggest real persons, and care to avoid inclusion of derogatory
false matter that is unnecessary to the artistic integrity of the
work, while not guarantees of nonliability, are mechanisms that
should be given consideration.

What about satire?

In satire, real people are placed in fanciful, exaggerated
contexts to make a satirical point. There is no question in satire
of who is described; the question is whether the exaggerated
statements qualify as libel.

Two cases illustrate the problem. In late 1968 after the election of President Nixon, then Los Angeles mayor Sam Yorty
who supported Nixon, let it be known that he was available for
a cabinet appointment. Paul Conrad, a political cartoonist for
the *Los Angeles Times*, portrayed the likelihood of such an
appointment in a cartoon picturing Yorty behind his desk on
the telephone while a number of attendants in white coats
entered his office. In the caption, Yorty says over the phone
"I've got to go now. . . . I've been appointed Secretary of
Defense and the Secret Service men are here." Not amused
Yorty sued for libel, claiming that the cartoon accused him of
being mentally unstable.[146]

In the second case, as part of its review of the highlights of
the year, a Boston magazine rated a local sportscaster "worst"
and said he was "the only newscaster in town who is enrolled
in a course for remedial speaking." He sued for libel.[147]

The courts ruled in both cases that the claims of libel could
not be sustained. In the Boston case, the Massachusetts Supreme Court declared:

> We conclude that a reader would not reasonably under-
> stand the statement that Myers "is enrolled in a course for
> remedial speaking" to be an assertion of fact. Taken in
> context, it can reasonably be understood to suggest that
> Myers should have been so enrolled. Even the latter state-
> ment may be hyperbolic. The author may have meant only
> that Myers' sports news reading needed improvement. On

either of these interpretations, the challenged publication states a critical judgment, an opinion.[148]

However, in another recent case the trial court ruled that whether a satiric reference to the plaintiff was a protected form of humor or a grievous libel had to be determined by a jury after a full-fledged trial:

> Humor, then, may well be a defense to a suit in libel, but the mere assertion that a statement was meant to be funny does not automatically absolve the utterer. Humor is intensely subjective. Blank looks or even active loathing may be engendered by a statement or cartoon that evokes howls of laughter from another. What is amusing or funny in the eyes of one person may be cruel and tasteless to someone else. There is always a thin line between laughter and tears. . . .
> Thus, the writer resorting to parody must be wary, for his shafts may miss the mark, and be cruel without purpose, inflicting real hurt where only laughter was intended. . . . It is difficult for a court to impose its own opinions as to the intent and impact of a purportedly humorous work. . . . Just as questions of what is truth, what is reasonable, or what is obscene are left to the collective judgment of a group of laymen serving on a jury, so the question of whether a particular statement is nonactionable humor or compensable libel should appropriately be left to the judgment of a jury.[149]

As in fiction, legal tests looking to falsity, like the actual-malice test, are essentially useless in cases of libel by satire, since satire is intentionally exaggerated and in that sense knowingly "false." Here too, a new legal test is required but has not been fully developed. One appropriate standard might be to consider satire as constitutionally protected expression of opinion that by definition can be neither true nor false.[150] Only in those rare cases where satire could not be considered opinion because of seemingly factual assertions should a court determine whether the author and publisher intended the satire to be taken as fact or acted recklessly about whether it could reasonably be so taken. Until such a test is adopted, the courts may continue to apply a falsity standard—in cases where falsity is just about the only issue not in dispute.

Can photographs and works of visual art be libelous?

Yes, although there have been comparatively few cases. In one famous case, an optical illusion in which the plaintiff's genitals appeared to be exposed resulted in a recovery for libel.[151] A more recent case involved a painting entitled *The Mugging of the Muse* in which several masked figures were portrayed mugging a female form while cherubs and the like hovered nearby. The plaintiffs, whose faces appeared on the masks, claimed that the painting accused them of being violent criminals. The artist claimed that his painting was an allegorical statement of his opinion that the plaintiffs were enemies of art. A jury sustained the plaintiffs' claims, and the trial judge upheld that verdict. But an appellate court reversed the judgment. The court accepted the jury's finding that the artist intended to, and did, portray the plaintiffs in the painting, and it assumed that a work of art can be libelous. Nonetheless, it held that the libel claim could not be sustained since the painting was clearly allegorical and as such should be considered a nonactionable statement of opinion.[152]

But the point remains that a person can successfully sue for libel by a work of visual art if he satisfies all the legal requirements discussed in this chapter.

Where can a creative person be sued for libel?

In theory at least, libel injury may occur wherever defamatory matter is circulated to persons who know the plaintiff and can be influenced by its publication. A statement published or broadcast in the mass media can cause injury almost anywhere. The "jurisdictional" question is whether circulation of the libel within a given locale (or "forum") has caused injury in that forum and whether the publisher's or author's contacts with the forum are sufficient to permit jurisdiction. It is generally held that circulation of a libel in a forum causes injury in the forum. Once actionable injury is established, the question becomes to what extent and on what basis a forum can legitimately reach out to assert jurisdiction over a nonresident. The limits of such jurisdiction are found in constitutional concept of due process and the First Amendment.

In 1984 the Supreme Court rendered two important decisions dealing with jurisdiction. In *Calder v. Jones*,[153] the actress Shirley Jones sued the *National Enquirer* and two of its employees in a state court in California. All of the defendants were Florida residents, and the two employees had extremely limited contacts with California. The Court found that the employees could be sued in California:

> The Due Process clause of the Fourteenth Amendment to the United States Constitution permits personal jurisdiction over a defendant in any state with which the defendant has "certain minimum contacts . . . such that the maintenance of the suit does not offend 'traditional notions of fair play and substantial justice.'" . . . In judging minimum contacts, a court properly focuses on "the relationship among the defendant, the forum, and the litigation."
>
> . . . .
>
> The allegedly libelous story concerned the California activities of a California resident. It impugned the professionalism of an entertainer whose television career was centered in California. The article was drawn from California sources, and the brunt of the harm, in terms both of respondent's emotional distress and the injury to her professional reputation was suffered in California. In sum, California is the focal point both of the story and of the harm suffered. Jurisdiction over petitioners is therefore proper in California based on the "effects" of their Florida conduct in California.[154]

In *Keeton v. Hustler Magazine, Inc.*,[155] a New York resident sued *Hustler*, an Ohio corporation, in federal court in New Hampshire. The plaintiff's only connection with New Hampshire was the circulation there of a magazine of which she was an editor. The defendant-publisher's only connection with that state was the monthly sale there of some ten thousand to fifteen thousand copies of its magazine. It was clear that the only reason the plaintiff had sued in New Hampshire was that state's 4-year statute of limitations for libel.

The Supreme Court found that the publisher could be sued in New Hampshire, noting in passing that "false statements of fact harm both the subject of the falsehood *and* the readers of the statement." The Court concluded: "The victim of a libel, like the victim of any tort, may choose to bring suit in any forum with which the defendant has certain minimum contacts. . . . Where, as in this case, [a publisher] has continuously and deliberately exploited the New Hampshire market, it must reasonably anticipate being haled into court there in a libel action based on the contents of its magazine."[156]

As a result of these decisions, a creative person who anticipates that her work will be circulated in a given state and that it could cause injury there can also anticipate the possibility of being sued in that state.

If an author or artist is sued in an out-of-state forum and cannot defeat jurisdiction, there is the possibility to "remove" the case to a federal court (as opposed to a state court) in the foreign jurisdiction, which may provide a more neutral and hospitable forum for the litigation, or to seek a change of venue to a more convenient forum or in the interests of justice.[157]

How do headlines, captions, and photographs present potential libel problems for the author or artist?

It is beyond the scope of this book to deal with libel and related problems in news reporting and news publication. But even authors who are not reporters should know that a libel claim may be based not only upon the author's work but its presentation in published form. If headlines, captions, or photographs are added, these can form the basis—alone or with the author's material—of a libel or privacy action. In fact, in some jurisdictions defamatory matter in a caption or headline is actionable even if the rest of the story explains away, or supports, the defamatory allegations.[158] In most jurisdictions, however, headlines and captions are read with the rest of the publication and will be actionable based on the meaning of the overall story. If headlines are particularly prominent and so unrelated as to damage the plaintiff's reputation separately, they may be separately actionable.[159] Accordingly, authors and artists should review material in its final form before publication or secure an indemnification for matter added by the publisher.

Is retraction a meaningful protection from a libel claim?

Not always. Especially in the context of book and magazine publication, retraction protection is often not practically or legally available, or will be of limited assistance in defeating or containing a libel claim. Nonetheless, authors and artists should be aware of this option.

As a matter of common (rather than statutory) law, retraction is often recognized as evidence of an innocent or nonactionable intent. It can assure the availability of a claim of privilege or at least limit damages. The law often prevents recovery of punitive damages if a retraction has been made. An effective retraction may also limit the actual harm caused by the initial publication.

There are retraction statutes in several states.[160] They differ widely, but most of them relate mainly or entirely to newspapers, broadcasters, and other "hot news" media. Most book publishers and many magazines could not meet their requirements since time limits for retraction typically range from 48 hours to 3 weeks.[161] The statute may also require prominent publication (say, on the front page) in a type size the same as or larger than the item retracted, requirements that cannot be met by a book publisher. Still, an offer of a retraction in a letter to the plaintiff, a public announcement, or a correction in a subsequent edition of a book can be made in appropriate circumstances; even if the retraction is technically not in compliance with the rules, it may be relevant in any ensuing libel litigation.

Are there any other special safeguards available to defendants in libel cases?

Yes. Because of the First Amendment implications inherent in every libel case, the courts, including the Supreme Court, and various state legislatures have established several important safeguards for libel cases that are not necessarily available in other kinds of cases.

In 1984, in *Bose v. Consumers Union*,[162] the Supreme Court held that appellate courts in libel cases have an obligation to "make an independent examination of the whole record" to be sure that "the judgment [after trial] does not constitute a forbidden intrusion on the field of free expression." As the Court put it:

> The question whether the evidence in the record in a defamation case is of the convincing clarity required to strip the utterance of First Amendment protection is not merely a question for the trier of fact. Judges, as expositors

of the Constitution, must independently decide whether the evidence in the record is sufficient to cross the constitutional threshold that bars the entry of any judgment that is not supported by clear and convincing proof of "actual malice."[163]

In 1986, in *Anderson v. Liberty Lobby, Inc.*,[164] the Supreme Court made an equally important ruling relating to *summary judgment* in a libel case (where the defendant moves for dismissal, based on the law alone, before trial). The Court held that the judge hearing that motion in an actual-malice case must evaluate the evidence presented by the plaintiff and decide whether the plaintiff has met his burden of showing by "clear and convincing" evidence that the defendant acted with actual malice. To deny the motion and permit the case to proceed to trial, the trial court must find that "a reasonable jury might find [based on that evidence] that actual malice had been shown with convincing clarity."[165]

In 1986 the Supreme Court also made it clear that the plaintiff in all libel cases, at least where a "media" defendant is involved, has the burden of proving the falsity of the allegedly libelous material.[166]

Finally, many states have enacted "shield laws," which provide under varying circumstances that journalists (which usually includes freelance authors of articles and books) cannot be compelled to disclose their confidential sources, even in the context of a libel suit based on material provided by that source. However, in such cases the courts may take other measures, such as preventing the defendants from claiming they had a reliable source for the material and instructing the jury that it can (but doesn't have to) infer that there was no source for that material.[167]

Because of the First Amendment aspects of every libel case, the courts have established important protections for defendants. At the same time, the courts have never seriously considered abolishing the right to sue for libel. It is also clear that at least some libel plaintiffs are able to overcome all the protections afforded libel defendants and are able to win substantial libel judgments. The current state of libel law—with elaborate protections for defendants and the possibility of substantial (including million-dollar) judgments for plaintiffs—have led many thoughtful groups and individuals to consider how libel law might be reformed.

What legal remedies are available to a successful libel plaintiff?

Essentially, only money damages. The Supreme Court has made it clear that because of the special threat to the freedoms protected by the First Amendment, the government may neither issue injunctions against the dissemination of libelous statements nor order a publisher to publish a retraction (or make space available for rebuttal) if the publisher does not wish to.[168]

What kinds of damages can be awarded in libel actions?

Special damages, general or compensatory damages, and punitive damages.

Special damages are out-of-pocket losses that the plaintiff can prove were sustained as a result of the libel; for example, loss of a job, fellowship, or scholarship, or psychiatric or medical expenses.[169]

General damages compensate the plaintiff for injuries that are not susceptible to precise calculation—in particular, injury to the plaintiff's reputation.[170] Before the Supreme Court's decisions in the *New York Times* and *Gertz* cases, the law was that once a plaintiff established libel, damage would be presumed without proof. In *Gertz*, however, the Court ruled that presumed damages are inconsistent with the First Amendment. A libel plaintiff (at least in cases involving writers, publishers, or other media) can recover only for proved "actual injury," although the Court went on to observe: "Suffice it to say that actual injury is not limited to out-of-pocket loss. Indeed, the more customary types of actual harm inflicted by defamatory falsehood include impairment of reputation and standing in the community, personal humiliation, and mental anguish and suffering."[171] In *Firestone*, the Supreme Court seemed to indicate that an award of compensatory damages could be sustained constitutionally in the absence of proof of any injury to reputation,[172] but some state courts, including New York appellate courts, have held as a matter of state law that a libel plaintiff cannot recover damages without proving injury to reputation.[173]

egregious conduct and to serve as a deterrent. In *Gertz* the
Supreme Court disapproved the general availability of punitive
damages. It held that they can be awarded only if the plaintiff
proves that the defendant acted with actual malice (i.e., with
knowledge that the statement was false or with reckless disregard of its truth or falsity).[174] The Court left open whether
punitive damages should be abolished in libel cases. A few
states have done so, but the majority continues to allow them.[175]

The fact remains that a significant number of large awards,
several in millions of dollars, have been made since *Gertz*.
However, most of those verdicts are being appealed, and a
number have been reduced or set aside. As of late 1990, only
a minuscule number of million-dollar libel awards have been
finally affirmed on appeal.[176]

What kinds of reforms have been proposed for the law of libel?

As a result of the elaborate substantive and procedural protections afforded to defendants in libel cases, many lawyers,
judges, and legal scholars have concluded that it is far too
difficult, time-consuming, and expensive for plaintiffs with
valid libel cases to prosecute those cases. At the same time, it
is believed by many, including some of the same people, that
current libel law is still too burdensome on libel defendants,
with the possibility in virtually every case of a money judgment
that could put many such defendants out of business.

To deal with these perceived deficiencies, several individuals
and groups have proposed various reforms. For example, Congressman Charles E. Schumer of New York introduced a bill
that would have made several major changes to that law.[177]
The essence of that bill, which the congressman ultimately
withdrew because of the widespread opposition it received,
would have provided for a simplified declaratory-judgment action as a substitute to the full-fledged suit that is now the
plaintiff's only option.

Similarly, in 1988, a select panel of lawyers, judges, and law
professors brought together by the Annenberg Washington
Program issued a report recommending changes to libel law,
including a provision allowing either party to convert the case
into one for a declaratory judgment in which many of the

constitutional and procedural safeguards now available to a libel defendant would not apply.[178]

Most recently, in July 1990, a draft of a new Uniform Defamation Act was given its "first reading" to the Conference of Commissioners on Uniform State Laws, a group established to propose uniform laws for adoption by all the states.[179] This draft proposed that the issues in libel cases be decided in two separate stages: first, the issues of publication, defamation, reputational harm, and falsity; then, such remaining issues as privilege, fault, and damages. The draft also provides that if the plaintiff prevails at the first stage (i.e., that she has been libeled by a false statement published by the defendant), the defendant can then make a "termination offer" to pay the plaintiff her costs of litigation (including attorneys' fees) and publish a retraction. If the plaintiff declines that offer and prevails at the second stage, she can recover neither attorneys' fees nor punitive damages. If the defendant declines to make such an offer and loses at the second stage, the plaintiff would be entitled to recover her attorneys' fees in addition to all other remedies.

All of these proposals have engendered a great deal of dispute and controversy, and it seems unlikely that any of them will be adopted in the foreseeable future. Nevertheless, some changes in the current law, including the abolition of punitive damages, seem overdue and at least possible in the near future.

What does the law mean by *privacy*?

There are probably few words that have as many, and as diverse, legal meanings. *Privacy* has come to mean the right of individuals to decide for themselves (i.e., without government interference) whether to use contraception or have an abortion.[180] The word also refers to the Fourth Amendment right to be free from "unreasonable searches and seizures" by the government. Federal and state privacy statutes are designed to protect the confidentiality of the governmental (and private) records that are maintained on just about all of us.

The word *privacy* has also (somewhat unfortunately and confusingly) come to refer to four categories of lawsuits, most against writers, publishers, and producers, for allegedly invading or violating the "right of privacy."[181] Those four categories are often referred to as *false light, private facts, appropriation,* and *intrusion.*[182]

What is a *false-light* invasion of privacy?

It is similar to libel. The main difference is that although the law of libel is designed to vindicate the subject's reputation, the false-light claim is designed to remedy injured feelings. A false-light invasion involves "publicity placing a person in a 'false light' in a manner which would be highly offensive to a reasonable person or 'a person of ordinary sensibilities.'"[183] The elements have been succinctly summarized as follows: "The statement must be made public, it must be about the plaintiff, it must be unprivileged, and it must be false. The element of falsity must be proved by the plaintiff and the falsity shown must be substantial and material."[184]

What are some false-light invasions?

The Supreme Court has considered two false-light cases, which provide useful examples. *Time, Inc. v. Hill*[185] arose from an article in *Life* magazine mentioning the opening of a new play about a family that was held hostage by three escaped convicts. The article indicated that the play was an account of the experiences of a named family some years earlier. The family sued, claiming that its experience was different from that portrayed in the play and that the *Life* article placed the family in a false and embarrassing light.

In 1967 the Supreme Court, by a 5–4 vote, held that "the factual reporting of newsworthy persons and events is in the public interest and is protected"[186] and that falsity is not enough to defeat that protection. Echoing its landmark *New York Times* libel decision three years before, the Court declared that "the constitutional protection for speech and press preclude [recovery for invasion of privacy] to redress false reports of matters of public interest in the absence of proof that the defendant published the report with knowledge of its falsity or in reckless disregard of the truth."[187]

In *Cantrell v. Forest City Publishing Co.*,[188] a woman and her son sued the publisher and reporter of a newspaper article on the impact on their family of the father's death some months before in a publicized bridge collapse. The article purported to reflect face-to-face interviews with the family, but the reporter had had no direct contact with them. The Supreme Court found that there was sufficient evidence to support a finding that the paper and reporter were guilty of actual malice (i.e., knowledge of falsity or reckless disregard of truth or falsity) so a false-light recovery could be justified.[189]

Cantrell was decided after the Court ruled in *Gertz* that private figures need not prove actual malice in libel cases. However, since proof of actual malice had been established, the Court did not address whether a false-light plaintiff is still required by the First Amendment to satisfy the actual-malice test in discussions of matters of "public interest," which is what the Court announced in the *Hill* case. Some lower courts and commentators have speculated that the *Hill* decision no longer applies to private-figure false-light cases,[190] but the answer will have to await word from the Supreme Court.

What is a *private-facts* invasion of privacy?
It has been defined as follows:

One who gives publicity to a matter concerning the private life of another is subject to liability to the other for invasion of his privacy if the matter publicized is of a kind that

(a) would be highly offensive to a reasonable person and

(b) is not of legitimate concern to the public.[191]

Unlike libel and false-light claims, which are made about false statements, the essence of this claim is that the statements are true.

Because a private-facts invasion must be "not of legitimate concern to the public" and the courts have given broad application to this "newsworthiness" aspect, it is rare that such claims against authors and publishers have prevailed.[192] Most successful cases have been brought against nonmedia defendants such as employers, bankers, and doctors who improperly disclosed embarrassing private facts about the plaintiffs.[193]

There have been exceptions, however, usually with plaintiffs who were once notorious but have receded into anonymity. In a celebrated 1931 case, a woman who had been a prostitute and a defendant in a sensational murder case changed her lifestyle, married, and dropped out of sight. Several years later, a movie based on her earlier life was released. The California courts upheld her private-facts claim of invasion of privacy.[194]

In a 1971 case,[195] an article about hijacking in *Reader's Digest* mentioned that the plaintiff had stolen a trunk in Kentucky and engaged in a gun battle with the police. The article did not indicate that the events had occurred 11 years earlier, after which the plaintiff had moved to California, started a family, and become a respected member of the community. The California courts upheld his claim, stating that while they approved complete reporting about current and past criminal activity, "the identity of the actor in reports of long past crimes usually has little public purpose."[196]

But many other cases have ruled that "where are they now?" features about once notorious or famous people are "newsworthy" and thus protected.[197] In general, courts will be more sympathetic to plaintiffs' claims if their earlier notoriety was involuntary than if it was of their choosing.

What is an *appropriation* invasion of privacy?

Much of it is not really a matter of privacy but the appropriation of a person's (often, a celebrity's) name or likeness for commercial benefit without consent or remuneration. Aspects of this branch of privacy law are often referred to as the *right of publicity*.[198] Noncelebrities have this right too, but their claims seem more closely related to "privacy" than "publicity" concerns.[199]

The Supreme Court has found that misappropriation or right-of-publicity claims do not inherently violate First Amendment rights. In the leading case, a performer whose act consisted of being shot from a gun prevailed in a suit against a television station that broadcast his act (which took all of 15 seconds) without consent or compensation.[200] The broadcaster asserted, to no avail, that the performance was newsworthy and therefore protected by the First Amendment.

Occasionally this branch of privacy law is applied (or misapplied) to editorial rather than commercial uses of a name or likeness. However, the law seems clear that appropriation invasion-of-privacy protection does not apply to communications about matters of legitimate public interest, as will be found in most nonfiction newspaper or magazine articles and books. In a recent case,[201] the plaintiff's photograph was prominently displayed on the cover of the *New York Times Magazine* to illustrate an article on "the black middle class." He was not named or otherwise referred to in the article, and he disagreed with portions of it. He sued for invasion of privacy under New York's "Right to Privacy" statute, but the New York courts rejected the suit, holding that the publication of his picture was a legitimate editorial use that did not violate any right of privacy recognized in that state.[202] Other courts have found that "fleeting" or "incidental" references to real people in works of fiction (or fictionalized nonfiction) do not violate their privacy or publicity rights.[203]

More difficult problems are presented where real people are portrayed other than fleetingly in substantially fictionalized contexts, including "docudramas." Fictionalized dialogue and events in a biography of a baseball star resulted in a privacy judgment in the star's favor,[204] and some courts have held that satiric performances, parodies, and imitations can violate the right of publicity, even when there is substantial independent editorial content in the material.[205]

Elizabeth Taylor once sued to stop an allegedly fictionalized TV movie of her life. However, the case was dropped when the movie was, and it is still not clear how that case would have come out.

What is an *intrusion* invasion of privacy?

It has been defined as follows: "One who intentionally intrudes, physically or otherwise, upon the solitude or seclusion of another or his private affairs or concerns, is subject to liability to the other for invasion of his privacy, if the intrusion would be highly offensive to a reasonable person."[206] In essence, this refers to wrongful conduct (rather than published work) by writers and media representatives: for example, breaking and entering,[207] surreptitious surveillance,[208] unauthorized physical presence,[209] and the kind of harassing pursuit that some writers and photographers have been known to engage in.

Photographer Ron Galella was found to have violated the right of privacy of Jacqueline Kennedy Onassis by the manner of his pursuit of photographs.[210] Reporters who place a hidden camera and microphone in a private place[211] or who enter a public restaurant[212] or hospital room[213] with cameras rolling and without permission have been found in violation of the intrusion privacy right. As a leading commentator has observed, "Crimes and torts committed in news gathering do not ordinarily receive special protection under the First Amendment."[214]

What other kinds of personal-injury claims can be asserted against creative people?

Although most of the claims assert either libel or invasion of privacy, and often both, other kinds of claims can be brought. The recent case of *Falwell v. Hustler Magazine, Inc.*[215] provides a good example of one such category. *Hustler* magazine published an ad parody that portrayed the Reverend Jerry Falwell as having had sex with his mother in an outhouse and getting drunk before preaching, among similar charges. The trial judge dismissed Falwell's privacy claims before trial, and the jury rejected Falwell's libel claims, finding that the parody's charges could not be taken as statements of fact about him. However, the jury did uphold Falwell's claim that the parody constituted the "intentional infliction of emotional harm" and awarded him $200,000 in damages.

A unanimous Supreme Court in 1988 overturned Falwell's victory, holding that the contents of the ad parody could not reasonably be understood as stating facts about Falwell and that therefore the First Amendment precluded recovery, despite the defendant's intention to cause the plaintiff pain and distress. But the Court did leave open, however slightly, the viability of such claims in the future, stating that such plaintiffs could recover for the intentional infliction of emotional distress when they can show in addition "that the publication contains a false statement of fact which was made with 'actual malice.'"[216]

Another kind of claim sometimes made against creative people arises under the general legal heading of *unfair competition*, which, like the notion of privacy discussed above, actually encompasses a variety of legal theories.

If an author writes a book or a dramatist writes a play or an artist creates an illustration that prominently features a particular organization, product, or trademark—for example, the Girl Scouts[217] or the Pillsbury "Doughboy"[218]—the people who control or own those entities could claim that those works "dilute" the distinctiveness of the entity's name or identity or create "confusion" whether they participated in or authorized the creation of those works. It is also possible that the use of someone else's trademark in the title or body of a work could give rise to claims of trademark infringement.[219]

These kinds of claims are usually unsuccessful since the courts generally believe that those legal theories should be reserved for "commercial" as distinct from "editorial" contexts.[220] Nevertheless, authors and artists who contemplate such uses should probably consider whether such claims could validly be made.

Finally, authors, publishers, and producers have been sued by people who claim to have been injured because of *errors* in a book (or other work)—for example, a recipe in a cookbook that calls for ten tablespoons of chili powder instead of one, or instructions in a do-it-yourself manual that would result in a serious explosion—and by people who claim that others were inspired to imitate something in a book or movie, including acts of physical violence that caused injury to those people.[221] In one recent case the publisher of *Soldier of Fortune* magazine was successfully sued because an alleged "hit man" had advertised his availability in the magazine and was hired through that ad.[222] In general, the courts will uphold claims based on actual dangerous errors in a work that result in foreseeable injury but will reject claims asserting that a victim or a third party might have been "inspired" or "induced" to cause injury because of something in a work.[223]

Who can be sued in a libel or privacy case?

The original writer or creator is always directly answerable, much as the driver of a delivery truck is answerable for any accident. An employer of the writer is also answerable, like the employer of a driver. The publisher-broadcaster may also be answerable, even if the writer is a freelance contributor, and individual editors, producers, and collaborators who participate in the creation of a work may be answerable.

It occasionally happens that a plaintiff sues the printer of a work, its distributor and retailer, and even the advertisers who have sponsored it. However, because of the Supreme Court's decision in *Gertz* requiring plaintiffs to prove that libelous statements have been published with fault by the defendant, it seems unlikely that such tangential defendants will be found liable.[224]

Who bears the costs of a libel or privacy case?

It depends on what we mean by *costs*, and on the relationships among the people and entities involved in the publication.

Costs has at least three meanings. First, there are the physical and emotional costs inevitably incurred in litigation. Second, there are the out-of-pocket costs of defending a lawsuit: lawyers' fees, investigators' expenses, and the like. And third, there may be an award of damages to the plaintiff.

Writers or artists who are sued for libel or invasion of privacy bear most of the emotional and physical costs. Their work gave rise to the suit, and their reputations and careers may be directly affected. They are most likely to be intimidated and frightened by a lawsuit (including fear of major financial loss) and least likely to be experienced and sophisticated in dealing with such matters. Publishers or other media outlets are probably more experienced in such matters and can take the suit in stride as an unavoidable part of their business.

As for out-of-pocket costs, much depends on the relationship between writer and publisher. A newspaper or broadcaster will almost always assume, at no cost to the writer, full responsibility for legal defense. And most usually a magazine or book publisher will assume the initial costs of a joint defense with a nonemployee writer, including providing lawyers to represent both. But this does not mean that such protection must be provided or that the publisher will not ultimately seek a contribution from the writer.

Finally, the original writer is almost always held responsible for some or all of any damages awarded to the plaintiff, at least in the absence of culpable conduct by the publisher. The writer may also be legally obliged to reimburse the publisher for damages the publisher has paid to the plaintiff.

In practice, however, the writer and publisher will often agree to share the ultimate liability. The publisher can usually afford the payment of damages much better, and it is increasingly common for publishers to be covered by insurance. Such coverage is increasingly common for writers, primarily through coverage obtained by the publisher.[225]

Many of these issues can be dealt with in the contract between the writer and publisher (see Chapter III).

What can a writer or artist do to minimize the risk of a libel, privacy, or other legal claim?

The first rule is to be careful and accurate. But as the Supreme Court has repeatedly recognized, errors are inevitable, as are libel and privacy suits arising out of these errors. Even complete accuracy does not guarantee no lawsuits since some plaintiffs will have a different understanding of the truth and others will bring suit for reasons other than the expectation of winning, such as using the suit as a way to deny the charges against them or to harass and intimidate the writer or publisher.

Responsible writers should retain the notes and tapes they have compiled in preparing their work to be able to demonstrate in any future litigation that they acted reasonably and without negligence or reckless disregard of the truth. (However, if the notes would disclose a confidential source, there is the countervailing risk that they may have to be produced in litigation.)

If the subject matter of a creator's work suggests the potential of a libel, privacy, or other claim—for example, accuses its subject of criminal or otherwise improper or unpopular activities—many creators and most major publishers and radio and TV stations will have the work reviewed by a libel specialist, usually a lawyer. The specialist should be able to isolate aspects of the work that can lead to legal liability and suggest ways to minimize legal exposure (e.g., by deft rephrasing or careful editing) and to prepare for the potential legal claim. (This is sometimes referred to as *libel vetting*.) Especially if the publisher does not provide such review, the creative person concerned about lawsuits should consider getting such a review on his own.

NOTES

1. *Gertz v. Robert Welch, Inc.*, 418 U.S. 323, 341 (1974) (quoting Justice Potter Stewart's concurring opinion in *Rosenblatt v. Baer*, 383 U.S. 75, 92 [1966]).

2. Justices Black and Douglas expressed their view in a number of concurring and dissenting opinions, including *New York Times v. Sullivan*, 376 U.S. 254 (1964); *Garrison v. Louisiana*, 379 U.S. 64 (1964); and *Curtis Publishing Co. v. Butts*, 388 U.S. 130 (1967). In the *Butts* case, the two justices succinctly stated that "it is time for this Court . . . to adopt the rule to the effect that the First Amendment was intended to leave the press free from the harassment of libel judgments." 388 U.S. at 172. See also Hentoff, *The First Freedom: The Tumultuous History of Free Speech in America* (1980).

3. *New York Times v. Sullivan*, 376 U.S. 254 (1964). This case represents what has been called the *constitutionalization* of libel law.

4. Legal commentators have written extensively on the *New York Times* case and its effect on libel law. Among the most informative and readable are Lewis, *Make No Law: The Sullivan Case and the First Amendment* (1991); Smolla, *Suing the Press: Libel, the Media, and Power* (1986); Lewis, "Annals of Law: The Sullivan Case," *The New Yorker*, Nov. 5, 1984; Kalven, "The New York Times Case: A Note on 'The Central Meaning' of the First Amendment," 1961 *Sup. Ct. Rev.* 191 (1961); Eaton, "The American Law of Defamation Through Gertz v. Robert Welch, Inc. and Beyond: An Analytical Primer," 61 *Va. L. Rev.* 1349 (1975); Hill, "Defamation and Privacy under the First Amendment," 76 *Colum. L. Rev.* 1205 (1976); and Sack, *Libel, Slander, and Related Problems*, ch. 1, (1980) ([hereinafter, Sack); and Sandford, *Libel and Privacy* (2d ed. 1991). The Sack and Sandford books contain comprehensive discussions of most of the issues mentioned in this chapter.

5. Defamation law is traditionally defined and governed by state (and not federal) law. While defamation law from state to state follows similar patterns, specific legal rules will vary, sometimes markedly, depending upon the state and issue. Although the courts have in recent years significantly changed some state rules in response to First Amendment requirements, the Supreme Court continues to allow the states considerable latitude to define their defamation laws within broad constitutional parameters. For a comprehensive comparison of current law state by state, see LDRC *50-State Survey 1990: Current Developments in Media Libel and Invasion of Privacy Law*, (Henry R. Kaufman, ed., 1990) (hereinafter, LDRC survey). The *LDRC 50-State Survey* is published annually.

6. The basic distinctions, if any, between libel and slander vary from state to state. In general, a slander claim is more difficult to maintain. Some states restrict slander claims to specific, narrowly limited types of defamation. Many states require proof of "special damages." In some

states the statute of limitations for slander (i.e., the time within which a claim can be asserted) is very short. All these distinctions assume that oral defamation is less widely disseminated and therefore less harmful. *See* Sack at 43–45. Slander claims are rare for the average author, but they can arise from oral statements made in the course of research or investigation before publication or during press conferences or other press and media interviews after publication.

7. *Restatement (Second) of Torts* §559 (hereinafter, *Restatement*) (1977). This "model" legal code, prepared by legal scholars, has been extremely influential in the development of libel law. *See also Prosser on Torts*, §111 at 739 (4th ed. 1979).

8. Seelman, *The Law of Libel and Slander in the State of New York* at 8, ¶18 (1933) (quoted in Eldredge, *The Law of Defamation*, at 32, §7 [1978]).

9. *Restatement* §571, comment g, lists murder, rape, treason, and operating a bawdy house as examples of crimes that if falsely alleged may give rise to a libel action. Most states require that the crime be one of "moral turpitude," so that false allegations of minor offenses such as parking violations would not be considered libelous.

10. See *Solly v. Brown*, 220 Ky. 576, 295 S.W. 890 (1927) (statement that plaintiff "is eat up with the clap" found to be defamatory per se); *Simpson v. Press Publishing Co.*, 33 Misc. 228, 67 N.Y.S. 401 (1900) ("To falsely say of one that he has leprosy is slander per se"). The imputation must be to a disease which would be likely to result in excluding the plaintiff from society. *See, e.g., Chuy v. Philadelphia Eagles Football Club*, 595 F.2d 1265 (3d Cir. 1979). Several courts have upheld libel judgments for plaintiffs who were falsely stated to be afflicted with AIDS. *See, e.g., McCune v. Neitzel*, 235 Neb. 754, 457 N.W.2d 803 (1990); *Snipes v. Mack*, 191 Ga. App. 233, 381 S.E.2d 318 (Ga. Ct. App. 1989); *see also, Van Straten v. Milkwaukee Journal*, 151 Wis.2d 905, 447 N.W.2d 105 (Wis. Ct. App. 1989).

11. Examples of statements that have been found defamatory per se include charges that a lawyer or physician is unqualified, *e.g., Nasr v. Connecticut General Life Ins. Co.*, 632 F. Supp. 1024 (N.D.Ill. 1986) (reference to physician as "quack"); *see also, Ridgeway State Bank v. Bird*, 185 Wis. 418, 202 N.W. 170 (1925) (statement that bank was insolvent); and *M'Millan v. Birch*, I Binn. 178 (Pa. 1806) (statement that the plaintiff, a minister, was "a liar, a drunkard, and preacher of the devil").

12. *Restatement* §574 treats an imputation of unchastity or serious sexual misconduct to either sex as defamatory. *But see Moricoli v. Schwartz*, 46 Ill. App. 3d 481, 361 N.E.2d 74 (1977) where the court held that

alleging that a male was a homosexual was not slanderous per se. In the light of contemporary social mores, which seem increasingly to accept the fact that many people are sexually active before marriage and that many others are gay, it may be questioned whether the imputation of unchastity or homosexuality will continue to be considered defamatory.

13. The distinction between defamation "per se" and "per quod" is discussed in this chapter, but since they are among the most complex elements of defamation law, not all aspects are considered. For a more complete treatment, see Sack at 94–112.

14. See *Morrison v. Ritchie & Co.*, Sess. Cas. 645 (Scot. 2d Div.) (1901–02), 39 Scot. L. R. 432 (1902) where an erroneous but seemingly innocent announcement of the birth of twins was found libelous because the parents had been married only one month.

15. See Eldredge, "The Spurious Rule of Libel Per Quod," 79 *Harv. L. Rev.* 733 (1966); Prosser, "More Libel Per Quod," 79 *Harv. L. Rev.* 1629 (1966). A number of states require proof of special damages in libel per quod cases. See *Restatement* §569, explanatory note (tent. draft No. 11, 1965). The other jurisdictions make no distinction between libel per se and libel per quod and thus only require proof of harm to reputation.

16. In those states, truth is not a complete defense to a claim of libel; the statement must not only be true but be published with "good motives" or for "justifiable ends." See, e.g., Mass. Gen. Laws Ann., ch. 231, §92 (1974); Kansas Const. Bill of Rights §Il. In light of the revolutionary changes in libel law in recent years, it seems unlikely that a true statement could ever be found libelous.

17. See, e.g., *Philadelphia Newspapers, Inc. v. Hepps*, 475 U.S. 767, 106 Sup. Ct. 1558 (1986) where the Supreme Court, speaking through Justice O'Connor, stated: "To ensure that true speech on matters of public concern is not deterred, we hold that the common-law presumption that defamatory speech is false cannot stand when a plaintiff seeks damages against a media defendant for speech of public concern." As of 1990, the Court has not addressed whether the same rule would apply to nonmedia defendants.

18. See, e.g., *Wehling v. Columbia Broadcasting System*, 721 F.2d 506 (5th Cir. 1983); *Guccione v. Hustler Magazine, Inc.*, 800 F.2d 298 (2d Cir. 1986), *cert. denied*, 479 U.S. 1091 (1987); *Liberty Lobby Inc. v. Dow Jones & Co.*, 838 F.2d 121 (D.C. Cir. 1988); *Robinson v. U.S.News & World Report, Inc.*, 16 Med. L. Rptr 695 (N.D. Ill. 1989).

19. *Milkovich v. Lorain Journal Co.*, 497 U.S. 1, 110 S. Ct. 2695 (1990).

20. 110 S. Ct. at 2706.
21. *White v. Fraternal Order of Police*, 909 F.2d. 512 (D.C. Cir. 1990) (emphasis in original); *see also, Diesen v. Hessburg*, 455 N.W.2d 446 (Minn. 1990), *cert. denied*, 111 S. Ct. 1072 (1991). For a case rejecting a claim of "libel by omission," *see Janklow v. Newsweek, Inc.*, 759 F.2d 644 (8th Cir. 1989).
22. 418 U.S. 323, 339–40 (1974).
23. *Id.* at 338–39.
24. *See e.g., Ollman v. Evans*, 750 F.2d 970 (D.C. Cir. 1984) (en banc); *Steinhilber v. Alphonse*, 68 N.Y.2d 283, 508 N.Y.S.2d 901, 501 N.E.2d 550 (1986).
25. *Ollman v. Evans*, supra n.24.
26. 110 S. Ct. at 2705.
27. *Id.*
28. *Id.* at 2706.
29. Before *Milkovich*, calling someone a Nazi or Communist was found to be a statement of fact in some cases and a statement of opinion in others. *Compare Potts v. Dies*, 132 F.2d 734 (D.C. Cir. 1942), *cert. denied*, 319 U.S. 762 (1943) (accusing plaintiff of pro-Nazi sentiments an expression of opinion), *with Holy Spirit Assn v. Sequoia Elsevier Publishing Co.*, 75 A.D.2d 523 (1st Dept. 1980) (statement that religion was "Nazi-style" a statement of fact). *See also Buckley v. Littell*, 539 F.2d 882 (2d Cir. 1976), cert. denied, 429 U.S. 1062 (1977) where the court found that a reference to William F. Buckley as a "fellow traveler" of "fascism" was a statement of opinion and not of fact but that a further statement that "like Westbrook Pegler, who lied day after day in his column about Quentin Reynolds and goaded him into a lawsuit, Buckley could be taken to court by any one of several people who had enough money to hire competent legal counsel and nothing else to do" was a statement of fact and not opinion, and was libelous.
30. *Milkovich, supra* note 19; *Cianci v. New Times Publishing Co.*, 639 F.2d 54 (2d Cir. 1980).
31. Sack at 157; *see Rinaldi v. Holt, Rinehart & Winston, Inc.*, 42 N.Y.2d 369, *cert. denied*, 434 U.S. 969 (1977) where a statement that a judge was "incompetent," based upon disclosed facts or examples, was held to be constitutionally protected opinion, while a statement that he was "probably corrupt" was held to be a factual statement because it strongly suggested to the ordinary reader undisclosed factual "undertones of conspiracy and illegality."
32. 360 F.2d 344 (5th Cir. 1966).
33. *Id.* at 348.
34. 398 U.S. 6 (1970).

35. *Id.* at 14.

36. *Hustler Magazine, Inc. v. Falwell*, 485 U.S. 46, 108 S. Ct. 876 (1988).

37. *See Edwards v. National Audubon Society*, 556 F.2d 113 (2d Cir.), *cert. denied sub nom. Edwards v. New York Times Co.*, 434 U.S. 1002 (1977).

38. *See, e.g., Kelley v. Johnson Publishing Co.*, 160 Cal. App. 2d 718, 325 P.2d 659 (1958). In most states, if a person is libeled and later dies, the cause of action for libel dies with the person. *See Gruschus v. Curtis Publishing Co.*, 342 F.2d 775 (10th Cir. 1965). In a few states, the dead person's survivors can continue a suit that was commenced before the plaintiff's death. *See Moyer v. Phillips*, 462 Pa. 395, 341 A.2d 441 (1975); *MacDonald v. Time, Inc.*, 9 Med. L. Rptr. 1025 (D.N.J. 1983).

39. *See, e.g., Continental Nut Co. v. Robert L. Berner Co.*, 345 F.2d 395 (7th Cir. 1965) (corporation can be libeled only by statements that attack its financial or business practices). Municipal corporations may not sue for libel. *See Sack* at 124–25.

40. *See, e.g., Washington Post Co. v. Kennedy*, 3 F.2d 207 (D.C. Cir. 1925) where a newspaper article about an accused forger was found to libel a person with the same name. The article identified the forger as a 40-year-old Washington attorney named Harry Kennedy. The successful plaintiff in the libel action was the only Washington attorney named Harry Kennedy. Even though the *Post* did not intend the story to refer to the plaintiff, he was able to prevail because his friends and acquaintances thought the article was about him. However, these results could well be different in light of the Supreme Court's requirement that allegedly libelous statements be published with "fault."

41. *But see Allen v. Gordon*, 86 A.D.2d 514, 446 N.Y.S.2d 48 (1st Dept.), *aff'd*, 56 N.Y.2d 780, 542 N.Y.S.2d 25 (1982) where it was held that the portrayal of a Manhattan psychiatrist named Dr. Allen in a nonfiction book was not "of and concerning" the only Manhattan psychiatrist named Allen. On the other hand, a fictional account of a "nude marathon therapist" that did not name the plaintiff and indeed attempted to change the character's name, description, and circumstances to avoid identification, was held to be of and concerning the plaintiff and therefore actionable. *Bindrim v. Mitchell*, 92 Cal. App. 3d 61, 155 Cal. Rptr. 29, *cert. denied*, 444 U.S. 984 (1979).

42. *See Restatement* §564A: "One who publishes defamatory matter concerning a group or class of persons is subject to liability to an individual member of it, but only if (a) the group or class is so small that the matter can reasonably be understood to refer to the member, or (b) the circumstances of publication reasonably give rise to the conclusion that there is particular reference to the member."

43. *See, e.g., Farrell v. Triangle Publications, Inc.*, 399 Pa. 102, 159 A.2d 734 (1960) (statement referring generally to the thirteen town commissioners found to be "of and concerning" an individual commissioner); *Kirkman v. Westchester Newspapers, Inc.*, 287 N.Y. 373, 39 N.E.2d 919 (1942) (statement that "union officials are feathering their nests" found to be "of and concerning" one of sixteen union officials). Cases that have not allowed individual members of a group to recover for defamatory statements about the group include *Granger v. Time, Inc.*, 568 P.2d 535 (Mont. 1977) (statement that "arson has become common" in Butte, Montana, because "people who are unable to sell their devalued buildings burn them for the insurance" found not to be of and concerning a Butte businessman who lost his building to fire since the statement could apply to over two hundred people) and *Kentucky Fried Chicken, Inc. v. Sanders*, 563 S.W.2d 8 (Ky. 1978) (article criticizing the quality of food served at Kentucky Fried Chicken found not to be of and concerning one particular franchise because there are more than five thousand franchises nationwide). *See also, Neiman-Marcus v. Lait*, 13 F.R.D. 311 (S.D.N.Y. 1952); *Owens v. Clark*, 154 Okla. 108, 6 P.2d 755 (1931).

44. *Restatement* §564A, comment b. *But see Brady v. Ottaway Newspapers, Inc.*, 84 A.D. 2d 226, 445 N.Y.S. 2d 786 (2d Dept. 1981), (twenty-five members of a group of "at least 53 unindicted police officers" were permitted to press their libel claim).

45. *See, e.g., Ostrowe v. Lee*, 256 N.Y. 36, 175 N.E. 505 (1931) where the dictation of a letter to a stenographer was held to be "publication."

46. *See Restatement* §578.

47. *Edwards v. National Audubon Society*, 556 F.2d 113, 120 (2d Cir.), *cert. denied sub nom. Edwards v. New York Times Co.*, 434 U.S. 1002 (1977). *See also Price v. Viking Penguin, Inc.*, 881 F.2d 1426 (8th Cir. 1989).

48. *See, e.g., Dickey v. CBS, Inc.*, 583 F.2d 1221 1225 (3d Cir. 1978) where a federal court of appeals rejected the "neutral reportage" privilege. The highest state court in Kentucky rejected the concept in *McCall v. Courier-Journal*, 623 S.W. 882 (Ky. 1981), and New York's highest court has affirmed a lower-court opinion declining to recognize it. *Hogan v. Herald Co.*, 8 Med. L. Rptr. 2567 (N.Y. 1982).

49. *See Restatement* §585, comment e. The extent of the privilege is illustrated in *Nadeau v. Texas Co.*, 104 Mont. 558, 69 P.2d 586 (1937) where the chief judge of the Montana Supreme Court wrote a "scandalous, scurrilous and defamatory" opinion about a defendant and his counsel. The opinion was so defamatory that the other justices of the court disclaimed responsibility for it. In fact, they ordered that the opinion "not [be] published in the reports of the decisions of this

court." The court, however, denied libel relief to the subjects of the attack because of the judge's absolute privilege. In *Arundel Corp. v. Green*, 75 Md. App. 77, 540 A.2d 815 (1988), the privilege was extended to statements made before and in anticipation of judicial proceedings. *See also, Campana v. Muir*, 786 F.2d 188 (3rd Cir. 1986); *Gatlin v. Jewel Food Stores*, 699 F. Supp. 1266 (N.D. Ill. 1988) (quasi-judicial board).

50. Members of Congress are not liable for defamatory statements made in relation to legislative activity. Article I, §6 of the Constitution states that "any Speech or Debate in either House shall not be questioned in any other Place." (Most states have constitutional or statutory provisions giving similar protection to state legislators.) In *Hutchinson v. Proxmire*, 443 U.S. 111 (1979), the Supreme Court interpreted the clause to protect all statements directly relating to the legislative process, but it excluded from the absolute privilege the dissemination of statements by a member of Congress through newsletters or press releases. In a press release, Senator Proxmire had given a "golden fleece award" to the National Science Foundation and other agencies for granting federal funds to Hutchinson, a research scientist who was examining the emotional behavioral patterns of certain animals. The Supreme Court held that Proxmire's press releases were not protected by the speech and debate clause of the Constitution because they were not part of the Senate's "deliberative process."

51. *See, e.g., Barr v. Matteo*, 360 U.S. 564 (1959) where the Supreme Court held that statements made by federal executive officials while acting in their executive positions were absolutely protected from defamation claims. Defamatory statements made by members of local legislative bodies or agencies are absolutely privileged in some states and enjoy only a qualified privilege in others. *Compare, e.g., O'Donnel v. Yanchulis*, 875 F.2d 1059 (3rd Cir. 1989) (statements made by a town supervisor absolutely privileged), *with Cohen v. Bowdoin*, 288 A.2d 106 (Me. 1972) (member of the board of selectmen in a Maine town was granted only a qualified privilege for accusing the plaintiff of lying at a town meeting).

52. *See Litman v. Massachusetts Mutual Life Insurance Co.*, 739 F.2d 1549 (11th Cir. 1984). The scope of a person's consent often presents problems. For example, in *Burton v. Crowell Publishing Co.*, 82 F.2d 154 (2d Cir. 1936), the court held that the plaintiff's consent to the use of a photograph of him did not include consent to the use of a particular photo he found defamatory. *See also, Exxon Corp. v. Schoene*, 67 Md. App. 412, 508 A.2d 142 (1986). Problems also arise in the area of implied consent. For example, in *Genglar v. Phelps*, 92 N.M. 465, 589 P.2d 1056 (Ct. App. 1978), the court held that the

plaintiff, by filling out a job application, consented to her present employer's making defamatory statements about her to her prospective employer.

53. *See Hutchinson v. Proxmire,* 443 U.S. 111, 127–28 (1979) where the Supreme Court stated that "precedents abundantly support the conclusion that a Member may be held liable for republishing defamatory statements originally made in either House." *See also Williams v. Williams,* 23 N.Y.2d 592, 298 N.Y.S.2d 473 (1969) (court proceedings).

54. The concept of qualified privilege was first set forth in an English case, *Toogood v. Spyring,* C.M.& R. 181, 193, 149 Eng. Rep. 1044, 1050 (Ex. 1834). Toogood, a repairman, was sent to the defendant's farm to make repairs. A defamatory statement was circulated by the defendant to the effect that instead of fixing anything, Toogood broke into the defendant's wine cellar. The court held that the statement was privileged, stating: "An action lies for the malicious publication of [false statements] unless it is fairly made by a person in the discharge of some public or private duty—or in the conduct of his own affairs. . . . In such cases the law affords a qualified defense depending upon the absence of actual malice. If fairly warranted by any reasonable occasion or exigency, and honestly made, such communications are protected for the common convenience and welfare of society."

55. A recent Supreme Court decision dealing with some of these issues is *McDonald v. Smith,* 472 U.S. 479, 105 S. Ct. 2787 (1985). *See also Langston v. ACT,* 890 F.2d 380 (11th Cir. 1989) (qualified privilege where "duty" to speak); *Marchesi v. Franchino,* 283 Md. 131, 387 A.2d 1129 (1978) (a statement to a supervisor complaining of improper sexual advances by a coworker held privileged); *Anderson v. Dun & Bradstreet Co.,* 543 F.2d 732 (10th Cir. 1976) (report of a credit-reporting agency protected by a qualified privilege). *But see Johnson v. Bradstreet Co.,* 77 Ga. 172 (1886) (qualified privilege not extended to a credit-reporting agency). The privilege extended to a credit-reporting agency may be overcome by showing that its investigation was conducted recklessly. *See, e.g., Brown v. Skaggs-Albertson's Properties, Inc.,* 563 F.2d 983 (10th Cir. 1977) where the court held that the owner of a grocery chain could be sued for libel because he stated to a check-verification agency that the plaintiff had "bounced" two checks when in fact the checks were returned because the plaintiff had failed to endorse them. The court found that the defendant was liable and awarded the plaintiff $20,000 compensatory damages and $10,000 punitive damages.

56. In recent cases in some jurisdictions, the fair-report privilege has been extended even more broadly to cover other kinds of official proceedings and even official files and documents. *See. e.g., Medico*

v. *Time, Inc.*, 643 F.2d 134 (3d Cir.), *cert. denied*, 454 U.S. 836 (1981). *But see Bufalino v. The Associated Press*, 692 F.2d 266 (2d Cir. 1982), *cert. denied*, 462 U.S. 1111 (1983) (author must actually have relied on the records or reports in preparing the material in question) and *Dameron v. Washington Magazine, Inc.*, 779 F.2d 736 (D.C. Cir. 1985) (published statements must make clear that they are based on the official report).

57. *Restatement* §611.

58. Sack explains the rationale for the fair-report privilege as follows: "The privilege finds persuasive support in the general social and political interest in permitting citizens to learn about the operations of their courts and other governmental agencies." Sack at 317. Authors and publishers are sometimes given a great deal of leeway in reporting official proceedings. *See, e.g., Binder v. Triangle Publications, Inc.*, 442 Pa. 319, 275 A.2d 53 (1971) (the phrase "bizarre love triangle" was held to be a fair and accurate report of testimony in a murder trial because the plaintiff had many lovers who lived with her and her husband from time to time). In other cases, however, courts have been remarkably strict in second-guessing the accuracy of reports of such proceedings. *See, e.g., Time, Inc. v. Firestone*, 424 U.S. 448 (1976).

59. *New York Times v. Sullivan*, 376 U.S. 254 (1964).

60. *Id.* at 269 (quoting *Roth v. United States*, 354 U.S. 476, 484 [1956]).

61. *Id.* at 270.

62. *Id.* at 271.

63. *Id.* at 271–72 (quoting *NAACP v. Button*, 371 U.S. 415, 433 [1962]).

64. *Id.* at 273.

65. *Id.* at 279.

66. *Id.* at 279–80.

67. *Reliance Insurance Co. v. Barron's*, 442 F. Supp. 1341, 350 (S.D. N.Y. 1977) (Brieant, J.).

68. *Garrison v. Louisiana*, 379 U.S. 64, 74 (1964).

69. *St. Amant v. Thompson*, 390 U.S. 727, 731 (1967) (Justice White quoting Justice Harlan's opinion in *Curtis Publishing Co. v. Butts*, *supra* note 2.)

70. *Id.* at 731.

71. *Gertz v. Robert Welch, Inc.*, 418 U.S. 323, 335 n. 6 (1974) (citing *St. Amant v. Thompson*, *supra* note 54). The Supreme Court's definition of *actual malice* has been said to focus on the defendant's subjective attitude toward the truth rather than on the defendant's attitude toward the plaintiff. This test has led to problems in other aspects of libel law. For example, in *Herbert v. Lando*, 441 U.S. 153 (1979), the Court dealt with the permissible scope of pretrial discovery in public-

official–public-figure libel cases. The plaintiff was a military officer who sued the producers of TV's "60 Minutes" because of an unflattering report. Herbert claimed that the producers deliberately edited the report to distort the truth insofar as he was concerned. The Court found that since he was required to prove actual malice, he should be permitted to inquire into the decision-making process of the editors of "60 Minutes."

72. *Newton v. National Broadcasting Co., Inc.*, 930 F.2d 662 (9th Cir. 1990).

73. *Garrison v. Louisiana*, 379 U.S. 64, 73–74 (1964). *See also Beckley Newspapers Corp. v. Hanks*, 389 U.S. 81 82 (1967) and *Greenbelt Cooperative Publishing Ass'n, Inc. v. Bresler*, 398 U.S. 6, 10–11 (1970) where the Supreme Court again rejected the common-law meaning of *malice* in actual malice cases.

74. *See, e.g., Gertz v. Robert Welch, Inc.*, 680 F.2d 527 (7th Cir. 1982), *cert. denied*, 51 U.S.L.W. 3613 (1983).

75. *St. Amant v. Thompson, supra* note 54, at 732 (1968).

76. *Harte-Hanks Communications, Inc. v. Connaughton*, 491 U.S. 479, 109 S.Ct. 2678 (1989).

77. *Id.* at 2686.

78. *Burnett v. National Enquirer*, 7 Med. L. Rptr. 1321 (Cal. Super. L.A. Co. 1981), *modified on appeal*, 144 Cal. App. 3d 991, 193 Cal. Rptr. 206, 9 Med. L. Rptr. 1921 (Cal. Ct. App. 1983).

79. 7 Med. L. Rptr. at 1321.

80. *Harte-Hanks Communications, Inc. v. Connaughton, supra* note 76.

81. *Id.* at 2698.

82. *Masson v. New Yorker Magazine, Inc.*, U.S. , 111 S.Ct. 2419 (1991).

83. *Gallman v. Carnes*, 254 Ark. 987, 497 S.W.2d 47 (1973).

84. *Corbett v. Register Publishing Co.*, 33 Conn. Supp. 4, 356 A.2d 472 (1975); *Times Publishing Co. v. Huffstetler*, 409 So.2d 112 (Fla. 2d DCA 1982); *Peisner v. Detroit Free Press*, 82 Mich. App. 153, 266 N.W.2d 693 (1978); *Pasculli v. Jersey Journal*, 7 Med. L. Rptr. 2574 (N.J. App. Div. 1981).

85. *Rebozo v. Washington Post Co.*, 637 F.2d 375 (5th Cir.), *cert. denied*, 454 U.S. 964 (1981).

86. *Marchiano v. Sandman*, 178 N.J. Super. 171, 174 (App. Div. 1981); *Moore v. Bailey*, 628 S.W.2d 431 (Tenn. App. 1981).

87. *Nader v. deToledano*, 408 A.2d 31 (D.D.C. 1979), *cert. denied*, 444 U.S. 1078 (1980); *Stripling v. Literary Guild*, 5 Med. L. Rptr. 1958 (W.D. Tex. 1979).

88. *Alioto v. Cowles Communications*, 430 F.Supp. 1363 (N.D. Cal. 1977), *aff'd*, 623 F.2d 616 (9th Cir. 1980), *cert. denied*, 449 U.S. 1102 (1982) (mayor); *Wanless v. Rothballer*, 115 Ill.2d 158, 503 N.E.2d

316 (1986) (county attorney); *Kidder v. Anderson*, 354 So.2d 1306 (La. 1978) (police chief); *Dally v. Orange County Publications*, 117 A.D.2d 577 (2d Dept. 1986) (deputy sheriff); *Dow v. New Haven Independent*, 549 A.2d 683 (Super. Ct. 1987) (superintendant of public schools); *Miller v. Nestande*, 192 Cal. App. 2d 191, 237 Cal. Rptr. 359 (App. 1987) (candidate for public office).

89. *Hutchinson v. Proxmire*, 443 U.S. 111, 119 n. 8 (1979); *see also Rosenblatt v. Baer*, 383 U.S. 75, 84–85 (1966).

90. *Compare Franklin v. Lodge No. 1108*, 97 Cal. App. 3d 915 *with Sewell v. Brookbank*, 119 Ariz. 422, 425, 581 P.2d 267, 270 (Ariz. Ct. App. 1978) where the court stated that "as far as the law of defamation is concerned, teachers are 'public officials.'" *See also Basaarich v. Rodeghero*, 24 Ill. App. 3d 889, 321 N.E.2d 739 (1974).

91. *Rosenblatt v. Baer, supra* note 9, at 85.

92. *Id.* at 87 n. 14. *Compare Hart v. Playboy Enterprises, Inc.*, 5 Med. L. Rptr. 1811 (D. Kan. 1979) (passage of 6 years did not render a federal narcotics agent a private figure), *with Jones v. Himstead*, 7 Med. L. Rptr. 2433 (Mass. Super. 1981) (former state senator who had not run for elective office since 1974 was found not to be a public official or public figure). *See also Contemporary Mission v. New York Times Co.*, 842 F.2d 612 (2d Cir. 1988).

93. *Garrison v. Louisiana*, 379 U.S. 64, 77 (1964).

94. *Monitor Patriot Co. v. Roy*, 401 U.S. 265, 277 (1971). *See also Rinaldi v. Holt, Rinehart & Winston, Inc.*, 42 N.Y.2d 369, *cert. denied*, 434 U.S. 969 (1977).

95. *Curtis Publishing Co. v. Butts*, 388 U.S. 130 (1967); *Associated Press v. Walker*, 388 U.S. 130 (1967).

96. *Rosenbloom v. Metromedia, Inc.*, 403 U.S. 29 (1971). A Philadelphia man was called "a main distributor of obscene material and a smut distributor" by a local radio station following his arrest for selling nudist magazines. He was later acquitted of the charge because his magazines were found not to be obscene. The distributor sued the radio station for libel and won $25,000 actual damages and $250,000 punitive damages after a trial. The federal court of appeals reversed the lower court, stating that because the plaintiff was involved in a matter of public concern, he was required to prove actual malice on the part of the radio station. The Supreme Court affirmed that decision. However, the members of the Supreme Court could not agree on a rationale for that decision; the justices wrote five separate opinions, none of which spoke for more than three of them.

97. 418 U.S. 323 (1974).

98. The two lower courts were following Justice Brennan's opinion in *Rosenbloom* where he stated that the actual-malice standard applied

to all reports of "events of public or general concern." *Rosenbloom* at 52.

99. 418 U.S. at 345.

100. *Id.* at 347.

101. According to the LDRC, three states have retained the actual-malice standard for private figure plaintiffs; two states have adopted a standard less stringent that actual malice but more demanding than simple negligence; and thirty-four states have adopted a negligence standard. *LDRC Bulletin No. 19* (1987). New York's "intermediate" standard is set forth in *Chapadeau v. Utica Observer-Dispatch, Inc.*, 38 N.Y.2d 196, 199, 379 N.Y.S.2d 61 (1975) where the state's highest court held: "Where the content of the article is arguably within the sphere of legitimate public concern the party defamed may recover [if he establishes], by a preponderance of the evidence, that the publisher acted in a grossly irresponsible manner without due consideration for the standards of information gathering and dissemination ordinarily followed by responsible parties."

102. 418 U.S. at 351.

103. *Id.* at 351–52.

104. *Id.* at 352.

105. *Id.* at 351.

106. *Gertz v. Robert Welch, Inc.*, 680 F.2d 527, 1769 (7th Cir. 1982), *cert. denied*, 51 459 U.S. 1226 (1983). This ruling was questioned by the appellate court, but since Gertz sought and was awarded punitive damages, he was required to prove actual malice in any event.

107. *Eastwood v. Superior Court*, 149 Cal. App. 3d 409, 198 Cal. Rptr 342, 10 Med. L. Rptr 1073 (1983).

108. *Carson v. Allied News Co.*, 529 F.2d 206 (7th Cir. 1976).

109. *Holy Spirit Association v. Sequoya Elsevier Publishing Co.*, 75 A.D.2d 523 (1st Dept. 1980).

110. *Nader v. deToledano* (D.C. Super 1977), *aff'd in part, rev'd in part on other grounds*, 408 A.2d 31 (D.D.C. 1979), *cert. denied*, 444 U.S. 1078 (1980).

111. *Buckley v. Littell*, 539 F.2d 882 (2d Cir. 1976), *cert. denied*, 429 U.S. 1062 (1977).

112. *Hustler Magazine, Inc. v. Falwell, supra* note 36.

113. *See, e.g., Clements v. Gannett Co.*, 83 A.D.2d 988 (4th Dept. 1981) (a man who was very active in local civic affairs was declared a "public figure for all purposes").

114. *Gertz v. Robert Welch, Inc.*, 418 U.S. 323, 345 (1974).

115. 424 U.S. 448 (1976).

116. *Id.* at 450.

117. *Id.* at 453–54.

118. 443 U.S. 111 (1979).
119. *Id.* at 116.
120. 443 U.S. 157 (1979).
121. *Id.* at 166.
122. *Id.* at 169 (concurring opinion).
123. Justice Blackmun argued in *Wolston* that the passage of time affects whether a person is a "public" or "private" figure because "the defamed party's access to the means of counterargument" may diminish with time. *Id.* at 170–71.
124. *Street v. National Broadcasting Co.*, 645 F.2d 1227 (6th Cir.), *cert. dismissed*, 454 U.S. 1095 (1981).
125. *Church of Scientology v. Siegelman*, 475 F.Supp. 950 (S.D.N.Y. 1979).
126. *Henderson v. Van Buren Public School*, 4 Med. L. Rptr. 1741 (E.D. Mich. 1978).
127. *Anderson v. Low Rent Housing Commission of Muscatine*, 304 N.W.2d 239 (Iowa 1981).
128. *Tavoulareas v. Washington Post Company*, 8 Med. L. Rptr. 2262 (D.D.C. 1982).
129. *Ali v. Daily News*, 8 Med. L. Rptr. 1844 (D.V.I. 1982).
130. *Torgerson v. Minneapolis Star and Tribune*, 7 Med. L. Rptr. 1805 (Minn. D.C. 1981).
131. *Joseph v. Xerox Corp.*, 594 F. Supp. 330 (D.D.C. 1984).
132. *Thomas v. News World Communications*, 681 F. Supp. 55 (D.D.C. 1988).
133. *Cassady v. Marcum*, 11 Med. L. Rptr. 2046 (Ky. Cir. Ct. 1984).
134. *Pring v. Penthouse*, 7 Med. L. Rptr. 1101 (D.C. Wyo. 1981), *rev'd*, 8 Med. L. Rptr. 2409 (10th Cir. 1982), *cert. denied*, 51 U.S.L.W. 3902 (1983).
135. *Tavoulareas v. Washington Post Company*, *supra* note 128.
136. *Cantrell v. American Broadcasting Co.*, 8 Med. L. Rptr. 1239 (N.D. Ill. 1982).
137. *Jenoff v. Hearst Corp.*, 7 Med. L. Rptr. 1081 (4th Cir. 1981).
138. *From v. Tallahassee Democrat*, 7 Med. L. Rptr. 1811 (Fla. D. Ct. App. 1981).
139. *See Silvester v. American Broadcasting Co.*, 839 F.2d 1491 (11th Cir. 1988); *Marcone v. Penthouse International, Ltd.*, 754 F.2d 1072 (3rd Cir.), *cert. denied*, 474 U.S. 864 (1985); *Clark v. American Broadcasting Co.*, 684 F.2d 1208 (6th Cir. 1982), *cert. denied*, 460 U.S. 1040 (1983).
140. *See generally* Silver, "Libel, The 'Higher Truths' of Art, and the First Amendment," 126 *U. Pa. L. Rev.* 1065 (1978) (hereinafter, Silver).

141. *Bindrim v. Mitchell*, 92 Cal. App. 3d 61, 155 Cal. Rptr. 29, *cert. denied*, 444 U.S. 984 (1979). Bindrim was awarded $50,000 compensatory damages and $25,000 punitive damages.
142. 432 N.Y.S.2d 536, 78 A.D.2d 723 (3d Dept. 1980). The court also found that one of the allegedly defamatory statements was rhetorical hyperbole and therefore a protected expression of opinion even if it had referred to the plaintiff.
143. 8 Med. L. Rptr. 2613 (1st Dept. 1982). The court also dismissed separate claims for "prima facie" tort, invasion of privacy, punitive damages, and attorneys' fees.
144. 8 Med. L. Rptr. 2409 (10th Cir. 1982), *cert. denied*, 51 U.S.L.W. 3902 (1983).
145. *See* Silver at 1069.
146. *Yorty v. Chandler*, 13 Cal. App.3d 467, 91 Cal. Rptr. 709 (1970). The court rejected Yorty's libel claim because it found the cartoon to be privileged as an expression of editorial opinion.
147. *Myers v. Boston Magazine, Inc.*, 6 Med. L. Rptr. 1241 (1980).
148. *Id.* at 1243.
149. *Salomone v. Macmillan Publishing Co., Inc.*, 97 Misc.2d 346, 350–52 (N.Y.Co. 1978), *rev'd on other grounds*, 77 A.D.2d 501, 429 N.Y.S.2d 441 (1st Dept. 1980).
150. *See* Silver at 1069 and Sack at 241–43.
151. *Burton v. Crowell Publishing Co.*, 82 F.2d 154 (2d Cir. 1936).
152. *Silberman v. Georges*, 8 Med. L. Rptr. 2647 (1st Dept. 1982). The court suggested that the libel claim would also fail for failure to prove defamatory meaning, fault, or injury. *But see Mullenmeister v. Snap-on Tools Corp.*, 587 F. Supp. 868 (S.D.N.Y. 1984) ("A drawing or photograph may libel as easily as a writing").
153. 465 U.S. 783, 104 Sup. Ct. 1482 (1984).
154. *Id.* at 788–89.
155. 465 U.S. 770, 104 S. Ct. 1473 (1984).
156. *Id.* at 780–81.
157. *See, e.g., Westmoreland v. CBS*, 8 Med. L. Rptr. 2493 (D.S.C. 1982) (transferring a suit by retired general Westmoreland against CBS and various CBS employees from South Carolina, where Westmoreland lived, to New York City).
158. *See generally*, Sack, "Common Law Libel and the Press," *Communications Law* (1989); Dill, *The Journalist's Handbook on Libel and Privacy* (1986) (hereinafter, Dill).
159. *See* cases cited in Sack at 56–57.
160. For a list of retraction statutes (with text) see Sack at 589–619 (app. IV); Dill, app. C.

161. Books, and sometimes "periodicals," are often not included in the list of covered publications. Generally the statutes are interpreted narrowly and would not be construed to cover media not listed. *See, e.g., Burnett v. National Enquirer,* 7 Med. L. Rptr. 1321 (Cal. Super. L.A. Co. 1981), *modified on other grounds,* 9 Med. L. Rptr 1921 (Cal. Ct. App. 1983).

162. 466 U.S. 485, 104 Sup. Ct. 1949 (1984).

163. *Id.* at 511.

164. 477 U.S. 242, 106 Sup. Ct. 2505 (1986).

165. *Id.* at 257.

166. *Philadelphia Newspapers, Inc. v. Hepps, supra* note 17.

167. For a discussion and listing of the various states' shield laws, see Dill app. B. In 1991 the Supreme Court held that the First Amendment does not preclude a lawsuit for damages by a source against a newspaper when then paper breached its promise to keep his identity confidential. *Cohen v. Cowles Media Co.,* U.S. , S. Ct. (1991)

168. On the issue of injunctions against the press, see *Near v. Minnesota* 283 U.S. 697 (1931), and a case of more recent vintage, *Reliance Insurance Co. v. Barron's,* 428 F. Supp. 200, 205 (S.D.N.Y. 1977) The Supreme Court has stated that any "prior restraint" of the press is "presumptively unconstitutional." *See, e.g., New York Times Co. v. United States,* 403 U.S. 713 (1971). Moreover, long before the First Amendment implications were fully recognized, courts declined to enjoin alleged libels on grounds of general equity. *See, e.g., Brandreth v. Lance,* 8 Page N.Y. Chanc. 24 (1839). *See generally,* Sack at 361–63. On the issue of government's power to order the press to publish anything, see *Miami Herald Publishing Co. v. Tornillo,* 418 U.S. 241 (1974) where the Supreme Court struck down as unconstitutional a Florida statute that required newspapers to publish replies by political candidates to published criticisms. Referring to that statute, the Court stated that "it has yet to be demonstrated how governmental regulation of this [editorial] process can be exercised consistent with First Amendment guarantees of a free press as they have evolved to this time." *Id.* at 258. Sack states that the "broad language" quoted above "appears to foreclose statutory forced retractions in the context of libel cases." Sack at 363.

169. *See Restatement* §575, comment b.

170. *See, e.g., Burnett v. National Enquirer Inc., supra* note 161.

171. 418 U.S. at 350.

172. *Time, Inc. v. Firestone,* 424 U.S. 448 (1976).

173. *Salomone v. Macmillan Publishing Co., Inc.,* 77 A.D.2d 501, 42 N.Y.S.2d 441 (1st Dept. 1980); *see also France v. St. Clare's Hospital*

82 A.D.2d 1, 441 N.Y.S.2d 71 (1st Dept. 1981); *Gobin v. Globe Publishing Co.*, 8 Med. L. Rptr. 2191 (Kan. 1982).

174. "In short, the private defamation plaintiff who establishes liability under a less demanding standard than stated by New York Times [i.e., actual malice] may recover only such damages as are sufficient to compensate him for actual injury." 418 U.S. at 350.

175. States that have abolished punitive damages in libel actions on First Amendment grounds include Massachusetts, Montana, and Oregon. Jurisdictions that do not permit punitive damages in any civil action are Louisiana, Nebraska, New Hampshire, Puerto Rico, and Washington. *See* LRDC survey at 600–603, 615.

176. One of the few million-dollar libel verdicts to be upheld on appeal is *Brown & Williamson Tobacco Corp. v. Jacobson*, 827 F.2d 1119 (7th Cir. 1987), *cert. denied*, 485 U.S. 993 (1988). One case was reported settled for $1.4 million because the newspaper defendant was not fully insured and literally could not afford to purchase the bond required to cover the jury's $9.2-million judgment in order to pursue an effective appeal. *Green v. Alton Telegraph Printing Co.*, 8 Med. L. Rptr. 1345 (Ill. App. 5th Dist. 1982).

177. Congressman Schumer's bill, and other proposals for reform of libel law, are discussed in Lewis, *Make No Law: The Sullivan Case and the First Amendment*, ch. 19 (1991).

178. *Proposal for the Reform of Libel Law: The Report of the Libel Reform Project of the Annenberg Washington Program* (1988).

179. News Notes, 17 Med. L. Rptr. No. 35 (Aug. 7, 1990).

180. *See Griswold v. Connecticut*, 381 U.S. 479(1965) (contraception); *Roe v. Wade*, 410 U.S. 113 (1973) (abortion).

181. The genesis for a legally recognized "right of privacy" in civil actions against publishers or authors was a law review article written a century ago by Samuel Warren and Louis D. Brandeis, who was subsequently a justice of the U.S. Supreme Court. The article, entitled "The Right to Privacy," appeared in 4 *Harv. L. Rev.* 193 (1890). The authors made the focus of their "privacy" concerns clear: "The press is overstepping in every direction the obvious bounds of propriety and of decency. Gossip is no longer the resource of the idle and of the vicious, but has become a trade, which is pursued with industry as well as effrontery. To satisfy a prurient taste the details of sexual relations are spread broadcast in the columns of the daily papers. To occupy the indolent, column upon column is filled with idle gossip, which can only be procured by intrusion upon the domestic circle. The intensity and complexity of life, attendant upon advancing civilization, have rendered necessary some retreat from the

world, and man, under the refining influence of culture, has become
more sensitive to publicity, so that solitude and privacy have become
more essential to the individual; but modern enterprise and invention have, through invasions upon his privacy, subjected him to
mental pain and distress, far greater than could be inflicted by mere
bodily injury." *Id.* at 196. For an interesting glimpse into the genesis
of the article, see Sack at 387–89.

182. The four categories, which are now widely recognized, were first
defined by Professor Prosser. See Prosser, *Handbook on the Law of
Torts*, §117 (4th ed. 1971).

183. Sack at 394 (quoting *Restatement* §652E).

184. Sack at 394 (citations omitted).

185. 385 U.S. 374 (1967).

186. *Id.* at 383 (quoting *Spahn v. Julian Messner, Inc.*, 18 N.Y.2d 324,
328 [1966]).

187. *Id.* at 387–88.

188. 419 U.S. 245 (1974).

189. *Id.* at 252–53.

190. *See, e.g., Rinsley v. Brandt*, 446 F. Supp. 850 (D. Kan. 1977) where
the court held that *Gertz* overruled the *Hill* decision and that only
public figures must prove actual malice in false-light privacy cases;
Dresbach v. Doubleday, 518 F. Supp. 1285 (D.D.C. 1981) (a "private
person" who was placed in a false light in a book about his brother
who was convicted of murdering their parents, a matter of legitimate
public concern, need only prove that the author's negligence resulted
in the inaccuracies in the book).

191. *Restatement* §652 D.

192. *See, e.g., Meeropol v Nizer*, 560 F.2d 1061 (2d Cir. 1977), *cert.
denied*, 434 U.S. 1013 (1978) (the children of Julius and Ethel Rosen-
berg cannot prevail in a suit challenging disclosures made about them
in a book concerning their parents' trial and electrocution); *Friedan
v. Friedan*, 414 F. Supp. 77 (S.D.N.Y. 1976) (feminist Betty Friedan's former husband fails in a privacy claim concerning a magazine
article about his former wife in which he was described and pictured).
One leading commentator has observed that "the concept of newsworthiness has largely swallowed up the tort." Hill, "Defamation and
Privacy Under the First Amendment," 76 *Colum. L. Rev.* 1205, 1255
(1976). *But see Forsher v. Bugliosi*, 26 Cal. 3d 792, 163 Cal Rptr
628, 608 P.2d 716 (1980) where the plaintiff, who was named in a
book about the Manson "family" murders, *Helter Skelter*, in connection with the murder of a defense attorney, was allowed to pursue a
private-facts case because his name had never appeared in the public
record and because he was never charged with any crime in connec-

tion with the murder. *See also Campbell v. Seabury Press,* 614 F.2d 395 (5th Cir. 1980); *Gilbert v. Medical Economics,* 665 F.2d 305 (10th Cir. 1981); *Dresbach v. Doubleday,* 518 F. Supp. 1285 (D.D.C. 1981).

193. *See, e.g., Horne v. Patton,* 291 Ala. 701, 287 So.2d 824 (1973) (doctor's disclosure of private medical facts to plaintiff's employer); *Beaumont v. Brown,* 401 Mich. 80, 257 N.W.2d 522 (1977) (employer's letter to the army disclosing private facts about the plaintiff).

194. *Melvin v. Reid,* 112 Cal. App. 285, 297 P. 91 (1931). The court held that although the retelling of the plaintiff's story was newsworthy, the film violated her right of privacy when it delved into her present situation and linked it to her past.

195. *Briscoe v. Reader's Digest Ass'n,* 4 Cal. 3d 529, 93 Cal. Rptr. 866, 483 P.2d 34 (1971).

196. 4 Cal. 3d at 537.

197. *See, e.g., Sidis v. F-R. Publishing Corp.,* 113 F.2d 806 (2d Cir.), *cert. denied,* 311 U.S. 711 (1940) where the court rejected the privacy claim of a former child prodigy who had not been in the public eye for over 25 years because it was a matter of public concern to see how he had developed his early genius.

198. For a fuller discussion of the right of publicity, see Gordon, "Right of Property in Name, Likeness, Personality and History," 55 *Nw. U. L. Rev.* 553 (1960); Felcher & Rubin, "Privacy, Publicity and the Portrayal of Real People by the Media," 88 *Yale L. J.* 1577 (1979); Pilpel, "The Right of Publicity," 27 *Bull. Copy. Soc.* 249 (1980). The term *right of publicity* was first used in this context by Judge Jerome Frank in *Haelan Laboratories, Inc. v. Topps Chewing Gum, Inc.,* 202 F.2d 866 (2d Cir.), *cert. denied,* 346 U.S. 816 (1953).

199. In *Roberson v. Rochester Folding Box Co.,* 171 N.Y. 538, 64 N.E. 442 (1902), the New York Court of Appeals refused to recognize a common law claim for commercial misappropriation. As a result, within a year, the New York legislature passed a "right of privacy" statute which was limited to creating a cause of action for such misappropriation. N.Y. Civil Rights Law §§50, 51. Similar statutes have been enacted in several other states.

200. *Zacchini v. Scripps-Howard Broadcasting Co.,* 433 U.S. 562 (1977).

201. *Arrington v. New York Times Co.,* 55 N.Y.2d 433, 449 N.Y.S.2d 941, 434 N.E.2d 1319 (1982), *cert. denied,* 51 U.S.L.W. 3533 (1983). The court also rejected a nonstatutory false-light claim and a claim for invasion of constitutional privacy rights.

202. For a later case to the same effect, see *Finger v. Omni Pub. Int. Ltd.,* 77 N.Y.2d 138, 564 N.Y.S.2d 1014 (1990). In contrast, in late 1991 the same court—New York's highest—held that the use of the

plaintiff-physician's photograph, name and professional title on a promotional calendar for the defendant's for-profit medical services business violated the New York privacy law. *Beverley v. Choices Women's Medical Center, Inc.*, 19 Med. L. Rptr. 1724 (1991).

203. *See, e.g., Meeropol v. Nizer, supra note 165; Bauman v. Anson,* 6 Med. L. Rptr. 1487 (Sup. Ct. N.Y. Co. 1980).

204. *Spahn v. Julian Messner, Inc.*, 21 N.Y.2d 124 (1967), *app. dism'd,* 393 U.S. 1046 (1969).

205. *See, e.g., Groucho Marx Productions, Inc. v. Day and Night Company,* 523 F. Supp. 485 (S.D. N.Y. 1981), *rev'd on other grounds,* 689 F.2d 31 (2d Cir. 1982) (but questioning the lower court's First Amendment holding); *Estate of Presley v. Russen,* 513 F. Supp. 1339 (D.N.J. 1981).

206. *Restatement* §652B.

207. *See, e.g., Pearson v. Dodd,* 410 F.2d 710 (D.C. Cir.), *cert. denied* 395 U.S. 947 (1969).

208. *See, e.g., Dietemann v. Time, Inc.*, 449 F.2d 245 (9th Cir. 1971) (hidden camera); *Nader v. General Motors Corp.,* 25 N.Y.2d 560 (1970) (wiretapping and eavesdropping).

209. *See, e.g., Florida Pub. Co. v. Fletcher,* 340 So.2d 914 (Fla. 1976) *cert. denied,* 431 U.S. 930 (1977).

210. *Galella v. Onassis,* 487 F.2d 986 (2d Cir. 1973).

211. *See Dietermann v. Time, Inc., supra* note 207.

212. *See LeMistral v. Columbia Broadcasting Syst.*, 61 A.D.2d 491 (1st Dept. 1978).

213. *See Barber v. Time, Inc.,* 348 Mo. 1199, 159 S.W.2d 291 (1942).

214. Sack at 443.

215. 485 U.S. 46, 108 S. Ct. 876 (1988).

216. 108 S. Ct. at 882.

217. *Girl Scouts of America v. Personality Posters Mfg. Co.*, 304 F. Supp 1228 (S.D.N.Y. 1969).

218. *Pillsbury Co. v. Milky Way Productions, Inc.*, 215 U.S.P.Q. 12 (D.D. Ga. 1981).

219. *See, e.g., Cliffs Notes v. Bantam Doubleday Dell Publishing Group* 886 F.2d 490 (2d Cir. 1989).

220. *See, e.g., Rogers v. Grimaldi,* 875 F.2d 994 (2d Cir. 1989).

221. In a recent case, the estate of a youth who committed suicide claimed that the lyrics of a song by the artist Ozzy Osborne induced the youth to kill himself. Although the lyrics did suggest suicide as an alternative to an unbearable life, the court dismissed the suit, holding that liability could not be established unless the suicide was a specifically intended or reasonably foreseeable consequence of the lyrics. The court also found that the lyric

were not a "call to action" (in this case, suicide) because the lyrics were not intended to be understood literally. *McCollum v. CBS, Inc.*, 249 Cal. Rptr. 187, 202 Cal. App. 3d 989 (Cal. App. 1988). Other cases involving claims of injury from published or broadcast material include *Cardozo v. True*, 342 So.2d 1053 (Fla. App. 2d DCA 1977) (injuries from recipe in cookbook) and *DeFillipo v. NBC*, 115 A.2d 1053 (R.I. 1982) (juvenile accidentally hanged attempting to duplicate stunt on the "Tonight Show").

222. News article, *New York Times*, Dec. 9, 1990, at A28, col. 1. A federal judge upheld a jury's verdict for $12.4 million against the magazine where it found that the plaintiff's father was killed as a result of a "gun for hire" advertisement in the magazine. In an earlier case, where a jury awarded $9.1 million for a death caused by a hired killer who was found through an ad in the same magazine seeking "high risk assignments," the verdict was overturned on appeal. *Eimann v. Soldier of Fortune Magazine, Inc.*, 880 F.2d 830 (5th Cir. 1989). In that decision, the federal court of appeals attempted to "balance" the risk of harm from such advertisements against the utility of advertising activity in general. As a result, while the court acknowledged that injury could result from such advertisements, it concluded that it would impose too high a burden on magazines to require them to investigate every ad that suggests that the advertiser might engage in illegal activities.

223. An important 1991 decision held that a publisher cannot be found liable under principles of "products liability" law for injuries sustained as a result of a person relying on material in a book. *Winter v. G. P. Putnam's Sons*, 936 F.2d 1033 (9th Cir. 1991). In that case, the plaintiff became severely ill after eating mushrooms that were picked in reliance on information contained in the defendants' *Encyclopedia of Mushrooms*. In rejecting the claim, the court held that products liability law only applied to tangible products and not to intangibles such as ideas and expression.

224. For a discussion of the potential defamation liability of various participants in the publishing process, including the original newspaper publisher, the subsequent paperback publisher, the original reporters, and the book's editor, *see Karaduman v. Newsday*, 51 N.Y.2d 531 (1980).

225. For a review of the availability of such insurance coverage for authors, see *Media Insurance: Protecting Against High Judgments, Punitive Damages and Defense Costs* at 461–91 (Practicing Law Institute, 1983). *See also*, Kaufman, *Trends in Libel*, ch. 1 in *The Cost of Libel: Economic and Policy Implications*, Dennis and Noam, eds. (1989).

V

Obscenity

The issue of obscenity has confounded the law for centuries. In the United States it has resulted in a clash between advocates of the greatest First Amendment freedom and those who believe that society has the power and duty to suppress at least some sexual expression in the name of public morality.[1]

In one sense, the forces of suppression appear to have prevailed. Despite the sexual liberation that characterizes our society today, the First Amendment (at least as interpreted by a narrow majority of Supreme Court justices) has been held to permit the enactment and enforcement of state and federal criminal and civil laws against sexually explicit expression, even though suppression of any form of expression is fundamentally inconsistent with the full exercise of First Amendment freedoms. In addition, the mere existence of such laws against obscenity almost inevitably has a "chilling effect" upon other forms of expression that are not obscene but could be prosecuted (and persecuted) in the mistaken belief that they are.

But in another sense it seems clear that authors and artists today have much more freedom of sexual expression than at any time since the early nineteenth century. Although obscenity laws have been held constitutional, they are permitted to operate only within relatively narrow guidelines. Those limitations, together with the increasing acceptance by large segments of the public of sexually explicit expression and the lack of enthusiasm on the part of most law-enforcement agencies for enforcing obscenity laws, has led to unprecedented freedom.

When obscenity laws are enforced today, the targets are usually the most extreme and distasteful sexual materials: child pornography or pictorial magazines devoted to explicit and often perverse or violent sexual conduct. The era when literary classics such as *Ulysses, Lady Chatterley's Lover, Fanny Hill*, or the works of the Marquis de Sade could effectively be banned and their authors and publishers prosecuted has passed and probably will not come again. Nonetheless, obscenity laws remain on the books and cannot be ignored by the author or artist whose work includes sexual subjects. This chapter will review the origins of today's obscenity law and how it is structured and enforced. It will also discuss those areas where authors and artists continue to be vulnerable to legal action.

Do obscenity and pornography mean the same thing?

They have somewhat different but related dictionary definitions.[2] *Obscenity* is the term used most frequently by the law, and it is the term that will be used in this chapter.

For these purposes, *obscenity* refers to the kind of sexually explicit expression that the Supreme Court has declared not protected by the First Amendment. Courts and legislatures have repeatedly (and almost entirely unsuccessfully) attempted to distinguish the obscene from nonobscene in definitions. But there is no one meaningful legal definition of obscenity today; indeed, the inability of the law to define and limit the legal concept of obscenity effectively is a major reason why the continued existence of any obscenity law seriously infringes First Amendment rights.

In addition to works that qualify as obscenity under the current law, the Supreme Court has also held that there are other kinds of (nonobscene) sexually oriented expression that can also be legally regulated and suppressed, including "child pornography" and "indecent" scatological speech when presented on the broadcast media when children are likely to be in the audience. These categories of speech will be discussed later in this chapter.

Why don't obscenity laws violate the First Amendment?

The First Amendment declares that Congress may pass "no law" abridging freedom of speech or of the press. Obscenity laws plainly do abridge such freedoms. Since writings and visual creations that contain sexual themes or explicit sexual depictions seem to be expression entitled to the protections promised by the First Amendment, what has happened?

The short answer is that the Supreme Court, the ultimate arbiter of what the Constitution means, has never held that the First Amendment is as absolute as it appears. The Court has proclaimed that certain categories of expression are beyond the protection of the First Amendment, including libel, incitement to riot, and "obscenity."[3] According to prevailing majorities of the Supreme Court over the past four decades, since obscenity is "without redeeming social value," it is not entitled to First Amendment protection.

How can you distinguish between the obscene and the nonobscene?

This task is made even more difficult by the fact that legal judgments about obscenity involve matters of morality and taste, which are inherently subjective. The elaborate legal formulations of the Supreme Court cannot mask the fundamental impossibility of providing meaningful guidance to authors and artists who deal with sexual themes. What follows is a review of today's legal structure that attempts to define what cannot be defined, with a brief look at the background and history of obscenity law.

Are there different kinds of obscenity laws?

Yes. Both criminal and civil laws deal with obscenity. Criminal laws typically make it a criminal offense to publish, sell, lend, or otherwise disseminate materials that are legally obscene. Also, exhibition of obscene matter, for example, in motion-picture theaters and even in art museums, may be prohibited, and the production (i.e., printing or manufacturing obscene materials) may be proscribed. Some criminal statutes are limited to "commercial" dissemination; others are not.

Authors and artists generally fall within the realm of commercial distribution, which does not depend on whether a profit has been made. Mere possession with the intent to disseminate may be considered a criminal offense.[4] However, private possession of obscene materials for personal use is recognized as constitutionally protected.[5] Advertising the availability of obscenity is also an offense under some statutes, regardless of whether the advertisement is obscene. But with increasing First Amendment protection for "commercial speech," including advertising, these provisions may be constitutionally suspect.[6]

Besides these offenses, which generally involve dissemination or advertising to adults, there are also criminal statutes dealing with distributing or displaying matter that is said to be "harmful to minors" and with creating or disseminating "child pornography," a category of sexually explicit materials subject to a different set of legal standards than obscenity.

Criminal obscenity offenses range from minor misdemeanors to serious felonies, depending upon the state or locality and the circumstances of the offense. Penalties range from fines to prison terms of many years. In addition, during the 1980s the federal government and at least twenty-seven states enacted RICO (racketeer-influenced and corrupt organizations) laws that create extremely harsh penalties for those who commit multiple obscenity violations.

What kinds of civil obscenity laws are there?

Many kinds. And while they do not threaten incarceration, they do provide a range of sanctions that can have an impact on rights of free expression equal to or greater than criminal penalties. They can also place a significant economic burden on the individuals and business interests subject to them. Civil obscenity laws and sanctions include

- Injunctions against publication, dissemination, or exhibition of materials found to be obscene
- Court orders closing business enterprises which produce, distribute, sell, or display material found to be obscene. Such padlock or nuisance-abatement laws can result in the seizure, forfeiture, or destruction of allegedly obscene materials
- Court orders requiring the "forfeiture" of assets—including books, magazines, movies, and other expressive materials that are not themselves obscene—if they are found to have been acquired in whole or in part as a result of the sale or dissemination of materials that are found obscene
- Licensing schemes providing for prior review and censorship of materials to be exhibited or disseminated
- Civil proceedings to determine obscenity before possible criminal prosecution
- Statutes regulating the display of and access to sexually explicit matter, particularly to children or unconsenting adults, often with criminal penalties for their violation
- Local zoning ordinances intended to limit, concentrate, or disperse sex-oriented businesses.

What levels of government can enact and enforce obscenity laws?

All levels: federal, state, and local. Their laws may overlap or be mutually exclusive. The U.S. Constitution, which governs the lawmaking power at all levels of government, has been interpreted by the Supreme Court to permit states and localities to deal with obscenity, but it has also imposed significant limits on this power.[7] Today's constitutional standards even accept the existence of inconsistent laws, so that materials nonobscene in one locality are obscene in another.

The Constitution permits state and local obscenity laws, but it does not require them. Nonetheless, almost all of the states and many local governments, have obscenity laws.[8] These laws are often similar, but there are differences, sometimes significant, from state to state and within states. Some states have adopted "statewide standards" or have precluded or preempted local control over obscenity. Although control of obscenity is essentially a local or state matter, there are important federal laws dealing with obscenity. The asserted justification for such laws is to control interstate distribution of obscenity and prevent circumvention of local and state obscenity laws.

Can an idea be obscene?

No. The law today does not permit prosecution of so-called thematic obscenity; indeed, it is generally believed today that under the First Amendment the law may not penalize any idea or opinion, no matter how offensive it may be to lawmakers or the people they represent. The Supreme Court has ruled that the First Amendment protects ideas from attack under the guise of obscenity regulation and has struck down as unconstitutional convictions based upon ideas advocated in a work, even if the work was sexually explicit. For example, the Court struck down a New York statute that permitted censorship of a movie deemed "sacrilegious"[9] and another under which a license for the motion-picture version of *Lady Chatterley's Lover* was denied because it presented adultery as appropriate behavior. In the latter case the Supreme Court declared:

> What New York has done, therefore, is to prevent the exhibition of a motion picture because that picture advocates an idea that adultery under certain circumstances

may be proper behavior. Yet the First Amendment's basic guarantee is of freedom to advocate ideas. The State, quite simply, has thus struck at the very heart of constitutionally protected liberty.

It is contended that the State's action was justified because the motion picture attractively portrays a relationship which is contrary to the moral standards, the religious precepts, and the legal code of its citizenry. This argument misconceives what it is that the Constitution protects. Its guarantee is not confined to the expression of ideas that are conventional or shared by a majority. It protects advocacy of the opinion that adultery may sometimes be proper, no less than advocacy of socialism or the single tax. And in the realm of ideas it protects expression which is eloquent no less than that which is unconvincing.[11]

What are the historical origins of our obscenity laws?

It may be a surprise that the suppression of explicit sexual materials is little more than a hundred years old. Although governmental censorship has existed throughout recorded history, it has been directed mostly toward political and religious heresy rather than obscenity. In Greek and Roman times, and indeed until a few centuries ago, sexual explicitness was widely accepted in popular literature, drama, and ballads. Bawdy stories often became vehicles for the presentation of religious themes. Governmental and religious censors, who plainly had no qualms about suppressing other speech that displeased them, apparently saw no need to bother with even the most licentious matter.[12]

In sixteenth-century England, with the advent of the printing press, the first system of book licensing was established. Here too, licensing was directed toward books dealing with sedition and heresy, and its principal purpose was not censorship but the protection of English printers and bookbinders from foreign competition. During the second half of the century, Puritanism became increasingly widespread, and the Puritans sought to purge England of everything they considered obscene. The tolerant attitude toward sexual materials that had marked almost every age began to change, and except for a brief period following the Restoration in 1660, the Puritan influence has continued to be felt.

But even the Puritan concern for the "intollerable corruption of common life and manners, which pestilently invadeth the myndes of many that delight to heare or read the said wanton woorkes," failed to specify what ought to be condemned. Books and pamphlets that would be considered hard-core pornography today circulated freely in England; if they lacked antireligious content they apparently violated no law.[13]

No obscenity legislation was enacted in England until 1824, and the first laws prohibited only exposing an obscene book or print in public places.[14] By 1857, however, "Lord Campbell's Act" generally prohibited the dissemination of obscene materials in England.[15]

How did obscenity law develop in the United States?

Although explicit sexual materials were in circulation throughout the American colonies, only Massachusetts had a law addressed to them,[16] and it was not until 1821, 110 years after its enactment, that anyone was prosecuted for violating the statute.[17] This does not mean that there was no censorship. The American colonies were closely governed by the British sovereign, and the British law of libel and slander, which made it a crime to criticize the government, was actively enforced.

Against this background of governmental suppression of speech and press, the American colonies won their independence and in 1789 adopted the Constitution, which was not ratified until the framers added the Bill of Rights (which made it clear that certain precious individual freedoms, such as freedom of press, speech, religion, and assembly, could not be abridged by the newly created government).[19]

In 1821 Vermont became the first state in the new Union to pass an antiobscenity statute,[20] and many other states soon followed. The first federal antiobscenity statute, passed in 1842, was directed toward importation,[21] and in 1865 Congress passed a statute prohibiting the sending of obscene materials through the mails.[22]

The apparently growing concern with obscenity notwithstanding, there was little enforcement of state or federal obscenity laws until 1868 when the New York legislature enacted a law prohibiting the dissemination of obscene literature. Shortly thereafter, a grocery-store clerk named Anthony Comstock began a one-man crusade to ensure that the law was vigorously enforced. Joined by the YMCA, he formed a national organization called the Committee for the Suppression of Vice. In 1873, largely in response to this crusade, Congress broadened the federal mail act[24] and named Comstock a special agent of the Post Office in charge of enforcing it. Many states without obscenity statutes passed them after 1873; by 1900, at least thirty states had some form of general prohibition against the dissemination of obscene materials.

This response to obscenity continued through the first 60 years of this century. Many books, plays, films, and works of art were suppressed as obscene, and countless others had to be obtained (and kept) secretly, on the assumption that they would be suppressed if discovered.

Throughout this period, the prevailing definition of *obscenity* was that set forth in the 1868 English case of *Regina v. Hicklin*,[25] in which the court declared that material was obscene if it tended "to deprave and corrupt those whose minds are open to such immoral influences and into whose hands a publication of this sort may fall." This decision meant that for the first time materials could be prohibited solely because of their sexual content, without their attacking the government or religious institutions, and that an entire work could be suppressed as obscene on the basis of a few passages or if it tended to "deprave and corrupt" only the most immature and susceptible. The *Hicklin* definition prevailed in the United States during the first third of the twentieth century.

How have the courts dealt with obscenity in this century?

The first seven decades saw an ever-increasing number of obscenity cases, and confusion about the legal definition of obscenity seemed to increase with every case. More and more courts came to be troubled by shortcomings of the *Hicklin* formulation and the distorted results it spawned. In a celebrated case where the federal courts ruled that James Joyce's classic *Ulysses* was not obscene and could be admitted into the United States,[26] the word *obscene* was defined as "tending to stir the sex impulses or to lead to sexually impure and lustful thoughts." Also, the court rejected the *Hicklin* definition and ruled that a finding of obscenity had to be based on a reading not of isolated passages but the whole book and on the effect of the whole book on a "normal person."

Despite such occasional victories during this period, direct First Amendment challenges to the validity of obscenity laws were unavailing. Other courts were not always as enlightened as the *Ulysses* court in rejecting the restrictive *Hicklin* rules. Books such as *Lady Chatterley's Lover* by D. H. Lawrence,[27] *An American Tragedy* by Theodore Dreiser,[28] and *God's Little Acre* by Erskine Caldwell[29] were found obscene. As late as 1953, the U.S. court of appeals in San Francisco upheld obscenity findings against Henry Miller's *Tropic of Cancer* and *Tropic of Capricorn* based on a consideration of isolated passages in those works.[30]

Nonetheless, by the early 1950s, some aspects of the *Hicklin* test had been substantially eroded, and the basic contours of later constitutionally based standards began taking shape. By 1950, the whole-work, or dominant-theme, standard was accepted by most American courts. Also, the average-person test was accepted by most courts, and the idea that the literary value of a work could be taken into consideration was becoming established. Finally, the doctrine of "community standards" was emerging, generally in a manner that recognized increased sexual tolerance.

What was the *Roth* case?

It was not until 1957, 166 years after the First Amendment was adopted, that the Supreme Court directly considered whether various state and federal antiobscenity laws were constitutional and if so, what kinds of materials could be suppressed as obscene. Its decision in *Roth v. United States*,[31] however, did not conclusively answer these questions.

Although many argued that all antiobscenity laws—at least in the absence of proof that obscenity presented a "clear and present danger" of antisocial conduct—were unconstitutional because they violated the First Amendment, a majority of the Supreme Court disagreed. The Court declared that obscenity was not the kind of material protected by freedom of speech and press, and therefore a showing of clear and present danger was not necessary to justify its suppression. As the Court put it in an opinion by Justice William J. Brennan, Jr.:

The protection given speech and press was fashioned to assure unfettered interchange of ideas for the bringing about of political and social changes desired by the people. All ideas having even the slightest redeeming social importance . . . have the full protection of the guaranties, unless they encroach upon the limited area of more important interests. But implicit in the history of the First Amendment is the rejection of obscenity as utterly without social importance.[32]

In defining obscenity, however, the *Roth* majority recognized a number of important principles that had been developing in the lower courts. First, it held that "sex and obscenity are not synonymous," and it seemed to suggest strongly that significant "art, literature and scientific works" must be constitutionally protected. Accordingly, it held that only materials that "appeal to the prurient interest" can be obscene. Second, the Court rejected the *Hicklin* isolated-passages approach and adopted the requirement that the obscenity judgment be based on the "dominant theme of the material taken as a whole." Third, the Court held that the obscenity judgment must be based upon the reactions of an average person, not a person peculiarly susceptible to immoral or lustful influences. Finally, the judgment had to be made by "applying contemporary community standards," thus seeming to assure, at least in a permissive era, progress toward fewer restraints upon protected expression.

Justices William O. Douglas and Hugo L. Black dissented, adhering to their nearly "absolutist" view that censorship of any pure expression, "unless so closely brigaded with illegal action as to be an inseparable part of it," was a violation of the First Amendment.[33] They rejected the effort to define which publications had value and which had not, a role they thought was reserved not to official censors but to the people.

In another case decided that year, the Court insisted that obscenity statutes be narrowly tailored to the evils they were intended to control. *Butler v. Michigan* concerned a statute that sought to forbid distribution of sexually explicit material to adults because of its potential harm to minors.[34] Though the material in question was explicit, it was not obscene. In an opinion by Justice Felix Frankfurter, the Court stated:

The State insists that, by thus quarantining the general reading public against books not too rugged for grown men and women in order to shield juvenile innocence, it is exercising its power to promote the general welfare. Surely, this is to burn the house to roast the pig. . . . We have before us legislation not reasonably restricted to the evil with which it is said to deal. The incidence of this enactment is to reduce the adult population of Michigan to reading only what is fit for children.[35]

What happened after *Roth?*

Perhaps inevitably, the Supreme Court found itself serving as the "supercensor" of obscenity in the United States. Ironically, in this role, it reversed most of the obscenity convictions that came before it. Moreover, the very basis for excluding obscenity from constitutional protection—its degree of "social importance"—became the means by which constitutional protection was accorded to an ever-broader range of sexually explicit materials. The Court was slowly but surely moving toward narrowing permissible obscenity regulation to "hard-core" pornography. In one case the Court established the important rule against "thematic obscenity."[36] In another, the requirement of "patent offensiveness" was articulated.[37] Then, in *Jacobellis v. Ohio*,[38] Justice Brennan first suggested that the concept of "utterly without redeeming social value," which was initially stated as the reason to deny constitutional protection, should be the benchmark for determining whether material can be constitutionally be prosecuted as obscene.

But the "utterly without redeeming social value" test was not accepted by the majority in *Jacobellis* or in the next important case, *Memoirs v. Massachusetts* (the *Fanny Hill* case).[39] In fact, it was never adopted by a majority of the Supreme Court. It nevertheless became the prevailing standard for judging obscenity until the Court's all-important 1973 decision in *Miller v. California*. As stated by Justice Brennan in *Memoirs*, for a work to be found obscene, it had to be proved that "(a) the dominant theme of the material taken as a whole appeals to a prurient interest; (b) the material is patently offensive because it affronts contemporary community standards relating to the description or representation of sexual matters; and (c) the material is utterly without redeeming social value."[40]

After *Memoirs*, fewer and fewer obscenity convictions were obtained in lower courts, and when they were obtained, they were often reversed on appeal. The Supreme Court continued to be unable to secure a majority for one legal definition of obscenity, as it candidly acknowledged in 1967 in *Redrup v. New York*.[41] But the Court continued to accept obscenity cases for review, and for the next 6 years the justices decided most obscenity cases by reviewing the material in private, applying their divergent standards, and when a majority decided that obscenity could not constitutionally be found, issuing orders summarily reversing convictions without writing opinions. These "*Redrup* summary reversals" were issued in thirty-one cases between 1967 and 1973.[42]

Two developments during this period further encouraged those who believed (and proclaimed) that the "end of obscenity" was at hand.[43] In a major 1969 case, *Stanley v. Georgia*,[44] the Supreme Court struck down a state law that made it a crime to possess obscene materials. "A state has no business," declared Justice Thurgood Marshall, "telling a man, sitting alone in his own house, what books he may read or what films he may watch. Our whole constitutional heritage rebels at the thought of giving government the power to control men's minds."[45] The Court ruled that this privacy right applied even if the obscenity of the material in question was uncontested. *Stanley* seemed to declare the end of legal censorship and for a brief period was so interpreted by several lower courts.[46] If a person has the constitutional right to read and view such materials in his home, they reasoned, there must also be a right to produce and sell the materials. But until the Supreme Court adopted or rejected this interpretation, it could hardly be considered settled law.

The second development was the report of a special commission created by Congress in 1967 "to investigate the gravity of [the traffic in obscenity and pornography] and to determine whether such materials are harmful to the public." In its report issued in 1970, the commission found "no evidence to date that exposure to explicit sexual materials plays a significant role in the causation of delinquent or criminal behavior among youth or adults" and that it "cannot conclude that exposure to erotic materials is a factor in the causation of sex crime or sex delinquency."[47] One of the commission's principal recommendations was that "federal, state and local legislation should not seek to interfere with the right of adults who wish to do so to read, obtain or view explicit sexual material" and that "federal, state and local legislation prohibiting the sale, exhibition, or distribution of sexual materials to consenting adults should be repealed."[48]

What happened in the *Miller* case?

In 1973 the Supreme Court managed to render its first majority opinion in an obscenity case since *Roth* in 1957. However, contrary to the trend of its recent cases, the recommendations of the president's commission, and the urging of many, the Court did not proclaim the abolition of obscenity laws. A new Court majority, composed substantially of Nixon appointees, formulated a new and to a significant extent more regressive definition of obscenity. The new standards were announced in a series of cases generally referred to by the name of one of them, *Miller v. California.*[49] With only limited elaboration since, the *Miller* formulation has remained the prevailing legal standard of obscenity.

How did the *Miller* majority justify the continued suppression of obscenity?

The *Miller* majority reiterated *Roth*'s conclusion that obscene materials are not protected by the First Amendment. It endorsed the asserted "legitimate interest in prohibiting dissemination or exhibition of obscene material when the mode of dissemination carries with it a significant danger of offending the sensibilities of unwilling [adult] recipients or of exposure to juveniles."[50] But it refused to limit the reach of obscenity law to unwilling adults and children. It found that the states have a strong "interest . . . in the quality of life and the total community environment . . . [and in] maintain[ing] a decent society."[51] In addition, it rejected the need for "conclusive proof of a connection between antisocial behavior and obscene material"[52] and thus rejected (implicitly) the findings by the president's commission to the contrary. It held that states could simply "assume" such a connection.[53]

The *Miller* majority expressed confidence that its new formulation of obscenity would provide "sufficiently specific guidelines to isolate 'hard core' pornography from expression protected by the First Amendment"[54] and thus resolve the problems of vagueness, uncertainty, and overbreadth that had plagued the Court, and the law of obscenity, for many years. Finally, the majority found no justification for "sound[ing] the alarm of repression" because of continued enforcement of laws against obscenity. "Public portrayal of hard-core sexual conduct for its own sake, and for the ensuing commercial gain," cannot be equated with "the free and robust exchange of ideas and political debate" that is protected by the First Amendment.[55] "We do not see the harsh hand of censorship of ideas—good or bad, sound or unsound—and 'repression' of political liberty lurking in every state regulation of commercial exploitation of human interest in sex."[56]

And with these considerations in mind, the majority proceeded to rewrite the law of obscenity.

What was the position of the dissenting justices in *Miller?*

Four justices dissented. Perhaps the most significant opinion was that of Justice Brennan, the author of the majority opinion in *Roth* (which first declared that there was such a thing as obscenity that could constitutionally be suppressed). Brennan admitted his past errors: "I am convinced that the approach initiated 16 years ago in *Roth* . . . and culminating in the Court's decision today, cannot bring stability to this area of the law without jeopardizing fundamental First Amendment values."[57] Emphasizing the inherent vagueness and ambiguity of all definitions of obscenity, Brennan declared that the First Amendment "demand[s] that 'sensitive tools' be used to carry out the 'separation of legitimate from illegitimate speech,'" and he "reluctantly conclude[d] that none of the available formulas [of obscenity], including the one announced today, can reduce the vagueness to a tolerable level."[58]

As long as such vagueness exists, Justice Brennan observed, obscenity laws fail to provide constitutionally required "notice" to persons potentially affected, invite "arbitrary and erratic [law] enforcement," and "chill" constitutionally protected expression. Accordingly, Justice Brennan urged the Court to reject the total suppression of obscenity, to protect fundamental First Amendment interests and to prevent the institutional havoc that was the result of 16 years of disagreement on the Court. He concluded:

> I would hold, therefore, that at least in the absence of distribution to juveniles or obtrusive exposure to unconsenting adults, the First and Fourteenth Amendments

prohibit the State and Federal Governments from attempting wholly to suppress sexually oriented materials on the basis of their allegedly "obscene" contents. Nothing in this approach precludes those governments from taking action to serve what may be strong and legitimate interests through regulation of the manner of distribution of sexually oriented material.[59]

But the majority had one more vote than the dissenters.[60]

What are the elements of the current legal definition of obscenity?

As defined by the *Miller* majority, expressive matter—including writings, photographs, art, dramatic works, motion pictures, and even live performances—can be considered legally obscene and therefore constitutionally subject to legal action, only if such matter meets of all the following requirements:

1. It must "depict or describe" certain explicit sexual conduct that has been defined as prohibited in applicable state or federal law.
2. The prohibited sexual depictions or descriptions must be "patently offensive" to an "average" person based upon "contemporary community standards."
3. "Taken as a whole," the material must appeal to the "prurient" interest, again when judged against contemporary community standards.
4. Taken as a whole, the material must also lack "serious" literary, artistic, political, or scientific value.[61]

In formulating these standards, the *Miller* majority expressly indicated that they could be applied constitutionally only to materials that constituted hard-core pornography.

What does "depict or describe" mean with reference to explicit sexual conduct?

In this first *Miller* guideline, it is not clear what "depict or describe" means in all contexts, but most usually it should be readily apparent to the author or artist.

Evidently, graphic materials such as paintings, photographs, or movies that present or represent sexual activities "depict" those activities. Moreover, under *Miller*, the depictions need not present "actual" sexual activities but may include "simulated" activities. *Simulated* presumably means that the depiction has the appearance of presenting sexual activity that may not actually be taking place.

The parallel concept of *description* makes it clear that the Court still considers that words alone can be found obscene. Indeed, that was the precise holding of another case decided along with *Miller*, *Kaplan v. California*.[62]

What sexual activities are included in the Supreme Court's definition of obscenity?

The court provided in *Miller* what it called "a few plain examples" of the hard-core sexual conduct that a state statute could consider in defining obscenity. These examples, which the Court indicated were not exclusive, were

1. patently offensive representations or descriptions of ultimate sexual acts, normal or perverted, actual or simulated
2. patently offensive representations or descriptions of masturbation, excretory functions, and lewd exhibition of the genitals[63]

One year later, in *Jenkins v. Georgia*,[64] the Court held that mere nudity was not enough to render materials obscene as it overturned a finding of the Georgia courts that the movie *Carnal Knowledge* was obscene. It also ruled that while the examples of sexual conduct provided in *Miller* "did not purport to be an exhaustive catalogue of what juries might find to be patently offensive, [they did] fix substantive constitutional limitations" on the "type of material subject to a determination [of patent offensiveness]."[65]

What constitutes "lewd exhibition of the genitals"?

This is not at all clear. Of the examples provided by the Supreme Court, "lewd exhibition of the genitals" is the most ambiguous.

It is clear from the *Carnal Knowledge* decision that "mere nudity" is not sufficient to constitute lewd exhibition, but this does little to clarify lewd exhibition. In fact, in the *Carnal Knowledge* case, the Court observed that the movie contained "no exhibition whatever of the actors' genitals, nude or otherwise."[66] Perhaps all that can confidently be concluded is that lewd exhibition is something more than mere nudity and less than sexual activity.

A leading commentator has provided what may be the best brief explanation of the distinction between mere nudity and lewd exhibition of the genitals, to the extent that any single statement can make sense of inherently subjective and hazy judgments:

> "Lewd exhibition of the genitals" . . . should be interpreted to include photographs which focus on, exaggerate, or emphasize the genitalia or "erogenous zones." It is this exaggeration or "highlight" on the genitalia which often distinguishes hard-core pornography from mere nudity. Similarly, hard-core pornography often emphasizes suggestive poses or lewdly intertwined bodies, even in the absence of actual sexual activity.[67]

Perhaps because lewd exhibition of the genitals is one of the most open-ended *Miller* guidelines, the Court in a subsequent statement on the subject emphasized the need to limit the definition. In discussing the possible "overbreadth" of a New York child-pornography statute which contained a lewd-exhibition provision, the Court recognized the potential ambiguity and "impermissible application" of the statute, stating: "Nor will we assume that the New York courts will widen the possibly invalid reach of the statute by giving an expansive construction to the proscription on 'lewd exhibition[s] of the genitals.'"[68]

How is *patent offensiveness* defined?

This standard too is inherently ambiguous and subjective. According to one observer, it is basically designed to ask Does this material go too far? Does it go beyond "the current level of society's acceptance of sexual depictions or descriptions?"[69]

The courts offer little guidance; as a result, judging patent offensiveness is often left to the trier of fact (the jury, or where there is no jury, the judge), which must determine, based upon its understanding of the "average" person's views and applying contemporary community standards, whether the material is patently offensive. It may, but need not, consider objective evidence on community standards. Its findings are subject to appellate review, but the scope of the review may be limited by the subjectivity of the issue.

Perhaps the best understanding of patent offensiveness is provided by the cases decided before *Miller* in which the concept developed. According to Professor Schauer, the Model Penal Code in 1962 introduced the concept of patent offensiveness as a requirement for obscenity.[70] The Code required that in addition to appeal to the prurient interest, the material had to "go substantially beyond customary limits of candor" in describing or depicting certain sexual activities. The same year, Justice John Marshall Harlan referred approvingly to this patent-offensiveness test and indicated that it required "affront" to "current community standards of decency."[71] Still later, a plurality in another Supreme Court case recognized and approved the Model Penal Code language and characterized it as requiring "a deviation from society's standards of decency."[72] Finally (before *Miller*), patent offensiveness was incorporated as the second of three elements of obscenity set forth by the plurality opinion in *Memoirs v. Massachusetts*, requiring proof that "the material is patently offensive because it affronts contemporary community standards relating to the description or representation of sexual matters."[73]

What is the meaning of *prurient interest?*

This requirement did not originate with *Miller*. The Court first used it in *Roth*, where it gave only dictionary definitions to explain what it considered prurient.[74] Unfortunately, these definitions include two inconsistent views of prurient appeal. The first requires an appeal to "shameful," "morbid," or "abnormal" interest in sex; the second requires merely an appeal to sexual response, lust, or desire. According to one commentator, it is probably the second definition that the Supreme Court has in mind,[75] although many courts have disagreed on the question.

Who is the "average" person who is to judge patent offensiveness and prurient appeal?

The purpose of this requirement is to ensure as far as possible that neither deviant nor overly sensitive or insensitive standards are brought to bear in judging obscenity.[76] The average-person test is a rejection of earlier legal standards that sought to protect the most sensitive members of the community, children and "weak-willed" adults.[77] These standards have been decisively rejected in American obscenity law, which now requires that the standard be based upon the reactions of an average adult.[78] As for materials intended for so-called deviant groups (e.g., sadomasochists, flagellists, or fetishists), it has been held that the average-person test must be modified to consider whether the materials appeal to the prurient interest of the groups for which they were intended.[79]

How are the contemporary standards of the local community to be defined and applied?

When the concept of contemporary community standards was first recognized by the Supreme Court in 1957,[80] it liberalized obscenity law, in effect, by permitting courts and juries to consider the increasing sexual tolerance in the community at large rather than looking to some fixed (and presumably more regressive) legal concept of obscenity. Application of community standards recognizes the possibility of change and reflects a desire to locate an external standard rather than rely solely on the personal judgments of the jury or judge. These are admirable ideals, but in practice it has proved difficult to define community standards either geographically or substantively.

The geographical debate has focused on national versus local standards. In the first important case to consider the issue, a national standard was proposed, but only for federal obscenity cases.[81] Then, in 1964, Justice Brennan proposed a national standard for all obscenity cases.[82] To allow a local standard, he argued, would create inconsistent standards that would chill free distribution of material nationwide. "It is, after all, a national Constitution we are expounding."[83] The proposed national standard was never adopted by a majority of the Court, nonetheless, national standards were generally applied by the lower courts.[84]

Miller decisively rejected national standards in favor of the standards of the local community: "It is neither realistic nor constitutionally sound to read the First Amendment as requiring that the people of Maine or Mississippi accept public depiction of conduct found tolerable in Las Vegas, or New York City."[85] The Court also disagreed with the idea that local standards would necessarily be more repressive than national ones

The majority viewed the test as something of a trade-off: Some local communities might be more restrictive, but a national standard might prevent those in more liberal communities from receiving materials they would have deemed acceptable.[86]

Most observers agree, however, that the potential dangers of a national community standard are hypothetical and that there is a real possibility that local standards will lead to inconsistent and unpredictable results and a tendency on the part of authors, artists, and their publishers and producers to distribute only what is acceptable to the more repressive communities.

Miller expressly requires that local community standards be applied in deciding the question of appeal to the prurient interest, but the Court did not expressly attach the community-standards requirement to the question of patent offensiveness. There seems no reason, however, to conclude that *Miller* intended to preclude such an attachment. Indeed, as one commentator has put it, "If anything, patent offensiveness is more susceptible to temporal and geographic variations than is prurient interest."[87] In contrast, local community standards are not to be applied to the question of serious literary value.[88] In an important 1987 case, the Supreme Court purported to clarify the application of this branch of the obscenity definition as follows: "The proper inquiry is not whether an ordinary member of any given community would find serious literary, artistic, political or scientific value in allegedly obscene material, but whether a reasonable person would find such value in the material taken as a whole."[89]

What is the significance of the "serious-value" test?

It remains the most effective protection for the author or artist who deals with sexual subjects. Even if a work is found to arouse prurient interest and to be patently offensive, the work is not obscene unless it is also established that the material, taken as a whole, "lacks serious literary, artistic, political or scientific value."[90] It is difficult to describe precisely what constitutes serious value, but it is clear under *Miller* that the value must be greater, "more predominant, more serious, and more pervasive throughout the entire work" than under the earlier "utterly without" requirement. A more careful examination of the work as a whole will now be required. As has been observed:

> What the addition of the "serious" element does is to allow the jury and the court to look beneath the argued or claimed value of the material to the relationship between the nonpornographic and the pornographic, and to the intent upon which the insertion of literary, artistic, political, or scientific material is based. If that intent is to convey a literary, artistic, political, or scientific idea or message, or to impart information, or advocate a position, then the purpose or intent is "serious" as the word appears to be used in *Miller*. If, on the other hand, it appears or is found that the purpose is to "dress up" or try to "redeem" otherwise obscene matter, sold or distributed for its obscenity rather than for its ideas or message, then the value is not "serious."[91]

Has the serious-value standard lowered the obscenity threshold to the point where legitimate works by serious authors and artists will be threatened? The answer is probably no, although several 1990 obscenity prosecutions (discussed below) may suggest a different answer for the years ahead. While obscenity prosecutions against even arguably serious works are relatively rare, they still occur. The cases since *Miller* have reached inconsistent results and do not form a basis for final conclusions. For example, a Louisiana case held that an issue of *Penthouse* magazine did not lack serious value where sixty-seven pages of the magazine contained "articles with serious value" while another ninety-six pages contained articles lacking serious value.[92]

But a federal appellate court found that similar issues of *Penthouse* and *Oui* magazines were obscene: "The issue is close but the numerous pictorials and obscene letters were not saved by articles possessing some literary merit."[93] Two cases found that the movie *Caligula*, although explicit and offensive, did not lack serious political or artistic value.[94]

What is the significance of the requirement that to be found obscene, a work must be "taken as a whole"?

The Supreme Court made this requirement explicit in *Roth*,[95] and *Miller* continued the requirement for the serious-value and prurient-appeal standards. It is important that an isolated passage or picture in an otherwise serious work cannot be taken out of context and viewed separately to find the work obscene. On the other hand, the courts have developed a rule that prevents a minimal or unrelated addition of material from "redeeming" a work that is otherwise obscene. As the Supreme Court put it in a memorable passage: "A quotation from Voltaire in the flyleaf of a book will not constitutionally redeem an otherwise obscene publication."[96] The whole-work rule tends to ensure that a careful evaluation of the literary, scientific, political, or artistic purpose and overall theme of a work will be made.

How have obscenity laws been applied in the 1990s?

For the most part, since *Miller* in 1973 and the *Carnal Knowledge* decision in 1974, obscenity laws have been applied to books, magazines, movies, and videotapes that most people would recognize as hard-core pornography. However, several widely publicized obscenity cases in 1990 served as vivid reminders that such laws can be applied to very different kinds of works.

In one of those cases, the Contemporary Arts Center in Cincinnati, Ohio, a nationally recognized art museum, and Dennis Barrie, its director, were criminally prosecuted under Ohio's obscenity laws because a retrospective exhibition of the works of the widely acclaimed photographer Robert Mapplethorpe included five photographs containing graphic sadomasochistic images and two depicting children with their genitals exposed. In an important pretrial ruling, the trial court refused to dismiss the charges on the ground that those works could not be found obscene as a matter of law.[97] The court also rejected the museum's contention that the taken-as-a-whole requirement meant that the 7 accused photographs had to be considered as part of and in the context of the entire 175-photo exhibition; the court interpreted that requirement to mean that each of those photographs had to be considered standing alone without any reference to the other (nonaccused) photographs that composed the exhibition.[98] But despite that ruling (among others that seemed to work against the defendants), after a full trial a conservative jury in one of the most conservative jurisdictions in the country found the defendants (and hence the challenged photographs) not guilty of obscenity.

In another major 1990 obscenity case, a federal district court judge in Fort Lauderdale, Florida, found the rap record album *As Nasty As They Wanna Be* by the group 2 Live Crew obscene.[99] Addressing itself to the album's lyrics, the court said that "the depictions of ultimate sexual acts are so vivid that they are hard to distinguish from seeing the same conduct described in the words of a book, or in pictures in periodicals or films."[100] Noting that those lyrics were combined with music, the court also observed, "The evident goal of this particular recording is to reproduce the sexual act through musical lyrics. It is an appeal directed to 'dirty' thoughts and the loins, not the intellect and the mind."[101]

In a lengthy written decision rendered after a nonjury civil trial in which the group sought a declaration that the album was not obscene (local authorities had threatened to prosecute criminally anyone who sold it), the court found that the album met all of the requirements for obscenity set forth in *Miller*. Applying his "personal knowledge" of the tastes and tolerance of the relevant community (the three coastal counties around Fort Lauderdale), the judge said (1) that "based on the graphic deluge of sexual lyrics and sexual conduct," he had "no difficulty in finding that [the album] appeals to a shameful and morbid interest in sex"; (2) that the lyrics were "patently offensive"; and (3) that those lyrics were "utterly without any redeeming social value."[102]

Just a few weeks later, however, in a state criminal prosecution in the same part of Florida that contended that the live performance of the contents of that album violated the state's obscenity laws, a local jury had no apparent difficulty acquitting the defendants of all charges.

The mixed results of these cases left it unclear whether further attempts would be made to apply obscenity laws to artistic expression that was far removed from the kind of hardcore pornography that had been the main target of obscenity prosecutions prior to these cases. In the meantime, however, those prosecutions did send a message to everyone who creates, disseminates, sells, or exhibits works that involve sexual subjects, or who creates, disseminates, sells, or performs musical works that contain sexual references or terminology (no matter how popular or highly regarded those works might be) that those works can still lead to criminal obscenity charges in any given American locality. It can only be hoped that any chill on free expression that that message creates will be quickly and definitively dissipated.

What "criminal state of mind" is required in obscenity cases?
Most criminal laws in this country require proof of some degree of criminal or evil intent (in legal jargon, *mens rea* or *scienter*).[103] It is obviously crucial in obscenity cases to know whether a defendant can be convicted without any specific knowledge that the materials are legally obscene. If no such proof is required, the risk of an obscenity conviction without the defendant's knowing he was taking that risk could substantially deter the publication and dissemination of perfectly legal materials.

The Supreme Court has held that some degree of criminal knowledge must be proved to establish an obscenity offense. In the leading case, *Smith v. California*, the Court found unconstitutional a Los Angeles ordinance that made it a crime for a bookseller to have obscene books in his bookstore.[104] The ordinance had no *scienter* requirement and thus would have imposed "strict liability" on the bookseller. The Supreme Court held that strict criminal liability is unconstitutional where First Amendment rights are involved, but it failed to define how much criminal knowledge the Constitution requires.

However, it has become clear since then that some general knowledge of the nature and character of the materials is all that is required and that it need not be proved that the defendant knew or believed the materials were legally obscene.[105] Unlike a bookseller, who may never have read or even glanced at many of the books in his store, the author or artist is obviously fully aware of the content of her work. Thus the current *scienter* requirements provide little protection to authors and artists who deal with sexual subjects.

What is *pandering*?
Pandering, a legal doctrine created by the Supreme Court, permits material to be found obscene, although its contents might not otherwise qualify, because of the way it is sold to the public.[106] Evidence that the advertising or marketing of

materials stresses their sexually provocative nature can be considered in deciding whether the materials are obscene, especially if the obscenity issue is "close." But materials that are clearly not obscene cannot be transformed into obscene materials, no matter how blatant the pandering.[107]

Authors and artists are usually not in a position to influence advertising and marketing decisions that may ultimately become evidence of pandering. Most publishing contracts and customary publishing practices leave these decisions to the publisher. Still, authors and artists of explicit materials that might be considered obscene should at least attempt to obtain some control over advertising or marketing as a protection against potential charges of pandering.

Are there special rules that apply to the distribution of sexual materials to children?

Yes; many. The definitions of obscenity discussed so far apply to the dissemination of obscene materials to the general (and predominantly adult) public. The author or artist whose materials are intended for or may be distributed to children should be familiar with the special legal standards that apply to the distribution of sexually explicit materials to children.

When the prevailing definition of obscenity looked to the reactions of the "peculiarly susceptible," there was no need for special concern for children. But when the law moved to the average-person test, children became a matter of considerable legal concern. In *Ginsberg v. New York*[108] the Supreme Court expressly approved the concept of *variable obscenity,* upholding New York's "harmful-to-minors" statute. Under such laws, materials that are not obscene for adults can be obscene if exposed to children. Since *Miller,* to be obscene for children, a work must be patently offensive for minors, appeal to the prurient interests of minors, and lack serious value for minors.[109]

The standard for obscenity is changed, but other procedural protections related to obscenity remain.[110] The Supreme Court has not squarely considered the variable-obscenity doctrine since *Miller,* and at least one commentator has expressed doubt that the concept can survive *Miller*'s strict focus on hard-core materials as the only permissible subject matter for obscenity laws.[111] However, parallel developments since *Miller* strongly suggest that the Supreme Court as now constituted will continue to uphold rules devised to protect children, whether or not the rules are logically supportable under *Miller*.[112]

What is child pornography and how does it relate to the general rules of obscenity?

The purpose of so-called child-pornography laws is not to limit the dissemination of materials to children (covered by harmful-to-minors laws) but to prevent the use of children in the production of pornographic materials. Thus *child pornography* is sexually explicit material that displays children engaging in actual (or simulated) sexual activities.[113]

Child-pornography laws attempt to proscribe such materials in two ways. First, they impose heavy criminal penalties for the use of children in the creation of sexually explicit (but not necessarily obscene) materials. It has not been argued seriously that such "use" laws violate First Amendment rights. Second, presenting far more serious First Amendment concerns, they make it a crime simply to publish or sell such materials, even if the publisher or seller had nothing to do with their production and the materials are not obscene.

In 1981 New York's highest court held that a New York statute that made it a crime to sell such nonobscene materials was unconstitutional.[114] But in 1982, in *New York v. Ferber*, the Supreme Court reversed that decision and held that child-pornography materials need not be legally obscene to be constitutionally suppressed.[115] In so ruling, the Court expressly created a new exception to First Amendment protection for such nonobscene materials, an exception that does not require the application of *Miller* standards.

It is beyond the scope of this chapter to discuss this at length, but it seems appropriate to note that the Supreme Court has limited the child-pornography exception to visual depictions of actual or simulated sexual activity being performed by children. Written material and visual work not based on actual activity by a minor are not covered by these laws. To the extent that authors and artists do not deal with such matters, they should not be affected by the new exception. However, it is also clear that such laws can affect works of serious value.[116]

In 1990, in *Osborne v. Ohio*,[117] the Supreme Court made it clear that it was strongly committed to upholding the enforcement of *Ferber*-inspired child pornography laws. At issue in that case was an Ohio law that made it a crime simply to possess child pornography. The defendant argued that the Supreme Court's 1969 decision in *Stanley v. Georgia*, which declared unconstitutional a state law that made it a crime to possess obscene materials, should apply to child pornography. The Supreme Court, in a 6–3 vote, rejected the argument:

> In *Stanley*, Georgia primarily sought to proscribe the private possession of obscenity because it was concerned that obscenity would poison the minds of its viewers. . . . We responded that "[w]hatever the power of the state to control public dissemination of ideas inimical to the public morality, it cannot constitutionally premise legislation on the desirability of controlling a person's private thoughts." . . . The difference here is obvious: the State does not rely on a paternalistic interest in regulating Osborne's mind. Rather, Ohio has enacted [the statute] in order to protect the victims of child pornography; it hopes to destroy a market for the exploitation of children. . . . Given the importance of the State's interest in protecting the victims of child pornography, we cannot fault Ohio for attempting to stamp out this vice at all levels in the distribution chain.[118]

What are "minors-access" and "minors-display" laws?

The desire to protect children is also manifested in laws designed to prevent children from being exposed to or having access to sexual (but not necessarily obscene) materials. Some of these laws make it a crime to sell sexually explicit materials in stores open to children unless the material is in some way bagged, stapled, or otherwise sealed.[119] Other laws require that the materials be kept out of the reach of children.[120] However phrased, they almost inevitably restrict adult access to materials that are seemingly entitled to the full protection of the First Amendment. They also result in a substantial impairment of the First Amendment rights of children.

The constitutionality of these laws has been tested by publishers, booksellers, and distributors. Although the Supreme Court has not yet directly considered the issue, three display or access statutes have been struck down as unconstitutional by lower courts. [121] A Georgia display law was invalidated because it prevented perusal by adults and limited the sale of constitutionally protected material to adults. [122] Protecting minors was held to be an inadequate justification for such severe interference with adults' First Amendment rights.

A Colorado display statute was invalidated because the court concluded that channels for the interchange of literary, political, artistic, and scientific ideas about sex were effectively closed by the statute and that its enforcement would regulate to a commercially unfeasible degree the activities of responsible members of the community."[123]

Likewise, a California court invalidated a display ordinance requiring that commercial establishments seal magazines or books containing sexually explicit but nonobscene pictures, keep them out of the reach of minors, or bar minors from entering the stores. [124] The ordinance would have affected display in drugstores, grocery stores, and newsstands in addition to adult bookstores. The court held that the sealing requirement infringed the freedom of adults to browse and that the entire impact of the statute denied children access to material which they had "an unfettered constitutional right to enjoy."[125] "Whether accompanied by parents or not," stated the court, minors "cannot be denied access to retail establishments which sell a wide variety of literature, or the necessities of life, simply because such establishments also sell some materials sought to be restricted."[126]

One state's access law did get to the Supreme Court in 1988, but the Court avoided a direct ruling on its constitutionality. [127] Virginia had a law making it a crime "to knowingly display for commercial purpose in a manner whereby juveniles may examine or peruse" any material that was "harmful to juveniles," which was defined to mean in part material that "is patently offensive to prevailing standards in the adult community as a whole with respect to what is suitable material for children" and "is, when taken as a whole, lacking in serious literary, artistic, political or scientific value for juveniles."[128] A number of organizations, including the American Booksellers Association and the Association of American Publishers, challenged the law claiming that it was unconstitutionally vague

and would result in forcing bookstores and the like to remove
from their shelves countless books that were concededly not
obscene for adults.[129]

Two lower federal courts declared the law unconstitutional,
and the state appealed to the Supreme Court.[130] That Court
decided that before it could pass on the law's constitutionality,
the Virginia Supreme Court should interpret and give specific
meaning to the law's provisions and establish what a bookseller
had to do to comply with it.[131] Ultimately, the Virginia Supreme
Court interpreted the statute narrowly, holding (1) that the
term *harmful to juveniles* had to be construed "in accordance
with the current United States Supreme Court definition of
obscenity"; (2) that "if a work is found to have a serious literary,
artistic, political or scientific value for a legitimate minority of
normal, older adolescents, then it cannot be said to lack such
value for the entire class of juveniles taken as a whole"; and (3)
that a bookseller could only be convicted under the law only
if he "knowingly afforded juveniles an opportunity to peruse
harmful materials" or, being aware that such an opportunity
existed, "took no reasonable steps to prevent the perusal of
such materials by juveniles."[132]

Given the much broader potential scope of the law, the
plaintiffs in the case determined that as thus interpreted, the
law posed no significant threat to their activities and to the
First Amendment rights of juveniles and adults. However,
the full extent of harmful-to-minors laws will have to await a
definitive ruling from the Supreme Court.

How do obscenity laws affect television?

For several reasons, especially industry self-regulation, obscenity laws have rarely if ever been applied to traditional radio
and television programming.[133] The advent of more explicit
programming, to some extent on regular broadcast channels
but especially on cable television, has changed this. Because of
its unprecedented frankness in dealing with sexual matters,
cable TV has emerged as one of the most heated battlegrounds
of free expression. The legal issues are complex and volatile,
involving not only how cable systems ought to be treated for
regulatory purposes but also the proper standards that should
govern the censorship of cable programming. The question of

who should define and enforce such regulations is also controversial.

Over-the-air broadcasters are subject to licensing and extensive regulation by the Federal Communications Commission; this regulation has been held not to violate the First Amendment rights of broadcasters, although similar government control over other media would be unconstitutional.[134] A dramatic example of the extent of such regulation is the Supreme Court's decision in *FCC v. Pacifica Foundation*,[135] sometimes called the "seven dirty words" case. The FCC had imposed sanctions on a radio station that aired a comedic monologue by George Carlin of "words you can't say on the public airwaves." Carlin's routine was clearly not obscene; in fact, it did not describe sexual activities. But even though vulgar language had previously been held not to qualify as obscenity,[136] a divided Supreme Court upheld the FCC's sanctions against such "indecent" language.[137] In so doing, the Court distinguished the standards applicable to broadcasting from those for other media because broadcasting is a "uniquely pervasive" medium that can intrude into the privacy of the home and be readily accessible to children.[138]

It is not yet clear whether extensive regulation of cable television is permissible, as it is for broadcasting. Many interest groups and politicians believe that the content of cable programming should be subject to the same degree of governmental regulation as the content of over-the-air programming, and these forces have succeeded in enacting numerous statutes and government directives aimed at such regulation. Many others, however, argue that cable is distinct from over-the-air broadcasting both technologically and in practice, especially since there is none of the "spectrum scarcity" that has traditionally justified broadcasting regulation. Moreover, cable viewers must choose to subscribe, and all cable systems are now required to offer devices to prevent access by children without parental supervision. Thus, it is argued, cable is more like a newspaper than over-the-air broadcasting and should be accorded the fullest First Amendment protection from governmental control.[139] For the most part, these forces have persuaded the courts to strike down as unconstitutional efforts to subject cable programming to the kind of regulation that might be permissible for over-the-air broadcasting.

In an important commercial pay-TV case, for example, the court held that cable should receive a higher degree of First Amendment protection than over-the-air broadcasting and declared unconstitutional a Utah statute that made it a crime to transmit "pornographic" or "indecent" material via cable.[140] The court found that the Utah statute failed to meet the *Miller* standards for obscenity and that the statute could be applied to such serious and nonobscene movies as *The Godfather, Being There, Annie Hall,* and *Coming Home.* It rejected the argument that indecency on cable should be treated like indecency on television or radio. As the court noted, "There is no law that says you have to subscribe to a cable TV service any more than you have to subscribe to The Salt Lake Tribune."[141] Other courts have reached similar conclusions, but it is still not clear whether these precedents will be accepted in other cable-TV cases and by the Supreme Court.

Public-access programming on cable presents even more complicated First Amendment issues. In 1984, Congress enacted comprehensive legislation designed to establish uniform national guidelines for the regulation of cable television.[14] Among other things, that law authorized cities (and other franchising authorities) to require a cable company to provide channels for programming originating from the general public and prohibited such authorities from exercising any editorial control over the content of such programming except to prevent the cablecasting of materials that are "obscene or are otherwise unprotected by the Constitution of the United States."[143] As of 1991, no cases had tested the full scope of these new national guidelines.

Are there other ways government can regulate the content of sexually oriented expression?

Thus far, we've seen that government can regulate sexually oriented speech if it meets the *Miller* test of obscenity, meet the *Ferber* test of child pornography, or under specified and limited circumstances meets the "indecency" test of the "seven dirty words" case. In addition, certain groups and interests are relentless seeking new and ostensibly more effective means to suppress sexual speech they do not like without having to meet the established requirements of the First Amendment.

Perhaps the most significant example of such efforts involve

n ordinance enacted in 1984 by the city of Indianapolis, Indi-
na, at the urging of some religious groups and certain out-
poken feminists, including Catherine MacKinnon, a law pro-
essor, and Andrea Dworkin, a writer.[144] That ordinance defined
he term *pornography* to refer to "the graphic sexually explicit
ubordination of women, whether in pictures or in words" if
he material met one of six further requirements, including that
vomen are "presented in scenarios of degradation" or "as sexual
bjects for domination, conquest, violation, exploitation, pos-
ession or use, or through postures or positions of servility or
ubmission or display."[145] Unlike the *Miller* test for obscenity,
he ordinance made no reference to prurient appeal; patent
ffensiveness; the standards of the community; or literary, artis-
ic, political, or scientific value. The ordinance contained elabo-
ate procedures to deal with alleged violations, and it author-
zed anyone injured by someone who had seen or read
ornography to bring a civil lawsuit for damages against the
naker or seller.[146]

The arguments for and against this approach were summa-
ized as follows by the federal appeals court that decided
vhether the statute was constitutional:

> Those supporting the ordinance say it will play an impor-
> tant role in reducing the tendency of men to view women
> as sexual objects, a tendency that leads to both unaccept-
> able attitudes and discrimination in the workplace and
> violence away from it. Those opposing the ordinance point
> out that much radical feminist literature is explicit and
> depicts women in ways forbidden by the ordinance and
> that the ordinance would reopen old battles. It is unclear
> how Indianapolis would treat works from James Joyce's
> *Ulysses* to Homer's *Iliad*; both depict women as submissive
> objects for conquest and domination.[147]

The federal district court that first heard the case, the federal
ppeals court that heard the first appeal, and the Supreme
Court all concluded that the ordinance was unconstitutional.
As the appeals court put it after setting forth the arguments for
nd against the ordinance:

> We do not try to balance the arguments for and against an
> ordinance such as this. The ordinance discriminates on

the ground of the content of the speech. Speech treating
women in the approved way—in sexual encounters "premised on equality." . . .—is lawful no matter how sexually
explicit. Speech treating women in the disapproved way—
as submissive in matters sexual or as enjoying humiliation—is unlawful no matter how significant the literary,
artistic, or political qualities of the work taken as whole.
The state may not ordain preferred viewpoints in this
way. The Constitution forbids the state to declare one
perspective right and silence opponents.[148]

Despite this stinging repudiation of the MacKinnon-Dworkin
approach to the regulation of sexually explicit speech, it may
be anticipated that those who want to suppress sexually explicit
speech will continue to seek new ways to accomplish that goal.
And ultimately it will be for the courts, including the Supreme
Court, to determine whether those efforts comport with the
rigorous requirements of the First Amendment.

**Apart from criminal laws addressed to the content of sexual
speech, how else can such speech be regulated and controlled?**
In a number of ways. Zoning laws can specify where and
how establishments offering sexually explicit materials may
be located. Licensing systems can require those offering such
material to obtain licenses before doing so. And laws can provide very drastic remedies against people and businesses found
guilty of violating obscenity laws. In all such cases, however,
the laws must be found consistent with the First Amendment
and other provisions of the Constitution.

What is involved in the zoning of sexual materials?
In 1976 a narrowly divided Supreme Court upheld a Detroit
zoning scheme that sought to "disperse" bookstores and theaters that specialized in sexually explicit (but not necessarily
obscene) materials.[149] The Court's plurality opinion declared:
"Even though the First Amendment protects communication
in this area from total suppression, we hold that the State may
legitimately use the content of these materials as the basis for
placing them in a different classification from other motion
pictures."[150] Then, at least temporarily, a 1980 decision of the
Court cast doubt on the future impact of the Detroit decision. In

Schad v. Borough of Mount Ephraim,[151] the Court invalidated a local ordinance that prohibited "live entertainment (including nude dancing) in any establishment." With reference to the zoning issue, the Court declared flatly that "when a zoning law infringes upon a protected liberty, it must be narrowly drawn and must further a sufficiently substantial government interest." The Court found that the borough's blanket prohibition of entertainment violated the First Amendment.

In 1986, however, in *City of Renton v. Playtime Theatres, Inc.*,[152] the Supreme Court made it clear that localities had broad power to use zoning laws to locate "adult" establishments however they wished so long as they didn't completely banish them. In that case, the city enacted a zoning ordinance that prohibited "adult motion picture theaters" from being located within one thousand feet of any residential zone, single- or multiple-family dwelling, church, park, or school.[153] The result of that ordinance was to limit all such theaters to one concentrated commercially zoned part of the city where there were few if any available places for them. The Court held that the city could rely on findings made by other cities concerning the adverse effects of adult establishments on children and community life, and it declared: "Cities may regulate adult theaters by dispersing them, as in Detroit, or by effectively concentrating them, as in Renton. . . . 'The city must be allowed a reasonable opportunity to experiment with solutions to admittedly serious problems.'"[154]

In response to the theatres' claim that the ordinance effectively meant that there would be no places available for them to be legally situated, the Court said:

That [the theatres] must fend for themselves in the real estate market, on an equal footing with other prospective purchasers and lessees, does not give rise to a First Amendment violation. And although we have cautioned against the enactment of zoning regulations that have "the effect of suppressing, or greatly restricting access to, lawful speech . . . we have never suggested that the First Amendment compels the Government to ensure that adult theaters, or any other kinds of speech-related businesses for that matter, will be able to obtain sites at bargain prices. . . . In our view, the First Amendment requires only that

Renton refrain from effectively denying [the theatres] a reasonable opportunity to open and operate an adult theater within the city, and the ordinance before us easily meets this requirement.[155]

In 1991, the Supreme Court rendered a much-discussed 5– ruling that a state law prohibiting complete nudity in publi was not unconstitutional under the First Amendment whe applied to establishments "that wish to provide totally nud dancing as entertainment."[156] Three of the justices in the major ity found that public nudity could be prohibited even if th nudity was "expressive" and thus within the scope of the Firs Amendment, in part because the law "furthers a substantia government interest in protecting order and morality."[157] fourth justice, Antonin Scalia, found that the law did not appl to expression at all and thus was not subject to any First Amend ment scrutiny.[158] The fifth justice in the majority, David Soutel said he found the law constitutional under the Court's prece dents approving the zoning of adult entertainment and that h would be disinclined to uphold the law if it was applied to play such as *Hair* or *Equus* that contained total nudity.[159] The fou justices in the minority agreed that the law violated the estab lishments' First Amendment right to present entertainmen that included nudity.[160]

What was the Meese Commission?

In 1985, at the request of President Reagan, his then attorne general, William French Smith, chartered a commission t "determine the nature, extent, and impact on society of pornog raphy in the United States, and to make specific recommenda tions to the Attorney General concerning more effective ways i which the spread of pornography could be contained, consisten with constitutional guarantees."[161] Eleven members of the com mission were appointed, including several outspoken oppo nents of sexually explicit materials. Its chair, Henry Hudson was a local prosecutor in Virginia who had actively prosecute(many obscenity cases before being appointed to head the com mission.[162] The commission was given a 1-year term and budget of only $500,000, which meant that it could not conduc any research or studies of its own. The commission held publi hearings throughout the country at which it heard from advo ates who supported and opposed the vigorous enforcement of obscenity laws, and in 1986 it rendered a voluminous report that included among its attachments numerous examples of the kind of hard-core sexual materials that were the subject matter of the report. By that time, Edwin Meese III was Attorney General, and the commission became identified with him.

What were the Meese Commission's conclusions?

Among other things, the commission found that "the predominant use of such material is as a masturbatory aid."[163] It also found that there was little risk that the enforcement of obscenity laws would result in the regulation of nonobscene legal speech.[164] It decided that it was a mistake to look at "all sexually explicit materials, or even all pornographic materials, as one undifferentiated whole," and it concluded that such materials should be considered in three separate subgroupings: sexually violent materials; nonviolent materials depicting degradation, domination, subordination, or humiliation; and nonviolent and nondegrading materials.[165]

With respect to sexually violent material, the commission concluded unanimously that the available evidence strongly "supports the hypothesis that substantial exposure to sexually violent materials . . . bears a causal relationship to antisocial acts of sexual violence and, for some subgroups, possibly to unlawful acts of sexual violence"[166] and to undesirable attitudinal changes, including increased acceptance of the "rape myth" (i.e., that women enjoy being coerced into sexual activity and being physically hurt during sex). The commission said: "We have found a causal relationship between sexually explicit materials featuring violence and these consequences, and thus conclude that the class of such materials, although not necessarily every individual member of that class, is on the whole harmful to society."[167]

With respect to the second category, nonviolent but degrading sexual materials, the commission reached similar conclusions, although admittedly with less confidence.[168] The commission also found that this category of material constitutes somewhere between the predominant and the overwhelming part of what is currently standard heterosexual pornography and is a significant theme in a broader range of materials not

commonly considered sufficiently sexually explicit to be pornc
graphic.[169]

With respect to the third category, nonviolent and nonde
grading materials, where the participants seem to be entirel
willing and occupy equal roles in a setting devoid of actual c
apparent violence or pain, the members of the commissio
reported that it "disagreed substantially about the effects c
such materials."[170] The commission believed that such material
constituted a small part of the larger universe of sexually explic
materials and concluded, "We are on the current state of th
evidence persuaded that material of this type does not bear
causal relationship to rape and other acts of sexual violence."[1
The commission discussed other kinds of alleged harm resultin
from such materials, including harm to the moral environmen
of society, but reached no conclusions concerning such harm

What recommendations did the Meese Commission make
The commission concluded that laws proscribing sexuall
explicit materials should not be repealed, thus disagreeing wit
the main recommendation of the 1970 president's commission
but it also concluded that new laws to define such material
were not required.[172] It called for enhanced prosecution c
sexually violent and nonviolent but degrading sexual materials
but it made no recommendations on the enforcement of law
against nonviolent and nondegrading sexual materials.[173] Th
commission was also divided, and made no recommendations
concerning the enforcement of laws against written but no
illustrated sexually explicit materials that are not aimed a
children.[174]

The commission was skeptical of zoning laws that simpl
moved outlets for sexually explicit materials from one part of
city to another, and it declined to adopt proposals that inde
cency standards should be applied to programs on cable TV.[17
In all, the commission propounded ninety-two separate recom
mendations, most of which designed to enhance or facilitat
the enforcement of existing obscenity laws.

What was the response to the Meese Commission's report
For the most part, the report was largely ignored if no
ridiculed, many observers being especially critical of its casua
and often inaccurate use of the available scientific evidenc

nd its willingness to make sweeping conclusions based on its nterpretation of that evidence and its assumptions and notions f "common sense." However, the commission's report proba- ly did provide encouragement to law-enforcement officials, specially on the federal level, and private groups who support he vigorous prosecution of sexually explicit materials, and it ertainly offered no help to those who support less prosecution.

Besides the First Amendment, are there other constitu- ional limitations on laws addressed to obscenity?

Yes. The fact that speech found obscene is not protected by he First Amendment does not mean that it can be regulated r suppressed in disregard of other constitutional protections. ndeed, a legal doctrine sometimes called *First Amendment lue process* has been developed to ensure that obscenity cases re handled with special deference to the First Amendment alues that are always implicated.[176]

Criminal obscenity laws are not the only means government as to deal with obscenity. Civil proceedings are also available. ne such proceeding enables the state to seek a judicial deter- nination that a work is obscene and an order enjoining its listribution and sale, with criminal action possible if the work is lisseminated in violation of the injunction.[177] The government emains able to censor obscenity, and the people who handle uch material are not confronted with the potentially drastic onsequences of a criminal prosecution. To this extent, "prior ivil proceedings" can be seen as protective of First Amend- nent rights. Many states have enacted legislation providing for rior civil proceedings, either voluntary or mandatory.[178]

Such civil proceedings are fraught with special perils, how- ver. A civil judgment of obscenity can result in subsequent criminal penalties. Moreover, civil actions result in prior re- traints against the exercise of free expression. Prior restraints ave traditionally been considered the most serious abridg- nents of First Amendment rights.[179] Civil judgments may also ead to the confiscation and forfeiture of valuable property. Because of these potentially severe penalties, several recent udicial decisions make clear the necessity for stringent proce- lural safeguards in such proceedings.[180]

In general, prior restraints—injunctions—against publica- ion are very rare in our legal system. They are permitted in connection with obscenity only because obscene matter is no considered entitled to the protection of the First Amendment But because nonobscene expression is fully protected by th First Amendment, careful procedures are constitutionally re quired before a prior restraint can be issued against obscenity

The leading case is *Freedman v. Maryland.*[181] In the 1960 Maryland was one of the few states that still maintained motion-picture licensing and censorship board. Although th Supreme Court in *Freedman* did not rule that such board were prohibited by the First Amendment, it declared that "an system of prior restraints of expression comes to this Cour bearing a heavy presumption against its constitutional valid ity."[182] The Court struck down the Maryland system and liste the minimum procedural safeguards that an obscenity censor ship statute must contain to comport with the Firs Amendment:

> Where the transcendent value of speech is involved, due process certainly requires that the State bear the burden of persuasion to show "that the appellants engaged in criminal speech." Second, while the State may require advance submission of films, in order to proceed effectively to bar all showings of all unprotected films, the requirement cannot be administered in a manner which would lend an effect of finality to the censor's determination. [B]ecause only a judicial determination in an adversary proceeding ensures the necessary sensitivity to freedom of expression, only a procedure requiring a judicial determination suffices to impose a valid final restraint. To this end, the exhibitor must be assured, by statute or authoritative judicial construction, that the censor will, within a specified brief period, either issue a license or go to court to restrain showing the film. Any restraint imposed in advance of a final judicial determination on the merits must similarly be limited to preservation of the status quo for the shortest fixed period compatible with sound judicial resolution. [T]he procedure must also assure a prompt final judicial decision, to minimize the deterrent effect of an interim and possibly erroneous denial of a license.[183]

The procedural requirements outlined in the *Freedman* cas have had far-reaching implications for obscenity law. The al

ence of such procedures led to the invalidation of a federal
postal statute that authorized refusal to deliver mail based on
a nonjudicial determination of obscenity[184] and state statutes
that allowed materials to be seized before judicial proceedings
had determined their obscenity.[185] In 1975 a city was held to
have unconstitutionally restrained a production of the musical
Hair because of a procedure that lacked the *Freedman* protections.[186] In 1990 the Supreme Court reaffirmed the importance
of the *Freedman* precedent, invalidating a licensing scheme
adopted by Dallas, Texas, because it "does not provide for an
effective limitation on the time within which the licensor's
decision must be made. It also fails to provide an avenue for
prompt judicial review so as to minimize suppression of the
speech in the event of a license denial."[187]

In 1976 the Supreme Court considered for the first time the
validity of a state's prior civil obscenity proceeding and held Alabama's approach constitutionally inadequate.[188] An Alabama
civil court had determined that a publication was obscene.
Thereafter one McKinney, who had no notice of the earlier proceeding, was convicted for selling the publication. When he tried
to challenge the determination of obscenity during his criminal
trial, the issue was held foreclosed by the prior civil action.

The Supreme Court overturned McKinney's conviction, stating that since he had no notice of the prior proceeding and no
opportunity to participate in it or challenge its findings, he
should be allowed to have the issue of obscenity fully reconsid-
ered at his trial.[189] In his concurring opinion, Justice Brennan
pointed out other difficulties inherent in civil obscenity proceedings and noted that because of the precious First Amendment values at stake, a civil obscenity proceeding should require a stricter standard of proof than the ordinary civil standard
of "preponderance of the evidence." "The hazards to First
Amendment freedoms inhering in the regulation of obscenity,"
he stated, require that the state "comply with the more exacting
standard of proof beyond a reasonable doubt."[190]

Unfortunately, Justice Brennan's position was subsequently
rejected by the Supreme Court, which held that proof beyond
a reasonable doubt is not required in a civil obscenity action.[191]
The Court did not specifically indicate whether an intermediate
standard such as proof by "clear and convincing evidence"
would be required but seemed to suggest strongly that the

states were free to choose the burden of proof in a civil obscenity action, including the least stringent standard, preponderance of the evidence.[192]

What are "nuisance-abatement" or "padlock" laws, and how do they comport with First Amendment due-process requirements?

A recent development in civil obscenity law has been the enactment of nuisance-abatement or padlock statutes in many cities and states.[193] These statutes invoke a civil court's power to impose unique far-reaching civil penalties on persons found to be in violation of its injunctions. Relying on traditional civil laws pertaining to public nuisances, several states have attempted to authorize "abatement" injunctions that operate not only against materials found obscene but against the premises where they were made or sold. In this way, a civil nuisance action can result in not only the suppression of obscene materials but also the closing of the bookstore that carries them. The Supreme Court has thus far declined to address the constitutionality of such laws, choosing instead to review them in light of the procedural requirements in *Freedman*.

For example, in 1980, in *Vance v. Universal Amusement Co. Inc.*,[194] two Texas nuisance statutes were applied to locations found to have been distributing obscene materials or showing obscene films. One statute authorized the mandatory closing of the premises for 1 year; the other authorized the granting of injunctions prohibiting the future commercial manufacturing, distribution, or exhibition of obscene material.

The Supreme Court held that the injunction statute violated the Constitution but avoided reviewing the premises-closing statute, since the lower court had held it inapplicable to obscenity cases.[195] The Court was clearly concerned with the issue of procedure. With respect to the injunction statute, the Court recognized

> (a) that the regulation of a communicative activity such as the exhibition of motion pictures must adhere to more narrowly drawn procedures than is necessary for the abatement of an ordinary nuisance, and (b) that the burden of supporting an injunction against a future exhibition is even heavier than the burden of justifying the imposition of a criminal sanction for a past communication.[196]

The Court did provide a strong indication that it had significant concerns about the broader First Amendment issues, stating in an important footnote:

> Any system of prior restraint "comes to this Court bearing a heavy presumption against its constitutional validity." The presumption against prior restraints is heavier and the degree of protection broader than that against limits on expression imposed by criminal penalties. Behind the distinction is a theory deeply etched in our law: a free society prefers to punish the few who abuse rights of speech after they break the law than to throttle them and all others beforehand. It is always difficult to know in advance what an individual will say, and the line between legitimate and illegitimate speech is often so finely drawn that the risks of freewheeling censorship are formidable.[197]

As for the procedural improprieties in the Texas statute, the Court noted that it authorized prior restraints of indefinite duration on material that had not been finally found obscene. "Presumably," the Court declared, "an exhibitor would be required to obey such an order pending review of its merits and would be subject to contempt proceedings even if the film is ultimately found to be nonobscene. Such prior restraints would be more onerous and more objectionable than the threat of criminal sanctions after a film has been exhibited, since nonobscenity would be a defense to any criminal prosecution."[198]

What are "RICO" laws, and how do they apply to obscenity cases?

In recent years the federal government and many states have enacted racketeer influenced and corrupt organizations, or RICO, laws. Originally designed to enhance law-enforcement efforts against organized crime, such laws provided drastically enlarged penalties for those who are found in either criminal or civil RICO proceedings to have participated in a "pattern" of specific criminal activity, which means three separate acts of the criminal activity within a 10-year period.[199] Among those new penalties was the "forfeiture" to the government of any real or personal property belonging to such persons traceable to the proceeds obtained from such criminal activity and/or

used to commit or to promote the commission of the activity
including the possibility of such forfeitures even before trial.[20]

The federal RICO law (and that of many states) include
obscenity crimes among those that can trigger such drastic
new remedies. In 1989, and again in 1990, cases involving the
forfeiture provisions of obscenity-based RICO cases reached
the Supreme Court.

In 1989, in *Fort Wayne Books, Inc. v. Indiana*,[201] the Court
declared unconstitutional the pretrial forfeiture provisions of
Indiana's RICO law. As authorized by that law, the county
sheriff had seized before trial all the contents of several adult
bookstores and padlocked the stores. Although the Court ex
pressly held that there was nothing unconstitutional about
subjecting obscenity offenses to the drastically enhanced penal
ties of RICO laws, it also held that the pretrial seizures could not
be squared with the Court's long-standing view "that rigorous
procedural safeguards must be employed before expressive
materials can be seized as 'obscene.'"[202] As the Court put it:

> Our cases firmly hold that mere probable cause to believe
> a legal violation has transpired is not adequate to remove
> books or films from circulation. . . . The elements of a
> RICO violation other than the predicate crimes remain to
> be established in this case; e.g., whether the obscenity
> violations by the three corporations or their employees
> established a pattern of racketeering activity, and whether
> the assets seized were forfeitable under the State's [RICO]
> statute. Therefore, the pretrial seizure at issue here was
> improper.[203]

The Court in the Indiana case did not directly address the
constitutionality of posttrial forfeiture of "expressive materials"
under RICO laws. However, in 1990, the Court was asked to
do just that. That case, *United States v. Pryba*,[204] involved a
federal RICO prosecution against the owners of nine video
rental stores and three bookstores in northern Virginia. The
prosecution involved the sale of little more than $100 worth of
allegedly obscene materials. After the defendants were con
victed, in addition to prison terms and substantial fines, the
trial court ordered the forfeiture of all the defendants' busi
nesses and their contents, including materials that were not
legally obscene.[205]

The federal court of appeals hearing the case upheld the forfeitures in their entirety. As that court stated:

> The forfeiture provided by [the federal RICO Act] does not violate the First Amendment even though certain materials, books and magazines, that are forfeited, may not be obscene and, in other circumstances, would have constitutional protection as free expression. There was a nexus established between defendants' ill gotten gains from their racketeering activities and the protected materials that were forfeited. The forfeiture did not occur until after defendants were convicted of violating various obscenity statutes and of participating in a racketeering activity, and until after it was established beyond a reasonable doubt that the proceeds from these criminal activities had been used to acquire the arguable protected publications.[206]

In October 1990, the Supreme Court declined to review that decision,[207] thus letting it stand and at best leaving for another case whether such drastic forfeitures of constitutionally protected expressive materials can be reconciled with the First Amendment.

What about censorship efforts by private individuals and groups?

The First Amendment, like the other provisions of the Bill of Rights, is addressed to the federal government and by judicial interpretation to state and local governments. But it does not apply to purely private conduct. As a result, there is nothing illegal or unconstitutional about a private publisher's or bookstore owner's refusing to handle any material based on its content, whether political, sexual, or otherwise. And there is nothing illegal or unconstitutional about a person's refusal to purchase, read, or view any material because of its content. Indeed, such decisions are a necessary and precious concomitant of the First Amendment's commitment to free speech and free thought.

As a result, the activities of private individuals and groups that seek to persuade and pressure members of the consuming public and publishers, retailers, networks, and advertisers, among others, to shun certain materials because of their sexual content are themselves protected by the First Amendment

unless they violate other laws unrelated to their message. Simi
larly, the decisions made by the targets of such efforts are
protected by the First Amendment, so that a television network
or chain of convenience stores that succumbs to such pressure
and decides to stop offering certain materials can do so withou
violating any law.

Of course, all such efforts are specifically intended to limi
(indeed to censor) the freedoms of those targets to acquire
publish, and disseminate materials based on their persona
choice and tastes. Those efforts are anathema to the true mean
ing and spirit of the First Amendment, whatever one may think
of the materials such people seek to suppress, and all such
efforts should be resisted and opposed as vigorously as if those
efforts emanated from the government.

Occasionally such efforts are made by organizations that are
created by or affiliated with governmental bodies or officials
For example, in *Bantam Books, Inc. v. Sullivan*,[208] the Supreme
Court declared unconstitutional informal actions taken by a
group called The Rhode Island Commission to Encourage Mo
rality in Youth, which was not a government agency but had
ties to the state's attorney general. As the Supreme Court put it,
"The direct and obviously intended result of the Commission's
activities was to curtail the circulation in Rhode Island of books
published by appellants. . . . Unless [the publisher] is permitted to sue, infringements of freedom of the press may too often
go unremedied."[209] In such cases, the courts have held that the
First Amendment prohibits informal and indirect efforts at
censorship by such quasi-governmental entities as fully as if
those efforts were made directly by the government.

Creative people should be vigilant of, and resist as vigorously
as possible, all efforts to restrict what they can create, what
publishers can publish and readers read, while recognizing the
rights of others not to create, publish, or read such materials.
Only in that way can the precious First Amendment rights of
all people be fully respected and implemented.

NOTES

1. Countless books, monographs, treatises, articles, and other writings
   deal with obscenity, and many of them discuss the impact of obscenity

laws upon freedom of expression. Particularly useful and influential are two works by Professor Thomas Emerson, *The System of Freedom of Expression* at 476–515 (1970) and "First Amendment Doctrine and the Burger Court," 68 *Cal. L. Rev.* 422 (1980); *see also* L. Tribe, *American Constitutional Law* at 656–70 (1978) (this leading general constitutional treatise is widely cited and provides a useful although brief treatment highly critical of the Supreme Court's failure to recognize First Amendment rights in the field of obscenity).

2. According to the *Random House College Dictionary* (1972), the meaning of *obscenity* is "1—That which is offensive to modesty or decency; lewd. 2—That which causes or intends to cause sexual excitement or lust. 3—That which is abominable or disgusting; repulsive: an obscene exhibition of public discourtesy.'" The definition of *pornography* is "Obscene literature, art or photography, esp. that having little or no artistic merit."

3. The classic statement summarily excluding obscenity, and certain other categories of expression, from First Amendment coverage appears in *Chaplinsky v. New Hampshire,* 315 U.S. 568, 571–72 (1942): "There are certain well-defined and narrowly limited classes of speech, the prevention and punishment of which have never been thought to raise any Constitutional problem. These include the lewd and obscene, the profane, the libelous, and the insulting or 'fighting' words. . . . It has been well observed that such utterances are no essential part of any exposition of ideas, and are of such slight social value as a step to truth that any benefit that may be derived from them is clearly outweighed by the social interest in order and morality." *See also Beauharnais v. Illinois,* 343 U.S. 250 (1952) (libel not covered by First Amendment).

4. *United States v. Reidel,* 402 U.S. 351 (1971); *United States v. Thirty-Seven (37) Photographs,* 402 U.S. 363 (1971).

5. *Stanley v. Georgia,* 394 U.S. 557 (1969). In 1990 the rule of the *Stanley* case was held inapplicable to the possession of child pornography. *Osborne v. Ohio,* 495 U.S. 103, 110 S.Ct. 1691 (1990).

6. *See, e.g., Carey v. Population Services International,* 431 U.S. 678 (1977) (a New York statute prohibiting advertising of contraceptives violated the First Amendment). The Supreme Court expressly rejected a contention that the advertisements could be prohibited as offensive or embarrassing, "at least where obscenity is not involved." The Court appeared to require a consideration of the obscenity of the advertisement and not of the material or transaction being promoted.

7. Legal limits on state and local power are reviewed later in the chapter in connection with *Miller v. California,* 413 U.S. 15 (1973) and related Supreme Court decisions.

8. State and local laws can vary, sometimes significantly, in their reac and severity and are constantly revised and reinterpreted, althoug they must adhere to the constitutional limits defined by the Suprem Court. The Media Coalition, an umbrella group that monitors obscen ity law developments, maintains an up-to-date collection of state an local laws. The Coalition is located at 900 Third Avenue, Suite 160(New York, NY 10022, (212) 891–2070.

9. *Joseph Burstyn, Inc. v. Wilson*, 343 U.S. 495 (1952). This was a Firs Amendment ruling, but the Court's rationale focused on the religiou freedom clause of the First Amendment: "It is not the business government in our nation to suppress real or imagined attacks upo a particular religious doctrine whether they appear in publications speeches, or motion pictures." *Id.* at 505.

10. *Kingsley International Pictures Corp. v. Regents*, 360 U.S. 684 (1959

11. *Id.* at 688–89.

12. For a brief review of the historical origins of American obscenit law, see generally Schauer, *The Law of Obscenity* at 1–29 (197((hereinafter, Schauer), and the historical materials cited in Schauer 2 n.3. This is by far the most useful authoritative single-volume tex on the law of obscenity and is a principal source for several part of this chapter. *See also, Report of the President's Commission o Obscenity and Pornography* (New York Times ed., 1970) (hereinafte *President's Commission Report*) at 348–54. Although the recommen dations of the *President's Commission Report* (which was accompanie by nine volumes of technical reports) have been largely ignored if n expressly rejected, it remains an invaluable source of information o obscenity. Also useful for background purposes is the *Final Report (the Attorney General's Commission on Pornography* (1986), als known as the Meese Commission.

13. For example, the first case to reach the law courts (rather than churc tribunals) refused to recognize obscenity as a common-law rather tha religious crime. *Queen v. Read*, Il Mod. Rep. 142, 88 Eng. Rep. 95 (1708).

14. The Vagrancy Act of 1824.

15. *See* Schauer at 6–7; *President's Commission Report* at 351.

16. *President's Commission Report* at 352.

17. *Commonwealth v. Holmes*, 17 Mass. 336 (1821) (assumed obscen libel was a common-law misdemeanor and upheld a conviction fo publishing an edition of *Fanny Hill*).

18. See Hentoff, *The First Freedom: The Tumultuous History of Fre Speech in America* at 55–76 (1980).

19. The First Amendment states: "Congress shall make no law respectin

an establishment of religion, or prohibiting the free exercise thereof; or abridging the freedom of speech, or of the press; or the right of the people peaceably to assemble, and to petition the government for a redress of grievances."

20. Laws of Vermont, 1824, ch. XXIII, No. 1, §23.

21. 5 Stat. 566, §28.

22. 13 Stat. 50 (1865).

23. 7 N.Y. Stats. 309 (1868).

24. 17 Stat. 598 (1873) (prohibiting the mailing of obscene publications), currently 18 U.S.C. §1461, still popularly known as the Comstock Act. A later statute extended the scope of federal jurisdiction over obscenity to any matter traveling through or via "interstate commerce." 29 Stat. 512 (1897), currently 18 U.S.C. §1462.

25. L.R. 3 Q.B. 360 (1868).

26. *United States v. One Book Called "Ulysses,"* 5 F. Supp. 182 (S.D.N.Y. 1933).

27. *People v. Dial Press*, 182 Misc. 416 (Magis. Ct. 1944).

28. *Commonwealth v. Friede*, 271 Mass. 318, 171 N.E. 472 (1930).

29. *Attorney General v. Book Named "God's Little Acre*," 326 Mass. 281, 93 N.E.2d 819 (1950).

30. *United States v. Two Obscene Books*, 99 F. Supp. 760 (N.D. Cal. 1951), *aff'd sub nom. Besig v. United States*, 208 F.2d 142 (9th Cir. 1953).

31. 354 U.S. 476 (1957).

32. *Id.* at 484.

33. *Id.* at 508–14.

34. 352 U.S. 380 (1957).

35. *Id.* at 383.

36. *Kingsley International Pictures Corp. v. Regents*, 360 U.S. 684 (1959).

37. *Manual Enterprises v. Day*, 370 U.S. 478 (1962).

38. 378 U.S. 184 (1964).

39. 383 U.S. 413 (1966).

40. *Id.* at 418.

41. 386 U.S. 767 (1967).

42. *See Miller v. California*, 413 U.S. 15, 22 n.3 (1973).

43. *See, e.g.*, Note, "Obscenity from Stanley to Karalexis: A Back Door Approach to First Amendment Protection," 23 *Vand. L. Rev.* 369 (1970); Katz, "Privacy and Pornography," 1969 *Sup. Ct. Rev.* 203 (1969); Comment, "Stanley v. Georgia: New Directions in Obscenity Regulation," 48 *Tex. L. Rev.* 646 (1970); "The Supreme Court, 1968 Term," 83 *Harv. L. Rev.* 7, 147 (1969).

44. 394 U.S. 557 (1969).

45. 394 U.S. at 565. Although there was no dissent in *Stanley*, there was no majority opinion. Justice Marshall's opinion announced the Court's judgment and was based upon constitutional protection for "mere private possession of obscene matter," *id.* at 559, with strong First Amendment overtones as well. Justices Stewart, Brennan, and White believed the conviction should be overturned because of an illegal search and seizure and did not join Justice Marshall in deciding the other constitutional issues. Justice Black adhered to his position that all obscenity laws are constitutionally impermissible under the First Amendment.

46. *See, e.g., Karalexis v. Byrne*, 306 F. Supp. 1363 (D. Mass. 1969) (principles of *Stanley* applied to theatres open only to "consenting adults"), *vacated and remanded*, 401 U.S. 216 (1971); *United States v. Thirty-Seven Photographs*, 309 F. Supp. 36 (C.D. Cal. 1970) (principles of *Stanley* applied to importation for personal use), *rev'd*, 402 U.S. 363 (1971).

47. *See President's Commission Report* at 32, 59; *see generally* 169–309. These findings have been widely criticized, primarily by those wishing to justify continued enforcement or enactment of obscenity laws. *See, e.g., President's Commission Report* at 456–505, 578–623 (dissenting report of Commissioners Hill, Link, and Keating).

48. *President's Commission Report* at 57.

49. 413 U.S. 15 (1973).

50. *Id.* at 18–19.

51. *Paris Adult Theatre I v. Slaton*, 413 U.S. 49, 58–60 (1973).

52. *Id.* at 6061.

53. Incredibly, the majority's only citation to the *President's Commission Report* was to the Hill-Link minority report. *Paris Adult Theatre I*, *supra* note 51, at 58 nn.7–8.

54. *Miller*, *supra* note 42, at 27.

55. *Id.* at 34, 35.

56. *Id.* at 35–36.

57. *Paris Adult Theatre I*, *supra* note 51, at 73.

58. *Id.* at 79, 84.

59. *Id.* at 113.

60. *Miller* was decided by a 5–4 vote, but this one-vote margin has held firm for almost two decades. With the retirement of Justice Brennan in 1990, and Justice Marshall in 1991, the Court has lost its most eloquent and effective voices against the restrictive and repressive atmosphere encouraged by *Miller* and the cases that followed it.

61. *See Miller v. California*, *supra* note 42. Each of these branches of the *Miller* definition of obscenity is explored in detail later in the chapter.

62. 413 U.S. 115 (1973). *Kaplan* involved a book that "contains no pictures.

It is made up entirely of repetitive descriptions of physical, sexual conduct, 'clinically' explicit and offensive." *Id.* at 116–17.

63. *Miller, supra* note 42, at 25.

64. 418 U.S. 153 (1974).

65. *Id.* at 160–61. Even depiction or description of sexual intercourse or other similar explicit sexual conduct is not per se "hard core" (and therefore obscene). According to Schauer at 112, although normal heterosexual intercourse may be found to be obscene, "most hard-core pornography emphasizes other sexual practices, such as homosexuality, bestiality, flagellation, sadomasochism, fellatio, cunnilingus, and the like."

66. *Jenkins v. Georgia, supra* note 64, at 161.

67. Schauer at 111–12.

68. *New York v. Ferber*, 458 U.S. 747 (1982).

69. Schauer at 104, 103. See also *United States v. Various Articles, Schedule 2102*, 707 F.2d 132 (2d Cir 1983).

70. Schauer at 102, citing A.L.I. Model Penal Code §251.4 (1962).

72. *Manual Enterprises v. Day*, 370 U.S. 478, 482 (1962).

73. *Jacobellis v. Ohio*, 378 U.S. 184, 191–92 (1964) (Brennan, J.).

74. 383 U.S. 413, 418 (1966).

75. *Roth v. United States, supra* note 31, at 487 n.20.

76. Schauer at 98.

77. See *Roth v. United States, supra* note 31, at 489–90.

78. *Compare* the "particular-sensibility" test of *Regina v. Hicklin*, [1868] L.R., 3 Q.B. 360, *with United States v. Levine*, 83 F.2d 156 (2d Cir. 1936) (reversible error to instruct a jury that obscenity must be judged in terms of its likely effect on "the young and immature, the ignorant and those who are sensually inclined").

78. The requirement of adult standards was made clear in *Butler v. Michigan*, 352 U.S. 380 (1957), where a statute was invalidated because it would have "reduce[d] the adult population to reading only what is fit for children." *Id.* at 383. *See also Pinkus v. United States*, 436 U.S. 293, 296 (1978) (reversing an obscenity conviction based on an instruction inviting the jury to consider "young and old . . . men, women and children" in determining the standards to be applied). But *Pinkus* permitted a jury to consider the "sensitive" and the "insensitive" in attempting to determine the standard for a hypothetical average person in the community, apparently on a theory that considering all persons in the community will lead to a correct appreciation of the views of an average person.

79. See *Mishkin v. New York*, 383 U.S. 502 (1966); *Hamling v. United States*, 418 U.S. 87, 128–30 (1974); *Pinkus v. United States, supra* note 78, at 301–3.

80. *Roth v. United States, supra* note 31, at 489.
81. *Manual Enterprises v. Day*, 370 U.S. 478, 488 (1962) (Harlan, J).
82. *Jacobellis v. Ohio*, 378 U.S. 184 (1964).
83. *Id.* at 195.
84. Indeed, according to Schauer, every federal court which considered the community standards issue after *Jacobellis* and before *Miller* selected a national standard. *See* Schauer at 119 n.19 and cases cited therein.
85. 413 U.S. 15, 32 (1973).
86. *Id.* at 32–33 n.13.
87. Schauer at 123.
88. *See, e.g., Penthouse International, Ltd. v. McAuliffe*, 7 Med. L. Rptr. 1798, 1802 (N.D. Ga. 1981): "It is clear that 'serious value' is not to be judged by the tastes of the 'average person' or measured in terms of 'community standards.'" *Miller v. California*, 413 U.S. at 30; *Smith v. United States*, 431 U.S. at 301.
89. *Pope v. Illinois*, 481 U.S. 447 (1987).
90. *Miller, supra* note 42, at 24. The list of "serious" values in *Miller*—literary, artistic, political and scientific—unlike the list of hard-core sexual activities, is said not to be by way of example but to be all inclusive. Still, the four categories should be viewed expansively; there appear to be other related values that will be expressly or implicitly recognized in appropriate cases. Certainly this would include serious "educational" value, a category which could be subsumed under one or more of the enumerated values. Schauer speculates that the Court may not have included educational value in order to avoid the suggestion that any educational aspect would satisfy the test, since any material, however obscene, would arguably teach a person something. Schauer at 142. Similarly, the omission of entertainment value should not be read as suggesting that serious works that are also entertaining are not protected. In fact, the Court has on many occasions held that entertainment is protected by the First Amendment, most recently in *Schad v. Borough of Mount Ephraim*, 452 U.S. 61 (1981) (applying First Amendment protection to live entertainment in a zoning case).
91. Schauer at 140.
92. *Louisiana v. Walden Book Company*, 6 Med. L. Rptr. 1696 (La. 1980).
93. *Penthouse International, Ltd. v. McAuliffe*, 610 F.2d 1353, 1372 (5th Cir. 1980). Serious value is particularly difficult to assess for magazines or other collections of generally unrelated poetry, short stories, or articles. It is not easy to judge such works as a whole, and

courts are put to the task of weighing the relative merits of more and less valuable matter.

94. *Mitchell v. Delaware,* 6 Med. L. Rptr. 1988 (Del. Super. 1980) (serious political value in movie *Caligula,* although it lacks serious literary, artistic, or scientific value); *Penthouse International, Ltd. v. McAuliffe,* 7 Med. L. Rptr. 1798 (N.D. Ga. 1981) (serious political and artistic, but not literary and scientific, value in *Caligula*).

95. *Roth v. United States, supra* note 31, at 489.

96. *Kois v. Wisconsin,* 408 U.S. 229, 231 (1972).

97. *City of Cincinnati v. Contemporary Arts Center,* No. 90-CRB 11700 A&B, filed Sept. 6, 1990 (order denying motion to dismiss).

98. *Id.*

99. *Skywalker Records, Inc. v. Navarro,* 739 F.Supp. 578 (S.D. Fla. 1990).

00. *Id.*

01. *Id.*

02. *Id.*

03. *See Lambert v. California,* 355 U.S. 225 (1957).

04. 361 U.S. 147 (1959). The requirement of scienter relates primarily to criminal laws; in general, it has limited relevance to civil obscenity regulations.

05. *Hamling v. United States,* 418 U.S. 87 (1974) (citing with approval *Rosen v. United States,* 161 U.S. 29 [1896]). *See also, Young v. Abrams,* 698 F.2d 131 (2d Cir. 1983).

06. The pandering doctrine was first fully developed in *Ginzburg v. United States,* 383 U.S. 463 (1966) and has been expressly upheld by the Supreme Court in two subsequent cases: *Hamling v. United States,* 418 U.S. 87 (1974), and *Splawn v. California,* 431 U.S. 595 (1977).

07. *See Papish v. Board of Curators of University of Missouri,* 410 U.S. 667 (1973) where the lower court found pandering but the Supreme Court reversed on the ground that the materials were clearly protected by the First Amendment. Pandering is not a separate criminal offense but merely "evidence" of obscenity. *See* Schauer at 80–87.

08. 390 U.S. 629 (1968).

09. *See* Schauer at 89.

10. This would include the requirement of specificity in statutory offenses defining matter harmful to minors; due-process safeguards; protections for ideas, vulgar language, or mere nudity; and limitation to sexually explicit matter rather than violence or other "thematic" obscenity. *See* Schauer at 89–91.

11. Schauer at 94–95.

112. *See, e.g., FCC v. Pacifica Foundation,* 438 U.S. 726 (1978); *New York v. Ferber,* 458 U.S. 747 (1982).
113. *See, e.g.,* N.Y. Penal Law §§263.00 *et seq.*
114. *People v. Ferber,* 52 N.Y. 2d 674 (1981).
115. *New York v. Ferber,* 458 U.S. 747 (1982).
116. *See, e.g., St. Martin's Press v. Carey,* 605 F. 2d 41 (2d Cir. 1979) which involved an unsuccessful attempt by the publisher of the sex education book *Show Me!* to enjoin enforcement of the New York statute against that book. After the Supreme Court upheld the statute, the publisher withdrew the book from circulation.
117. *Osborne v. Ohio, supra* note 5.
118. *Id.* at 1696–97.
119. *See, e.g.,* City of Paramount, Calif., Ord. No. 478, Paramount Mun. Code, Chapter 11A, *discussed in American Booksellers Association v. Superior Court,* 8 Med. L. Rptr. 2014 (Cal. Ct. App. 1982).
120. *Id.*
121. *American Booksellers Association v. McAuliffe,* 7 Med. L. Rptr. 2281 (N.D. Ga. 1981); *American Booksellers v. Superior Court, supra* note 119; *Tattered Cover, Inc. v. Tooley,* Case No. 81 CV 9693 (Dist. Ct. Denver Co.) (unreported decision of Jan. 7, 1982).
122. *American Booksellers Association v. McAuliffe, supra* note 119.
123. *Tattered Cover, Inc. v. Tooley, supra* note 121.
124. *American Booksellers Association v. Superior Court, supra* note 119.
125. *Id.* at 2017–18.
126. *Id.* at 2017.
127. *Virginia v. American Booksellers Association, Inc.,* 484 U.S. 383 (1988).
128. Va. Code §18.2–391(a) (Supp. 1985).
129. *American Booksellers Association, Inc. v. Commonwealth of Virginia,* 802 F.2d 691 (4th Cir. 1986).
130. *Id.*
131. *Virginia v. American Booksellers Association, Inc., supra* note 127.
132. *Commonwealth v. American Booksellers Association, Inc.,* 236 Va. 168, 372 S.E.2d 618 (1988).
133. But see a small number of Federal Communications Commission proceedings cited in *FCC v. Pacifica Foundation,* 438 U.S. 726, 740 n.16 (1978).
134. *Compare Red Lion Broadcasting Co. v. FCC,* 395 U.S. 367 (1969) (upholding FCC broadcast regulations on "fairness," personal attack, and political editorializing against a First Amendment challenge) *with Miami Herald Publishing Co. v. Tornillo,* 418 U.S. 241 (1974) (overturning on First Amendment grounds a state statute requiring

a kind of public access to newspapers to reply to political positions espoused in those papers).

35. 438 U.S. 726 (1978).

36. *See, e.g., Cohen v. California,* 403 U.S. 15 (1971).

37. Justices Brennan, White, Marshall, and Stewart dissented, making this another of the Supreme Court's narrow 5–4 decisions. The opinion was even more divided in that two of the justices in the majority (Powell and Blackmun) dissociated themselves from a key portion of the majority opinion that would have endorsed different levels of protection depending upon a judicial analysis of the "value" of the expression. Compare Part IV(B) of Justice Stevens' majority opinion with Part II of Justice Powell's concurring opinion.

38. 438 U.S. at 748.

39. This position was recently advocated in a major paper issued by the National Cable Television Association.

40. *Home Box Office, Inc. v. Wilkinson,* 8 Med. L. Rptr. 1108 (D. Utah 1982). *See also Community Television of Utah, Inc. v. Roy City,* No. NC 82–01221 and NC 82–0171J (D. Utah 1982), 9 Med. L. Rptr. No. 24, "News Notes," July 12, 1983.

41. 8 Med. L. Rptr. at 1117–18.

42. 47 U.S.C. §§521 *et seq.*

43. *Id.* at 532.

44. *American Booksellers Association, Inc. v. Hudnut,* 771 F.2d 323 (7th Cir. 1985).

45. Indianapolis Code, §16–3(q).

46. *Id.*

47. *American Booksellers Association, Inc. v. Hudnut, supra* note 144, at 325.

48. *Id.*

49. *Young v. American Mini Theatres,* 427 U.S. 50 (1976).

50. *Id.* at 70–71.

51. 452 U.S. 61, 68 (1981). See also *Basiardanes v. City of Galveston,* 682 F.2d 1203 (5th Cir. 1982); *Alexander v. City of Minneapolis,* 798 F.2d 936 (8th Cir. 1983); *CLR Corp. v. Henline,* 702 F.2d 637 (6th Cir. 1983).

52. *City of Renton v. Playtime Theatres, Inc.,* 475 U.S. 41 (1986).

53. *Id.* at 44.

54. *Id.* at 52.

55. *Id.* at 54.

56. *Barnes v. Glen Theatre, Inc.,* 111 S. Ct. 2456, 59 U.S.L.W. 4745 (1991).

57. *Id.* at 4748.

158. *Id.*
159. *Id.* at 4751.
160. *Id.* at 4752.
161. *Attorney General's Commission on Pornography Final Report* (1986
162. *Id.*
163. *Id.* at 266.
164. Id. at 269.
165. *Id.* at 321.
166. *Id.* at 326.
167. *Id.* at 329.
168. *Id.* at 331.
169. *Id.* at 334.
170. *Id.* at 337.
171. *Id.*
172. *Id.*
173. *Id.* at 377.
174. *Id.* at 382–84.
175. *Id.*
176. *See* Monaghan, "First Amendment 'Due Process,'" 83 *Harv. L. Re*
     518 (1970).
177. Chief Justice Burger, in *Paris Adult Theatre I v. Slaton*, 413 U.
     49, 55 (1973), approved a prior civil injunction proceeding institute
     by the state of Georgia, stating that "such a procedure provides a
     exhibitor or purveyor of materials the best possible notice, prior
     any criminal indictments, as to whether the materials are unpr
     tected by the First Amendment and subject to state regulation
     Justice Douglas, dissenting in *Miller*, also endorsed such civil pr
     ceedings: "Until a civil proceeding has placed a tract beyond th
     pale, no criminal prosecution should be sustained." 413 U.S. at 4
178. An example of a "mandatory" civil proceeding requiring a civil dete
     mination of obscenity before any criminal action can be commence
     is Mass. Ann. Laws, ch. 272, §28c. An example of a nonmandato
     proceeding is Ala. Code Title 14, §374.
179. *See, e.g., New York Times Co. v. United States*, 403 U.S. 713 197
     (the "Pentagon Papers" case).
180. *See, e.g., Blount v. Rizzi*, 400 U.S. 410 (1971); *Roaden v. Kentuck*
     413 U.S. 497 (1973); *Lee Art Theatre v. Virginia*, 392 U.S. 636 (196
     (per curiam).
181. 380 U.S. 51 (1965).
182. *Id.* at 57.
183. *Id.* at 58–59.
184. *See, e.g., Blount v. Rizzi*, 400 U.S. 410 (1971).

185. *See, e.g., Roaden v. Kentucky,* 413 U.S. 497 (1973); *Lee Art Theatre v. Virginia,* 392 U.S. 636 (1968) (per curiam).

186. *Southeastern Promotions Ltd. v. Conrad,* 420 U.S. 546 (1975).

187. *FW/PBS, Inc. d/b/a Paris Adult Bookstore II v. City of Dallas,* 493 U.S. 215, 110 S. Ct. 596, 606 (1990).

188. *McKinney v. Alabama,* 424 U.S. 669 (1976).

189. *Id.* at 676–77.

190. *Id.* at 683–84.

191. *Cooper v. Mitchell Brothers,* 454 U.S. 90 (1981) (per curiam) (nuisance abatement). As might be expected, Justice Brennan dissented, along with Justices Marshall and Stevens, although Justice Stevens did not express his views on the First Amendment issue.

192. *Id.* The Court sent the case back to the California state courts, which then adopted the clear-and-convincing-evidence test as required by both state and federal constitutional law. 128 Cal. App. 3d 937, 180 Cal. Rptr. 728 (Ct. App.), *cert. denied,* 103 S. Ct. 259 (1982).

193. *See, e.g.,* arts. 4666, 4667, Texas Revised Civil Statutes, discussed in *Vance v. Universal Amusement Co., Inc., infra* note 194.

194. 445 U.S. 308 (1980).

195. *Id.* at 314 n.8.

196. *Id.* at 315–16.

197. *Id.* at 316 n.13.

198. *Id.* at 316.

199. *See* 18 U.S.C. §§1961 *et seq.*

200. *Id.*

201. 109 S. Ct. 916 (1989).

202. *Id.* at 927.

203. *Id.* at 929.

204. *United States v. Pryba,* 900 F.2d 748 (4th Cir.), *cert. denied,* U.S. , 111 S. Ct. 305 (1990).

205. *United States v. Pryba,* 678 F. Supp. 1225 (E.D.Va. 1988).

206. *United States v. Pryba, supra* note 204, at 755.

207. 111 S. Ct. 305 (1990).

208. 372 U.S. 58 (1963).

209. *Id.* at 64, n.6.

VI
Business and Tax Matters Affecting Creative People

Authors, artists, and other creative people who sell their work or otherwise derive a financial benefit from it are "in business" and must make decisions about the way they conduct their businesses. They are also taxpayers—on the federal, state, and perhaps local level—and should be aware of how tax laws affect them and what steps they can take to minimize their taxes. Also, alas, they will all die and should be concerned about the estates they will leave behind.

A full discussion of these issues is beyond the scope of this chapter. Instead, we will discuss some of the most common business, tax, and estate questions that affect creative people.

What are the available ways of doing business?
One creative person can conduct business as a *sole proprietorship* or as a *corporation*. If the creative person joins forces with one or more colleagues, a third method, a *partnership*, is available.

What is a sole proprietorship, and how is it different from a corporation?
A sole proprietorship, the way of doing business used by most creative people, means that the author or artist is in business for herself, period. There are no other business entities (except, perhaps, agents or galleries) that stand between such creators and everyone they deal with, including the purchasers of their work.

This is the simplest form of doing business, but it may not be the wisest or the most economical for every creator. A sole proprietor is personally responsible for everything he does, including purchasing supplies, renting a studio, hiring assistants or other staff, and countless other everyday activities. If debts cannot be paid, there is an accident in the studio and someone is hurt, or an assistant defrauds a publisher or a gallery, the sole proprietor may be held personally liable, with creditors or victims collecting what is due from the proprietor's personal income and assets. This unlimited personal liability is a principal reason why many people prefer to do business as a corporation, where the individual's liability is more limited. If the risks of unlimited liability are not significant or can be insured, incorporation becomes less attractive.

Corporations are separate entities for tax purposes, and creative people who incorporate must prepare separate returns and pay separate taxes for the corporation and for themselves as individuals (unless they become what is known as an "S" corporation, in which event the corporation's finances are deemed to pass directly to the individual shareholder; this is discussed further below). However, because of the difference in tax rates between corporations and individuals, and other differences in tax law, a creative person who incorporates may pay less total tax than would have been paid as a sole proprietorship. (Tax laws affecting creative people are discussed later in this chapter.)

Incorporation involves expenses that a sole proprietorship does not. It is a more cumbersome way of doing business, and many creative people will not get significant tax or other benefits from it. Those who are in doubt about whether to incorporate should consult an accountant or lawyer familiar with such matters.

What does incorporation entail?

A corporation is in a sense a legal fiction—an entity created by the law that exists only in the eyes of the law. It cannot be seen or touched or talked to. It can conduct business, and hire and fire employees, but only if and when the people who own it tell it to.

Although it is more complicated than a sole proprietorship, a corporation is relatively easy to create. Forming one does not require the services of a lawyer. Essentially, one need only choose a corporate name, make sure the name is available by checking with the appropriate state agency (usually the secretary of state), prepare appropriate documents (the forms for which can usually be obtained from the agency), and deliver them with the necessary fees to the agency.

In most states, it is legal (and common) for a corporation to have only one shareholder, who is also its board of directors

and staff. The individual, having formed a corporation, nee
not involve anyone else in the conduct of its business. To
the outside world, she would look no different from the sole
proprietorship through which that business was conducted the
day before. But to the law and to those with whom the corpora
tion does business the differences are real and important.

Individual shareholders, directors, and employees of corpo
rations are generally not personally liable for the debts o
obligations of the corporation. Creditors, accident victims, o
the like can look only to the corporation for satisfaction, and
the assets a small corporation has available to provide tha
satisfaction are usually far more limited than those owned by the
individual. In effect, shareholders are insulated from persona
liability in many (but not necessarily all) of those situations in
which the sole proprietor would be fully liable. There would
be no such insulation for accidents actually caused by the indi
vidual or where the individual personally guaranteed paymen
of the corporation's obligations, which is frequently required
for small corporations.

The corporate structure works like this: Mary Artist has jus
formed Mary Artist, Inc. She becomes its only shareholder. A
such, she elects the board of directors, which consists solely o
herself. As the board of directors, she designates herself a
president and secretary (indeed the entire staff) and as the
authorized check signer on the corporate bank account. She
opens that account in the name of the corporation with a deposit
of, say, $250 of her own money, which is treated as paymen
for the shares of stock issued to her (which is how she became
the sole shareholder). A work schedule and salary are agreed
upon, with perhaps even a written employment contract, and
Mary goes to work. Legally, she now works for the corporation,
not herself. The paintings she creates belong to the corporation
which can decide when and for how much to sell them. Pro
ceeds from sales belong to the corporation and are used to pay
Mary's salary, the corporate rent, and other bills for her studio
and supplies. If any profits remain, they can be applied in a
number of ways.

The corporation and Mary must each file a separate income
tax return. Mary has to report only the salary she receives from
the corporation, and the corporation can deduct that salary
from its reported income. It can also deduct many other uses

of its income: for example, fringe benefits such as health and life insurance for Mary, placing part of the gross income in profit-sharing or pension plans for Mary's benefit, or mounting an exhibition of Mary's work. In this way, Mary can control her personal reportable income and at the same time enjoy fringe benefits that the corporation can deduct from its taxes, benefits that might not be deductible by Mary if she acquired them as a sole proprietor.

Incorporation can provide meaningful tax benefits in some cases. But such benefits are much less significant, even nonexistent, for the individual who must use a limited income just to make ends meet.

What about partnerships?

Partnerships are essentially sole proprietorships consisting of more than one proprietor. They do not provide the limited-liability protection of corporations; indeed, each partner can be held liable for obligations incurred by the others in the course of the partnership business. And they do not provide some of the tax advantages available from corporations. But they do enable several persons to pool their resources for their mutual benefit and to share profits and losses in accordance with any formula they choose.

How do tax laws treat creative people?

Prior to the Tax Reform Act of 1986, which made significant changes to this country's tax laws, those laws were decidedly unfriendly to creative people. And although that adverse treatment was for a while somewhat alleviated, by 1990 it became clear that that kind of treatment will once again be an unpleasant fact of life for all creators.

Under long-standing provisions of our federal tax law, works created by authors, artists, and other creative people are not considered "capital assets" and thus are not entitled to "capital-gains" treatment under those laws. More specifically, the law provides that "a copyright, a literary, musical, or artistic composition, a letter or memorandum, or similar property held by . . . a taxpayer whose personal efforts created such property" is ineligible for capital-gains treatment.[2] What this means is that when an artist sells a painting or an author grants publishing or movie rights to a book, his income (or "profit," or "gain") from that sale is treated as "ordinary income" for federal tax purpose and not as a "capital gain," which would be the case if the sam artist sold a similar work that he purchased from another artist

Prior to the 1986 changes, the applicable tax rates for ordi nary income were substantially higher than for capital gains and the creator selling her work had to pay taxes on those sale at those much higher rates. The 1986 Act drastically reduce the applicable rates for ordinary income and thus effectivel removed the difference between the rates for ordinary incom and capital gains. As a result the taxes payable by an artist o the sale of a work would be the same as if the work wer considered a capital asset. To that extent, the previous discrep ancy in treatment was eliminated.

However, since sales of taxpayer-created works are still de nied capital-gains treatment and since by 1991 it has becom clear that income-tax rates on ordinary income (but not capita gains) will be ever-increasing, that equality of treatment wil prove a temporary phenomenon. Once again, creative peopl who sell or grant rights in their own works will be forced to pa significantly higher taxes (all in the year the income is received than would be the case if capital-gains treatment were availabl for those sales. In the view of many, the creations of authors artists, and other creative people, particularly where they hav required much time and effort to produce and where thei value may appreciate substantially after they are created bu before they are sold, should be treated as capital assets.

How are royalties, fees, and other income received by cre ative people treated?

As with the funds received from the sale of a work, fund received by creative people as compensation for the grant o rights to a work or for creative services rendered (whethe in the form of royalties, fees, salary, profit participation, o otherwise) are also treated as ordinary income in the year suc funds are received. This too can create special burdens o creators; for example, an author who puts in 10 or even 20 year working on a book, during which she lives on savings or part time work and then enters into a publishing contract with substantial advance against royalties, has to pay income tax o the full amount of the advance in the year in which it wa eceived with no ability to "average" that tax over a period of years (as was possible before the Tax Reform Act of 1986).

The "fair market value" of prizes, awards, and the like must be treated as ordinary income.[3] The Tax Reform Act of 1986 significantly restricted the prior rather generous treatment of fellowships and scholarships, under which they were generally excluded from taxes. Now only candidates for degrees can exclude such funds from their reportable income and only to the extent that they are to be used for tuition, fees, books, and supplies required for coursework.[4] Any portion of a scholarship or fellowship that represents payment for teaching, research, or other services must be reported as income.[5]

Creative people who are self-employed and engaged in a trade or business (discussed further below) are also responsible for the federal self-employment tax that is imposed on all self-employed income, including royalties, for the purposes of old-age, survivors, disability and hospital insurance benefits (Social Security benefits).

What is an "S" corporation?

Under certain circumstances, a creative person can elect to incorporate his business but still be treated for federal tax purposes as an individual and not as a corporation. In this way, he gets the other benefits of incorporation, including limited legal liability, while avoiding the requirements of paying both corporate and individual taxes. There are a number of rules and regulations that must be complied with, but if they can be satisfied, choosing "S" treatment is often a wise course for creative people.[6]

When are a creator's expenses deductible?

Like all taxpayers, creative people (as individuals or corporations) may deduct their "ordinary and necessary expenses incurred during the taxable year in carrying out any trade or business."[7] This presupposes that the creator is engaged in the "trade or business" of creating works. The test is whether the creator's primary purpose and intention in engaging in the activity is to make a profit, and that expectation need not be a reasonable one so long as it sincere and not a sham. Indeed, one court went out of its way to emphasize that this test would be met even if there was no realistic expectation of profit:

That the objective, not the expectation, of making a profit is to govern determinations on whether a taxpayer is engaged in a business or a hobby, and the two criteria are not the same. One may embark upon a venture for the sincere purpose of eventually reaping a profit but in the belief that the probability of financial success is small or even remote. He therefore does not really expect a profit, but nonetheless is willing to take the gamble. . . . It cannot be gainsaid the "the activity actually is engaged in for profit"—that it was undertaken "with the objective of making a profit."[8]

Moreover, the absence of income does not prevent an enterprise from being classified as a trade or business. Also, an individual may engage in more than one trade or business. To this extent, the tax laws make it possible for creative people to deduct their creative expenses even while they engage in other jobs or professions and even if they don't have income from those creative efforts in the years in which they deduct those expenses.

It is not always easy to know whether an author or artist will be treated as a trade or business, but the Internal Revenue Code contains a presumption that if gross income exceeded expenses in 3 of the previous 5 years, the taxpayer is in business and can deduct expenses.[9]

If the creator qualifies as a trade or business, she can deduct expenses directly from gross income (on Schedule C) without having to itemize them (on Schedule A). This is preferable from a tax point of view to having to treat those expenses as (Schedule A) itemized deductions, which (if the expenses are deductible at all) would be the case if "trade or business" treatment is not available.

What if a creator doesn't qualify as a trade or business?

Even if the creator doesn't qualify as a trade or business, he can deduct expenses incurred in the creation of a work if those expenses are incurred "for the production . . . of income."[10] However, those expenses must be itemized on Schedule A, and creators who do not itemize deductions will not be able to take those deductions. Also, there are specific limits and restrictions on the permissible amounts of such deductions. The Internal Revenue Service has set forth nine factors that are to be considered in determining whether expenses were incurred for the production of income,[11] which factors have been summarized as follows:

> In order for creative activity to qualify as being carried on primarily for the production of income, all the circumstances of the transaction are considered. The taxpayer's intent to produce income from the writing or artistic activity is not by itself sufficient. The relevant factors are the intention of the [creative person], the record of prior gain or loss, the relation between the type of activity and the principal occupation of the individual and the uses to which the writing or artwork is put. Obviously, similarities exist between the criteria for determining if an activity is a trade or business. The difference, however, is in the scope of the activities to be considered.
>
> The entire enterprise is considered when determining if a [creative person] is engaged in [a trade or business]. . . . However, a single transaction may be carried on for the production of income. Thus, although qualification under the production of income provision does not have the same tax advantages as qualification under the trade or business provisions, qualification is somewhat easier.[12]

What if a creator's expenses do not qualify for either "trade or business" or "production of income" treatment?

Under such circumstances, the "hobby-loss" rules apply.[13] Under those rules, a creator can claim deductions for the expenses incurred while pursuing his or her creative activity, but only to the extent that the gross income derived from that activity during the tax year exceeds the deductions that he or she is otherwise allowed to claim. As with expenses incurred for the production of income, there are limitations and restrictions on the extent to which hobby expenses are deductible. The key factor that indicates that a creative person is engaged in a hobby and not a trade or business or working for the production of income is the lack of a bona fide expectation-objective of realizing a profit.

**Are there any special requirements for a creator's deduc-
tions?**

The Tax Reform Act of 1986 attempted to change the way a
creative person could claim deductions for expenses.[14] Essentially, those changes required creative people to keep elaborate
records of their expenses and to allocate those expenses to the
various works on which they were incurred. Thus, somehow
an author had to allocate among her works her expenses for
typing paper or computer disks, and an artist had to allocate
her expenses for paints, brushes, and easels. These changes
were strongly protested by creative people and their organizations, and by 1988, they were substantially alleviated.[15] Under
legislation enacted in that year, those allocation requirements
do not apply to "qualified creative expenses" incurred by "freelance authors, photographers, and artists." Those expenses are
defined as any expense "which is paid or incurred by an individual in the trade or business of such individual (other than as an
employee) of being a writer, photographer, or artist, and . . .
which, without regard to this section, would be allowable as a
deduction for the taxable year." That section contains definitions of the terms *writer, photographer,* and *artist*: "any individual if the personal efforts of such individual create (or may
reasonably be expected to create)" a "literary manuscript, . . .
a photograph or photographic negative or transparency . . .
[or] a picture, painting, sculpture, statue, etching, drawing,
cartoon, graphic design, or original print edition."[16]

What kinds of expenses are deductible?

To be deductible, expenses must be "ordinary and necessary." This requirement has been described as follows:

> That is, in general, they must be normal, usual, and cus-
> tomary in the business in which the individual is involved,
> whether one is an author or in any other business. *Ordi-*
> *nary* might be defined as an expense that arises with some
> degree of consistency in the business of the individual
> involved, and *necessary* means that it is appropriate or
> helpful to the development or conduct of the trade or
> business. I think there is one other criterion that the
> expense would probably have to satisfy—it must be reason-

able. Assuming that all of these three criteria were established, the expense would be deductible against the current income of the individual involved.[17]

Many expenses incurred by creative people are clearly deductible. These would include expenses for supplies and equipment; travel and lodging expenses while on business; rent, utilities, and other office- or studio-related expenses; and salaries, fees, and other payments made to assistants, models, and others. Similarly, fees paid to agents, representatives, galleries, and the like would be deductible. But other expenses may be more questionable, including especially those for a home office and for entertainment. Now, only 80 percent of expenses incurred for meals and entertainment expenses are deductible, and only if the expense was "directly related" to "the active conduct of the taxpayer's trade or business."[18]

To be able to deduct expenses for a home office, the Code requires that (1) the space be used exclusively for business; (2) it be used for business purposes on a regular basis; (3) it must be the principal place of the business being conducted there; and (4) the taxpayer cannot deduct expenses that exceed the gross income from the business use, so that if there is no income, there can be no such deductions.[19]

Expenses incurred for taking courses and attending conferences will be deductible if they are intended to maintain or improve the creator's work, but not if their only purpose is to enable the individual to *become* a creator.

What if a creator wants to donate a work to charity?

A creative person is free to donate works to charitable organizations. However, because the works of a creative person are not considered capital assets, the tax law imposes severe restrictions on the amount the creator can claim as the value of the work contributed. Essentially, the value will be limited to the amounts actually expended by the artist in the creation of the work (i.e., his "cost basis" in the work).[20] Thus, even if the work is worth thousands or perhaps millions of dollars in the marketplace, the creator may claim only his actual costs for the work. As a result, there is a real and unfortunate disincentive to creators to donate works to charitable organizations.

What can creative people do to minimize tax burdens?

First, they should keep detailed records of their deductible expenses, including reference to the business purpose of the expense if it is not self-evident. If they don't and there is an audit, the claimed deductions may be disallowed.

Second, they can take advantage of tax-saving programs that are available to all. For example, sums placed in self-employed "Keogh" retirement plans or Individual Retirement Accounts (IRA) are deductible from current income and are not taxable until the individual takes them out, usually at retirement when income and tax rates are presumably lower. The appreciation of and income earned on the funds is not taxable until the money is taken out.

Third, they can take steps to control the income they receive in a given year. An author can arrange with a publisher, or an artist with a gallery, not to be paid more than a fixed amount in a given year. If tax is paid on the "cash basis" (income as received, which is what most taxpayers do), there will be no tax on income not yet paid by the publisher or gallery. Such arrangements may minimize tax exposure, but they have drawbacks: It is unlikely that the publisher or gallery will agree to pay interest, or enough interest, on sums held, and the author or artist will lose money because of this; also, the publisher or gallery may go out of business or otherwise become insolvent and be unable to pay.

Finally, creators can transfer works and/or some or all of their copyright interests in works to other people by what the law calls *inter vivos* (between living people) transfers. Under current law, gifts of up to $10,000 (in cash or other assets) to any recipient in any year can be made without any gift-tax liability. If correctly done, such transfers can not only shift the tax liability for the income or gains subsequently realized from those works from the donor (giver) to the donee (receiver) but also reduce the value (and tax liability) of the creator's estate at the time of her death (discussed further below). However, it should be noted that as a result of the Tax Reform Act of 1986, it is no longer possible to obtain income-tax advantages by transferring works or rights to minor children since that law provided that the net unearned income of a child under the age of 14 in excess of a relatively nominal amount is subject to tax at the top marginal rate of the child's parents.[21]

What can a corporation do to minimize taxes?

Corporations, at least those with limited income, generally pay lower tax rates than individuals. Moreover, corporations pay taxes only on profits (i.e., the amount that remains after salaries, expenses, and retirement investments, etc.). With proper planning, it is possible that the corporation will pay little or no tax and that the author or artist will pay significantly less tax than he would have paid as a sole proprietor. However, as the taxable income of the corporation increases, which means that the applicable tax rate also increases, the amount of total tax savings will decrease, and the tax benefits of incorporation become less significant.

The corporation can control the amount it pays the individual each year, thus giving better foreknowledge and control of the individual's taxable income. The corporation can also control *when* sums are paid (e.g., as salary or dividends) so that they are received at a time most advantageous to the creative person. (There are also tax benefits on fringe benefits, as discussed earlier in the chapter.)

Finally, corporations can create pension and profit-sharing plans to defer and minimize taxes. Like individuals' Keogh and IRA plans, these plans segregate and invest moneys on which the employee does not have to pay taxes until later. Since 1982, the amount of money that may be placed in tax-deferred pension plans is the same for individuals and corporations.

These proposals are fraught with technical requirements that must be complied with. The services of an accountant or lawyer will probably be necessary. If done properly, they can bring significant savings to the creative person.

What about a creative person's estate?

Estate problems, particularly those of artists, are significant. As one commentator has noted:

The accumulated life's work of the working artist is [most] troubling. Most working artists do not focus on the problems that will be presented to their estate in disposing of their work in an effective way. If the artist has achieved limited public acceptance prior to death, the issue is not a major one. The Internal Revenue Service may ignore concern as to the value of the work for estate tax purposes and may permit a modest estate the value claimed without any dispute. If, however, the artist had publicly reported sales in any significant numbers, the problem can be acute and if the family of the artist has any concern in perpetuating the name of the artist—and generating any significant proceeds by the sale of his work—the problem can be severe and the methods of solving the problem can have substantial disparate results.[22]

The problem is that for federal estate-tax purposes, the assets of the decedent must be valued as of the date of death (or 6 months thereafter). If an artist leaves a significant number of works, including many that may have been created years earlier, difficult and crucial issues of valuation are presented. How is the "fair market value" of those works to be determined? The answer to that question can often spell the difference between a devastating estate-tax exposure and one that can be managed. In the early 1990s the federal estate-tax marginal rate on estates valued over $600,000 began at 37 percent and increased to a top rate of 55 percent on estates with a net valuation of $3 million.

A high estate tax will create severe burdens and pressures on the estate, which may be forced to sell works immediately to pay the tax. Naturally, a forced sale does not maximize the income of the estate, nor does it otherwise serve the reputation and future value of the work well. The Internal Revenue Code has provisions that would enable an estate to defer the payment of estate taxes under certain circumstances, particularly if specified percentages of the estate are attributable to a "closely held business."[23]

Recent changes in federal tax law have reduced estate-tax burdens for many. The amount of an estate that will be "exempt" from federal estate tax has been increased to $600,000, which means that estates up to $600,000 pay no estate taxes. Similarly, the *marital exemption* (i.e., the inheritance of a surviving spouse that will be exempted from estate tax) has been revised so that the entire inheritance is now exempt. This means that there will be no estate tax payable when the first spouse dies, with full estate taxes payable on the survivor's estate at the time of that spouse's death.

When created works are inherited, the tax "basis" for those

works is their value at the time of inheritance. This means that any appreciation in the value of those works prior to the creator's death will not be the tax responsibility of the person inheriting the work; that person will have to pay tax only on the amount of the increase in the value of the work after the creator's death when that work is sold by the person inheriting the work.

What about copyrights in a creator's estate?

As was discussed in Chapter II, ownership of a work does not automatically include ownership in the copyright in that work, and vice versa.[24] As a result, creators and their estate planners should take special care in disposing of the copyrights in works as well as the works themselves, and it should be remembered that the work can go to one recipient (perhaps a museum) and the copyright in the work to another heir entirely.

As also discussed in Chapter II, under some circumstances the U.S. Copyright Act may override provisions in a creator's will; for example, where a work is in its first term of copyright under the 1909 Copyright Act at the time of the creator's death.[25] In such cases, the Copyright Act spells out who will be entitled to the renewal term of that copyright, regardless of the provisions of the creator's will.[26]

What should creators do to plan their estates?

All creative people, but especially those who may leave sizable estates on their death, should plan now for the disposition of their work and payment of estate taxes when they die. They should have wills that dispose of their estates in an orderly way consistent with their desires, and they should have those wills planned and drafted by professionals who are knowledgeable and experienced in the special problems presented by the estates of creative people. They should also consider transfers or gifts during their lifetime that may serve the best interests of their families and their work. In their wills they may name special executors or curators to handle the disposition of their work, but special care should be taken not to appoint persons who may have a conflict of interest with respect to the work, such as the creator's publisher or gallery owner.[27]

NOTES

1. For a comprehensive discussion of many of the matters discussed in this chapter, see Lerner & Bresler, *Art Law: The Guide for Collectors, Investors, Dealers, and Artists* (Practicing Law Institute, 1989) (hereinafter, Lerner & Bresler); Duffy, *Art Law: Representing Artists, Dealers, and Collectors* (Practicing Law Institute, 1977); Davidson & Blue, *Making It Legal: A Law Primer for the Craftmaker, Visual Artist, and Writer* (1979); Horwitz, ed., *Law and the Arts* (Lawyers for the Creative Arts, 1979); and Crawford, *The Writer's Legal Guide* (1977).
2. Internal Revenue Code (IRC) §1221(3).
3. IRC §74.
4. IRC §117.
5. *Id.*
6. *See* IRC §1361 *et seq.*
7. IRC §162.
8. *Dreicer v. Commissioner of Internal Revenue*, 665 F.2d 1292, 1299–1300 (D.C. Cir. 1981).
9. IRC §183(d).
10. IRC §212.
11. I.R.S. Reg. §1.183–2(b); Federal Tax Guide Reports ¶1997B (CCH, 1991).
12. Federal Tax Guide Reports ¶13,126 (CCH, 1991).
13. IRC §183.
14. IRC §263A.
15. IRC §263A(h).
16. *Id.*
17. Remarks of Francis Neuwirth, C.P.A., at Symposium on Taxation sponsored by the Authors Guild on December 8, 1881, copies of which are available from the Guild.
18. IRC §274.
19. IRC §280A.
20. IRC §170(e).
21. IRC §63(c)(5).
22. Feldman, "Marketing Fine Art: Selling the Right Thing the Wrong Way," *Communications and the Law*, Vol. 1, No. 1, at 71.
23. IRC §§6166, 6166A.
24. See Chapter II.
25. See Chapter II.
26. Also as discussed in Chapter II, the Copyright Act grants to certain identified survivors of a creator the right to terminate grants or transfers of copyright interests in a work at specified times. Thus, any bequests

of copyrights in a creator's will would presumably be subject to such termination rights.

27. See *Matter of Rothko*, 43 N.Y.2d 305 (1977), where the executors of the estate of the artist Mark Rothko were found to have violated their "fiduciary" duty to the estate by selling works in the estate to themselves. The Authors Guild's Symposium of Author's Wills and Estates, published in the Guild's Spring 1983 *Bulletin*, contains an extensive discussion of issues raised in connection with the wills and estates of creative people.

Appendix A
Resources: Where to Go for More Information and Help

Numerous books, articles, and other materials dealing with the issues discussed in this book have been published in the last decade or so. In addition, there are many organizations involved in those issues that may be able to assist the reader with particular problems. This Appendix includes a brief selection of those resources, with indications of where further resources can be found.

FOR THE VISUAL ARTIST

Published Resources

By far the most comprehensive and current published resource for virtually all aspects of the law applicable to visual artists is *Art Law: The Guide for Collectors, Investors, Dealers, and Artists*, by Ralph E. Lerner and Judith Bresler, published in 1989 by Practicing Law Institute, New York, NY. This book contains clear and detailed discussions of the issues touched on here, as well as many others, together with numerous checklists, form agreements, and important state and federal legislation, among other useful resources. It should probably be the first place to look for further information about legal issues relating to visual artists.

Other helpful books that deal with such issues include Feldman & Weil, *Art Works: Law, Policy, Practice* (1974), revised in a two-volume edition as Feldman, Weil & Biederman, *Art Law: Rights and Liabilities of Creators and Collectors* (1986); Duffy, *Art Law: Representing Artists, Dealers and Collectors* (1977); DuBoff, *The Deskbook of Art Law* (1977 & Supp. 1984); Merryman & Elsen, *Law Ethics and the Visual Arts* (2d ed. 1987); Hodes, *Legal Rights in the Art and Collectors World* (1986); Caplan, *The Business of Art* (1989); and Watson, *The Business of Art* (1988).

Tad Crawford, a New York lawyer, is the author or coauthor of several books of potential interest to visual artists, including *Legal Guide for the Visual Artist* (1987); *Business and Legal Forms for Fine Artists* (1990); and, with Eva Doman Bruck, *Business and Legal Forms for Graphic Artists* (1990). The latter two books contain several useful forms and negotiating checklists.

Organizations

Volunteer Lawyers for the Arts, as its name suggests, provides legal assistance to creative artists and materials on legal subjects of concern to artists. Its main office is located at 1285 Avenue of the Americas, Third Floor, New York, NY 10019, (212) 977–9270, and it has numerous chapters throughout the United States.

Other organizations represent the interests of various categories of artists. They include Artists Equity Association, 3726 Albermarle Street N.W., Washington, DC 20016, (202) 244–0209 (deals with issues affecting rights of artists generally, with primary emphasis on the fine arts); Foundation for the Community of Artists, 280 Broadway, Room 412, New York, NY 10007, (212) 227–3770 (concerned with artists' rights and publishes a useful newspaper, *Artworkers' News*); Graphic Artists Guild, 30 East 20th Street, Room 405, New York, NY 10003, (212) 982-9298 (leading organization representing interests of graphic artists, with chapters throughout the country; publishes numerous publications and conducts seminars, etc.); and Society of Illustrators, 128 East 63rd Street, New York, NY 10021, (212) 838-2560 (concerned with issues relating to illustrators; conducts programs and shows; publishes valuable reference works).

FOR THE PHOTOGRAPHER

Published Resources

A comprehensive resource for photographers is *Selling Your Photography: The Complete Marketing, Business and Legal*

Guide, by Arie Kopelman and Tad Crawford, published in 1980 by St. Martin's Press, New York, NY. Especially useful are the detailed appendixes, which include extensive information on how and where to obtain grants; a list of professional organizations and associations; and an exhaustive bibliography of books and periodicals organized by their principal subject matter.

Other valuable resources for photographers include *ASMP Professional Business Practices in Photography, 4th Ed.*, (American Society of Magazine Photographers, 1986); Tad Crawford, *Legal Guide for the Visual Artist*; *Photography— What's the Law?*, (rev. ed., Robert M. Cavallo & Stuart Kahan, 1979); and DuBoff, *The Photographer's Business and Legal Handbook* (1989).

Organizations

The American Society of Magazine Photographers, 205 Lexington Avenue, New York, NY 10016, (212) 889-9144, is a national membership organization representing photographers who work in communications media such as advertising, industrial, journalism, and related fields. In addition to its main office in New York, it has chapters in Atlanta, Boston, Chicago, Houston, Los Angeles, Philadelphia, San Francisco, and Seattle. It makes available various materials of interest to professional photographers.

Other organizations that might prove helpful include Volunteer Lawyers for the Arts, discussed above; International Center of Photography, 1130 Fifth Avenue, New York, NY 10028, (212) 860-1777, a cultural organization that offers seminars and courses; and Professional Photographers of America, 1090 Executive Way, Des Plaines, Illinois 60018, (312) 299-8161, a membership organization representing portrait, wedding, commercial, and industrial photographers.

FOR THE WRITER

Published Resources

An indispensable resource for all writers who want to be published is the fourth edition of Judith Appelbaum's classic,

How to Get Happily Published, published in 1992 by Harper Collins, New York, NY. In addition to its wise and helpful discussions of all aspects of the publishing process, including self-publishing, this book contains over fifty pages devoted to resources (subdivided into useful sections to be most accessible and helpful to the writer who needs help). These resources include references to hundreds of published books and articles, as well as exhaustive lists of people, places, and programs that may assist writers with specific problems.

Other valuable works for writers seeking further information about the issues discussed in this book include Levine, *Negotiating an Author's Book Contract: A Guide for Authors, Agents and Their Lawyers* (1987); Crawford, *Business and Legal Forms for Authors and Self-Publishers* (1990); Goldfarb & Ross, *The Writer's Lawyer: Essential Legal Advice for Writers and Editors in All Media* (1989); Bunnin & Beren, *The Writer's Legal Companion* (1988); Polking, ed., *Writer's Friendly Legal Guide* (1989); Mungo, *Lit Biz 101: How to Get Happily, Successfully Published* (1988); and two books by Richard Curtis, a New York literary agent: *Beyond the Bestseller: A Literary Agent Takes You Inside the Book Business* (1990) and *How to Be Your Own Literary Agent* (1983).

Organizations

Among the numerous organizations that serve the interests of writers, probably the most significant are The Authors Guild, Inc., 234 West 44th Street, New York, NY 10036, (212) 398-0838; PEN American Center, 568 Broadway, New York, NY 10012, (212) 334-1660; and American Society of Journalists and Authors, 1501 Broadway, Suite 1907, New York, NY 10036, (212) 997-0947—all of which disseminate useful materials and conduct valuable programs.

FOR THE DRAMATIST

Published Resources

There are relatively few books that deal with the legal and business concerns of dramatists. A legal treatise, *Entertainment*

Industry Contracts, edited by Donald C. Farber, contains (in Volume 2) various dramatists' agreements, useful commentary, and a valuable resource guide that lists theatre licensing companies, small performing-rights licensing companies, unions, writers' and producers' organizations, the sections of the New York State Attorney General's Office that deals with theatrical productions, and Broadway, regional, and institutional theatres. Another treatise, *Lindey on Entertainment, Publishing and the Arts*, 2d ed., contains a separate section on plays, including several form agreements with annotations that refer to other legal and other resources. In addition, the Dramatists Guild, Inc., makes available agreements for most types of commercial and noncommercial productions. For first-class productions, the Guild's Approved Production Contract is the standard for the industry. For other types of productions, the Guild's agreements are less pervasive but nevertheless represent what it believes such agreements should contain from the dramatist's point of view.

Organizations

The Dramatists Guild, Inc., 234 West 44th Street, New York, NY 10036, is the principal organization dealing with issues of concern to playwrights. Another organization, the Association of Authors' Representatives, has a separate component that deals with issues of concern to representatives of dramatists. It is located at Ten Astor Place, New York, NY 10003, (212) 353-3709.

FOR THE SCREENWRITER

Published Resources

The Writers Guild of America's Basic Agreement is the single most important reference for screenwriters. It can be obtained from the WGA (see below). Unfortunately, that agreement is not as clear and intelligible as one might hope. There are several books that deal with that agreement, one of the most useful of which is *The Motion Picture and Television Business:*

Contracts and Practices. In addition, *Entertainment Industry Contracts* and *Lindey on Entertainment, Publishing and the Arts,* 2d ed., contain sections on motion pictures, including form agreements and annotations concerning many of their provisions. Other sources that may prove useful to screenwriters are Walter, *Screenwriting: The Art, the Craft, the Business of Film and TV Writing* (1988); Granger, ed., *Screenwriters Guild: (Almost) Everything You Need to Get Your Script Produced* (1987); and Field, *The Screenwriter's Guide to Hollywood* (1989).

Organizations

The most important organizations for screenwriters are the east and west offices of the Writers Guild of America (the dividing line is the Mississippi River). The east office is located at 555 West 57th Street, New York, NY 10019, (212) 245-6180. The west office is located at 8955 Beverly Boulevard, Los Angeles, CA 90048, (213) 550-1000.

FOR MORE ABOUT COPYRIGHT

The U.S. Copyright Office, which is part of the Library of Congress, is the government agency that administers copyrights. It publishes the official forms that must be used to file copyright registrations and other documents, and it makes available a number of other resources that are extremely helpful in explaining those forms, the policies and procedures of the office, and the fundamentals of copyright law. It also publishes an extensive bibliography of published works that deal with copyright issues. The Copyright Office can be reached at Library of Congress, Washington, DC 20559, and its telephone number is (202) 479-0700; a special "hotline" number, (202) 707-9100, is available for ordering specific circulars and forms.

Probably the best-known and most comprehensive treatise on copyright law is the four-volume *Nimmer on Copyright,* which is updated regularly and can be found in most law libraries. Other useful, and more accessible, works on copyright include *The Copyright Book,* by William Strong (1990) and *How to Protect Your Creative Work,* by David A. Weinstein

(1987). The latter book contains appendixes of copyright forms and form agreements.

FOR MORE ABOUT LIBEL AND INVASION OF PRIVACY

The Libel Defense Resource Center (LDRC), as its name suggests, compiles and publishes a wealth of information about libel and invasion-of-privacy law and cases, including a comprehensive state-by-state review of the applicable laws in all the states, *LDRC 50-State Survey: Current Developments in Media Libel and Invasion of Privacy Law*. The LDRC is located at 404 Park Avenue South, New York, NY 10016, (212) 889-2306.

Other useful resources are Bruce W. Sandford, *Libel and Privacy*, 2d ed. (1991); Robert D. Sack, *Libel, Slander and Related Problems* (1980); Rodney Smolla, *Suing the Press: Libel, the Media and Power* (1986); and Richard Labinkski, *Libel and the First Amendment: Legal History and Practice and in Print and Broadcasting* (1987).

FOR MORE ABOUT OBSCENITY

There are numerous organizations directly concerned with the issues that arise as a result of this nation's obscenity laws. Among those organizations are Media Coalition, 900 Third Avenue, Suite 1600, New York, NY 10022, (212) 891-2070, a coalition of several major trade associations in the publishing field that closely follows developments in obscenity law and publishes materials about those developments; American Booksellers Foundation for Free Expression, 137 West 25th Street, New York, NY 10001, (212) 463-8450, a branch of the trade association that represents most bookstores in the United States and publishes useful materials about obscenity-law issues; and the Office for Intellectual Freedom of the American Library Association, 50 East Huron Street, Chicago, IL 60611, (312) 944-6780, which publishes a comprehensive and invaluable bimonthly *Newsletter on Intellectual Freedom* that provides in-depth coverage of current developments in obscenity matters.

Among the countless books that have been written in recent years on obscenity and censorship issues, two of the most useful are *The Law of Obscenity,* by Frederick Schauer, and *Pornography in a Free Society,* by Gordon Hawkins and Franklin E. Zimring. In addition, *United States of America vs. Sex: How the Meese Commission Lied About Pornography,* by Philip Nobile and Eric Nadler, provides a detailed critique of the methodology and conclusions of the report of the Meese Commission on Obscenity that was released in 1986. Also, two extremely valuable pamphlets, *Sense & Censorship: The Vanity of Bonfires* and *Sense & Censorship: The Vanity of Bonfires—Resource Material on Sexually Explicit Material, Violent Material and Censorship: Research and Public Policy Implications,* both written and compiled by Marcia Pally and published in 1991 by Americans for Constitutional Freedom and the Freedom to Read Foundation, cogently discuss many contemporary issues in the obscenity area, including the claimed connection between sexually explicit materials and antisocial conduct.

Appendix B
"Red Flag" Words

The following selected "red flag" words and expressions* are typical of the numerous words and expressions that may lead to a libel lawsuit if not carefully handled by writers.

addict
adulteration of products
adultery
alcoholic
altered records
atheist

bad moral character
bankrupt
bigamist
blacklisted
blackmail
boozehound
bribery
brothel
buys votes

cheats
child abuse
collusion
confidence man
corruption
coward
crook

deadbeat
defaulter
divorced

double-crosser
drug abuser
drunkard

ex-convict

fawning sycophant
fraud

gambling den
gangster
gay
graft
groveling office seeker

herpes
hit man
hypocrite

illegitimate
illicit relation
incompetent
infidelity
informer
insider trading
intemperate
intimate
intolerance

Jekyll-Hyde personality

* From: *Sanford's Synopsis of Libel and Privacy*, 4th ed., by Bruce W. Sanford. Copyright © 1991 by Scripps Howard. Reprinted by permission.

kept woman
Ku Klux Klan

Mafia
mental disease
mobster
moral delinquency
mouthpiece

Nazi

paramour
peeping Tom
perjurer
plagiarist
pockets public funds
profiteering
prostitute

scam
scandalmonger
scoundrel
seducer
sharp dealing

shyster
slacker
smooth and tricky
smuggler
sneaky
sold influence
sold out
spy
stool pigeon
stuffed the ballot box
suicide
swindle

thief

unethical
unmarried mother
unprofessional
unsound mind
unworthy of credit

vice den
villain

Any words or expressions imputing

A loathsome disease
A crime, or words falsely charging arrest or indictment for
    or confession or conviction of a crime
Anti-Semitism or other religious, racial or ethnic intol-
    erance
Connivance or association with criminals
Financial embarrassment (or any implication of insolvency
    or want of credit)
Lying
Membership in an organization which may be in disrepute
    at a given time
Poverty or squalor
Unwillingness to pay a debt